Praise for
*The Letters of Minerva Mirabal
and Manolo Tavárez*

"Minerva Mirabal and Manolo Tavárez are martyrs of the Dominican struggle against tyranny and oppression, but they were also two human beings deeply in love with each other. Through this superb and careful translation of their letters and the powerful evocations of their daughter, Heather Hennes brings to the English-speaking public this very necessary book. A must-read!"

—Ramón Antonio Victoriano-Martínez, author of *Rayanos y Dominicanyorks: La dominicanidad del siglo XXI*

"An original and significant addition to the history and literature of the Dominican Republic, as it translates a collection of historically significant letters exchanged between two major figures in the struggle to end the infamous, long-lasting, widely condemned Trujillo dictatorship."

—Elizabeth Horan, editor and translator of Gabriela Mistral's *Motivos: The Life of St. Francis*

"Beautiful, sad, revelatory, and inspiring, this book offers English-language readers a glimpse into a revolutionary relationship, the beginnings of the radical movement that ended the Trujillo dictatorship in the Dominican Republic, and leftist mobilization in Latin America. A timely and important contribution to Dominican historiography and the study of dictatorship, resistance, and revolution that also reminds us of the very real exigencies of memory and reconciliation."

—Elizabeth S. Manley, author of *The Paradox of Paternalism: Women and the Politics of Authoritarianism in the Dominican Republic*

The Letters of Minerva Mirabal and Manolo Tavárez

THE LETTERS OF
Minerva Mirabal and Manolo Tavárez

Love and Resistance in the Time of Trujillo

MINOU TAVÁREZ MIRABAL

INTRODUCTION AND TRANSLATION BY
HEATHER HENNES

Foreword by Michelle Bachelet Jeria

Originally published in Spanish as
Mañana te escribiré otra vez. Minerva y Manolo. Cartas

University of Florida Press
Gainesville

Publication of this work made possible by a Sustaining the Humanities through the American Rescue Plan grant from the National Endowment for the Humanities.

"Letter On The Road" by Pablo Neruda, translated by Donald D. Walsh, from *The Captain's Verses*, copyright ©1972 by Pablo Neruda and Donald D. Walsh. Reprinted by permission of New Directions Publishing Corp.
"La carta en el camino," *Los versos Del Capitán* © Pablo Neruda, 1952 and Fundación Pablo Neruda

Introduction and Translation copyright 2022 by Heather Hennes
Originally published in Spanish as *Mañana te escribiré otra vez. Minerva y Manolo. Cartas*
All rights reserved
Published in the United States of America

27 26 25 24 23 22   6 5 4 3 2 1

Library of Congress Cataloging-in-Publication Data
Names: Tavárez Mirabal, Minou, 1956– author. | Mirabal, Minerva, 1926–1960, author. | Tavárez, Manolo, 1931–1963, author. | Hennes, Heather, translator, author of introduction. | Bachelet, Michelle, 1951– author of foreword.
Title: The letters of Minerva Mirabal and Manolo Tavárez : love and resistance in the time of Trujillo / Minou Tavárez Mirabal, introduction and translation by Heather Hennes, foreword by Michelle Bachelet Jeria.
Other titles: Mañana te escribiré otra vez : Minerva y Manolo : cartas. English
Description: 1. | Gainesville : University of Florida Press, 2022. | Originally published in Spanish under the title Mañana te escribiré otra vez : Minerva y Manolo : cartas. Santo Domingo : Fundación Hermanas Mirabal, 2013. | Includes bibliographical references and index.
Identifiers: LCCN 2021054503 (print) | LCCN 2021054504 (ebook) | ISBN 9781683402626 (hardback) | ISBN 9781683402725 (paperback) | ISBN 9781683402640 (pdf) | ISBN 9781683403159 (ebook)
Subjects: LCSH: Mirabal, Minerva, 1926–1960—Correspondence. | Tavárez, Manolo, 1931–1963—Correspondence. | Dominican Republic—History—1930–1961. | BISAC: POLITICAL SCIENCE / World / Caribbean & Latin American | BIOGRAPHY & AUTOBIOGRAPHY / Social Activists | LCGFT: Personal correspondence.
Classification: LCC F1938.5.M56 T3813 2022 (print) | LCC F1938.5.M56 (ebook) | DDC 972.9305/3—dc23/eng/20211129
LC record available at https://lccn.loc.gov/2021054503
LC ebook record available at https://lccn.loc.gov/2021054504

University of Florida Press
2046 NE Waldo Road
Suite 2100
Gainesville, FL 32609
http://upress.ufl.edu

To my brother Manolo
and of course to
Minerva Victoria, Minou,
Talía, Camila Minerva, and
Manuel Aurelio

Contents

List of Figures · xi
Acknowledgments · xiii

Introduction to This Edition · 1
Heather Hennes

Translator's Note · 35
Heather Hennes

THE LETTERS OF MINERVA MIRABAL AND MANOLO TAVÁREZ

Foreword · 43
Michelle Bachelet Jeria

To My Parents · 44
Minou Tavárez Mirabal

Part I. Courtship: August 1954–October 1955 · 51
Part II. Marriage: 1956–1958 · 207
Part III. Letters in Prison: 1959–1960 · 227
Part IV. The Final Letter, 1960–1963 · 255

Glossary · 265
Bibliography · 279
Index · 283

Figures

0.1. Mirabal Reyes family tree xv
0.2. Tavárez Justo family tree xvi
0.3. María Teresa, don Enrique and doña Chea at their home in Ojo de Agua xvii
0.4. Portrait of Patria, Dedé, and Minerva xviii
0.5. Manuel Tavárez Ramos with all of his children in 1962 xviii
0.6. Map of the Dominican Republic 9
1.1. Telegram from Minerva to Manolo, August 3, 1954 51
1.2. Minerva with a perm. Letter from Minerva to Manolo, November 1954 52
1.3. The first photo that Manolo gave Minerva. Letter from Manolo to Minerva, January 18, 1955 52
1.4. Dedé, Hortensia, Minerva, Patria, and Jaime Enrique in Ojo de Agua, 1955 53
1.5. Manolo with his cousin Isabelita Justo on the day of his graduation, February 25, 1955 53
1.6. Minerva driving a Jeep, with friends 54
2.1. Manolo and Minerva's wedding on November 20, 1955 207
2.2. Manolo, Minerva, María Teresa, Leandro, and Patria in Montecristi 208
2.3. Manolo and Minerva, pregnant with Minou, on the staircase to their home in Montecristi, 1956 208
2.4. Minerva and Manolo with newborn Minou on September 1, 1956 209
2.5. Manolo with Minou on her first birthday 209
2.6. Minerva with Manolo on the day she graduated with her law degree on October 28, 1957 210

3.1. Founding members of the 14 of June Movement 226
3.2. Letter from Minerva to Manolo, written in prison on the back of an insert for toothpaste, 1960 227
3.3. Letter from Manolo to Minerva, written in prison on paper from cigarette packaging, 1960 228
3.4. Bust of Minou that Minerva sculpted while in prison, 1960 228
4.1. Memorial card from the Mass celebrated on November 24, 1961, the first anniversary of the deaths of Patria, Minerva, and María Teresa Mirabal and Rufino de la Cruz 255
4.2. The widowers of the Mirabal sisters, photographed in prison, 1960 256
4.3. Manolo and Minou on the day of her First Holy Communion in August, 1961 256
4.4. Manolo addressing a crowd as leader of the 14 of June Political Party 257
4.5. Noris González Mirabal, Manolo, doña Chea, Jaime David Fernández Mirabal, Manolito, Jacqueline Guzmán Mirabal, and Raúl González Mirabal at the house in Conuco 257
4.6. Minou at two months. The note that Minou wrote to her father just before his death 262
4.7. The letter-snail sent by Manolo to his daughter Minou the day he was assassinated 263
4.8. Doña Chea Reyes with her daughter Dedé and her nine grandchildren, 1981 264

Acknowledgments

I owe a debt of gratitude to the many individuals who helped make this edition possible. First and foremost, to Minou Tavárez Mirabal for entrusting me with her words and those of her parents and for providing invaluable insights along the way. I hope to have honored them through this translation. Likewise, thank you to Manuel E. Tavárez Justo and the Fundación Hermanas Mirabal for supporting this project and for granting rights to the text and images.

I am extremely grateful to Stephanye Hunter at the University of Florida Press. Her enthusiasm and support for this project, and in particular her many helpful comments on multiple drafts, have been invaluable. Her guidance and encouragement as editor have helped me to grow professionally and have made the process enjoyable.

Likewise, many thanks go to the readers whose thoughtful feedback has helped shape this project. In particular, Nicole Harris, Maggie Chapman, Eric Hennes, and John King treaded through the initial drafts and provided much encouragement. Arturo Victoriano Martínez supported the project from the start and provided thoughtful feedback that helped shape the text. I also owe a debt of gratitude to one external reviewer who remains anonymous and who held me to a high standard for the translation. This individual's candid feedback was the impetus that pushed me to work through the translation even more and to grow as a novice translator. Finally, I am greatly indebted to Elizabeth Manley for her extremely detailed, insightful and encouraging feedback, as well as her own scholarship, which helped inform the text. The introduction in this volume would be significantly less substantial were it not for her suggestions and encouragement.

I am also grateful to those who have granted permission to reproduce texts and images that appear in this volume. The Fundación Hermanas Mirabal provided the vast majority of the images, as well as the rights to translate the text. Many thanks to Irina Miolán of Miolán Graphic Design for facilitating my access to these images. I am also grateful to the Fundación Manolo Tavárez Justo and to Milvio Pérez for granting permission to reproduce photographs. María Margarita Moreno Montalvo, Matilde Suescún and Natalia Suescún graciously granted permission to reproduce the late Nicolás Suescún's lovely translation, "Song of the Profound Life" ("Canción de la vida profunda") by Colombian poet Miguel Ángel Osorio, known as Porfirio Barba Jacob. And I thank Teresa Pinto at the Agencia Literaria Carmen Balcells, Christopher Wait at New Directions, and the Fundación Neruda for granting permissions to reproduce Donald Devenish Walsh's translation of Pablo Neruda's "La carta en el camino" ("Letter on the Road").

This project was made possible by the financial support of my home institution, Saint Joseph's University in Philadelphia, which granted me a sabbatical for the academic year 2018–2019, for which I am extremely grateful. The University has also provided other forms of financial support for my professional development and for the development of this publication. Of course, it is the support of my dear colleagues in the Department of Modern and Classical Languages that has seen me through this project. And finally, many thanks go to Lisa Chicchi for making my amateurish graphics look professional.

On a personal note, I am thankful to Dr. Otilio Portorreal, collaborator in the 14 of June Movement, for introducing me to the story of the Mirabal Sisters, and to David Portorreal for helping me to learn more about his father's story and the story of their generation. Much of my desire to tell this story stems from my deep affection for Otilio, who was always very supportive of me.

Last, but never, ever least, many thanks go to my family. To my parents, Leo and Sara Hennes: I am only able to do this work because you have loved, supported, taught, and sacrificed for me and my brothers all our lives. To you: all my love and gratitude. To my daughters, Olivia and Elena González de Echávarri: thank you for your patience as I worked through draft after draft and for inspiring me to do my best. The story of the Tavárez Mirabal family moved me as it did because, thanks to you, I can understand that deep, undying connection between mother and daughters. And to my beloved husband, Javier González de Echávarri: you helped me work through countless phrases; you have been by my side all along the way; and you have made it possible for me to dedicate myself to this project. Many thanks and all my love.

Heather Hennes

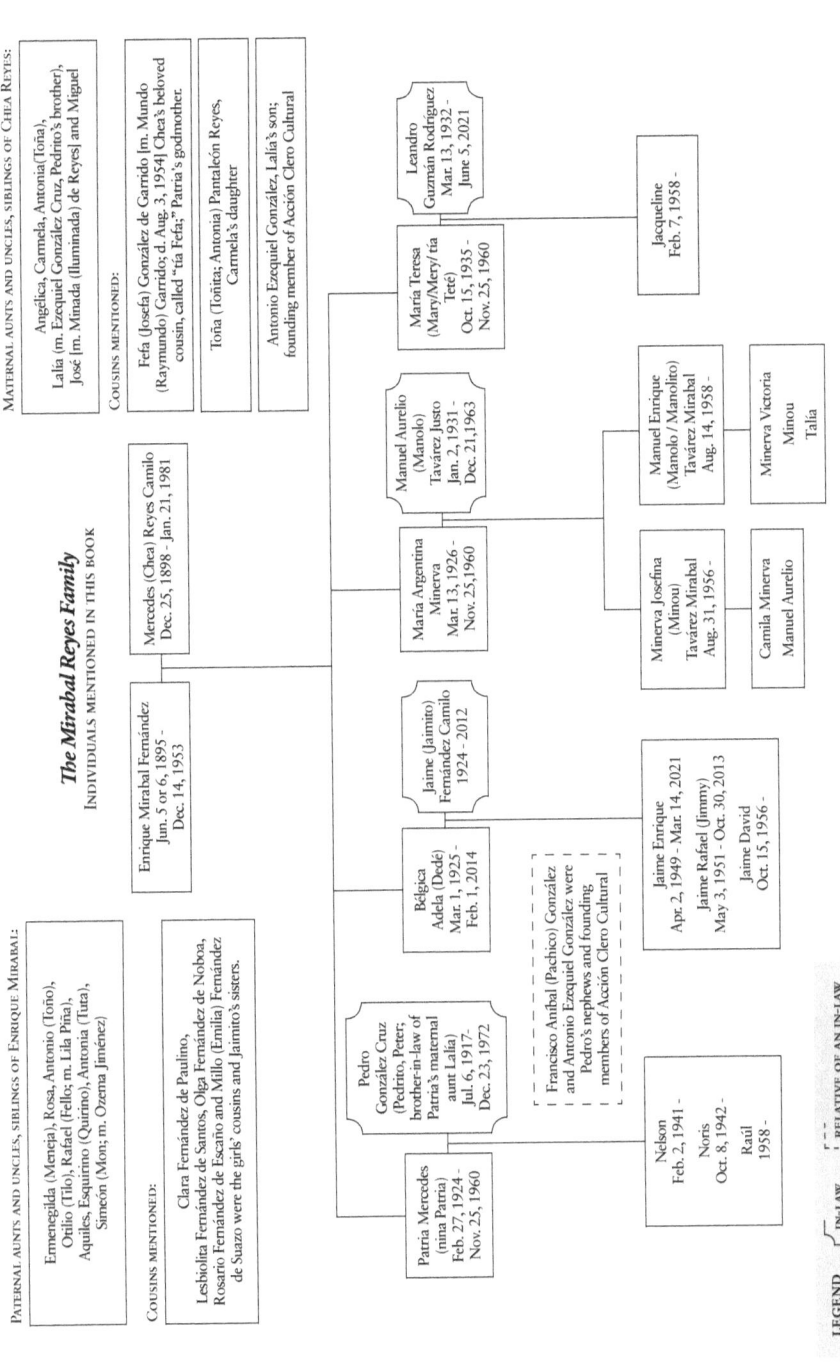

Figure 0.1. Mirabal Reyes Family Tree. Created with the help of Lisa Chicchi, Saint Joseph's University.

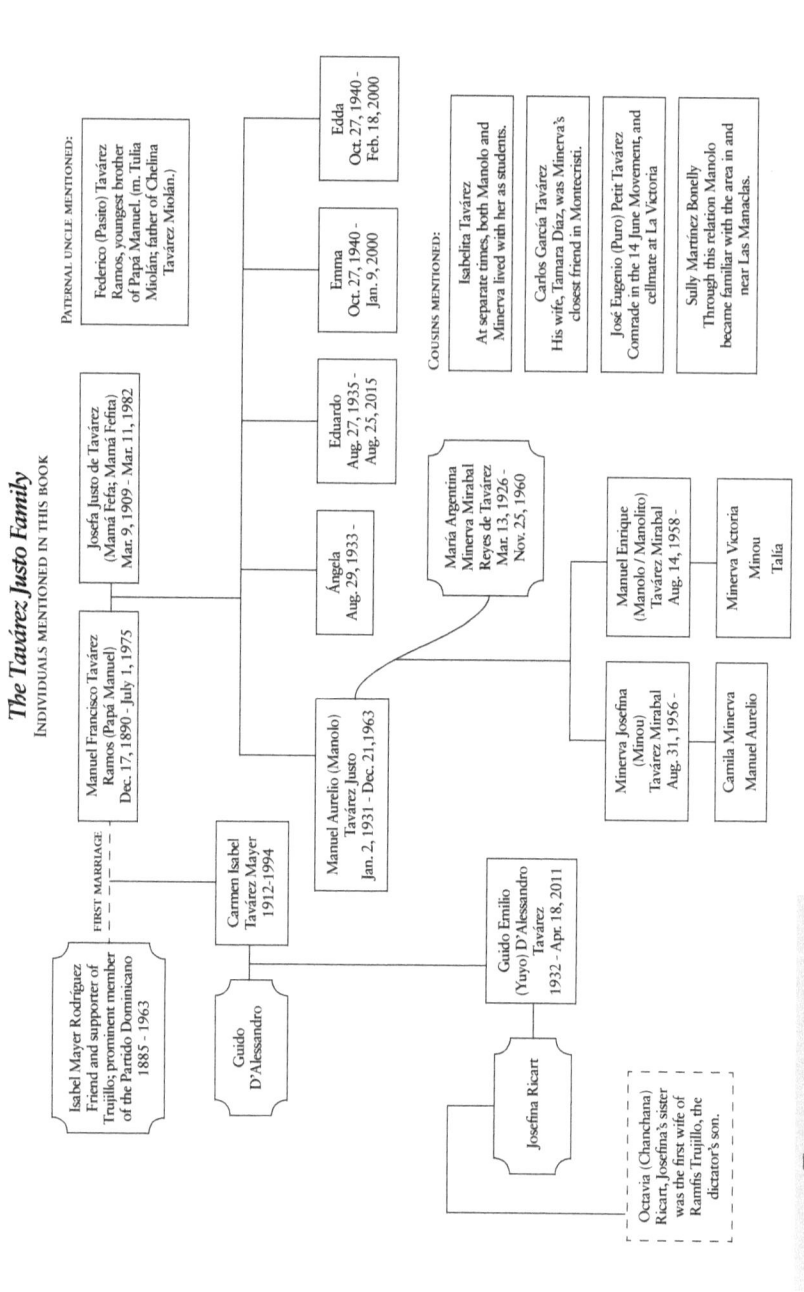

Figure 0.2. Tavárez Justo Family Tree. Created with the help of Lisa Chicchi, Saint Joseph's University.

Figure 0.3. María Teresa, don Enrique and doña Chea at their home in Ojo de Agua. Courtesy of the Fundación Hermanas Mirabal.

Figure 0.4. Portrait of Patria, Dedé, and Minerva. Courtesy of the Fundación Hermanas Mirabal.

Figure 0.5. Manuel Tavárez Ramos with all of his children in 1962. *From left to right*: Eduardo and Emma Tavárez Justo, Carmen Tavárez Mayer, don Manuel, Manolo, Ángela, and Edda Tavárez Justo. Courtesy of the Fundación Hermanas Mirabal.

Introduction to This Edition

Heather Hennes

Known as "Minou," Minerva Josefina Tavárez Mirabal (b. 1956) is an important political leader in the Dominican Republic. Aside from her background as a university professor and philologist, she has served as undersecretary of foreign relations (1996–2000), congresswoman (2002–2016), founder of the political party Opción Democrática, and vice president of the political party Alianza País. She served as president of Parliamentarians for Global Action and recently joined the Board of Directors of the Trust Fund for Victims at the International Criminal Court. She staunchly advocates for greater democracy, a reining in of clientelism and corruption, and an end to impunity for those who have violated human rights.

She is also internationally known as the daughter of Minerva Mirabal (1926–1960) and Manolo Tavárez (1931–1963), martyred national heroes who were taken from Minou and her brother when they were young children. Minou was three years old in 1960 when her parents, aunt, and uncles were imprisoned and tortured for their leadership in an underground resistance movement against the Dominican dictator Rafael Trujillo Molina (1891–1961). Later that year, her mother, two aunts, and their driver were brutally murdered in what Trujillo's henchmen tried to pass off as an accident. Minou was only seven when her father was executed for his militant opposition to the leadership of the Triumvirate installed by the 1963 military coup. But as she reaffirms in this journey through her parents' personal correspondence, she was there. She was shaped by her parents and the lives they shared together, and she, in turn, formed part of their now legendary lives.

In her foreword to *Mañana te escribiré otra vez,* former Chilean president and internationally known human rights advocate Michelle Bachelet captures the significance of this book: Dominican lawyers and revolutionaries Minerva Mirabal and Manolo Tavárez are "heroes of Latin American dimensions" who continue to inspire many in the struggle for democracy and social justice. One need only visit the Memorial Museum of Dominican Resistance in Santo Domingo to appreciate their transcendence as national icons who represent the courage and sacrifice of the thousands of Dominicans who actively opposed Trujillo's dictatorship over three decades (1930–1961). Their story resonates with people across the region and across the world precisely because it reflects the experiences of so many. Still, until now, much of their story has been silenced, victim of the regime that took their lives, but also of their mythification in the popular imaginary. This mythification and martyrization obscures their complexity and fullness as individuals, as well as the life experiences they had in common with many of us. It blurs our understanding of their activism and its legacy. In this volume, their letters and their daughter's memories bring them back in their fullness and challenge us to see that they were like us in many ways. They challenge us to ask where the injustices are in our own lives and where we might find the courage to oppose them.

In this book, Minou Tavárez Mirabal, who continues her parents' struggle for democracy, shares their intimate correspondence and guides us on a journey into life under the repressive Trujillo dictatorship in the Dominican Republic. The memoir with which she frames her parents' 117 letters and telegrams from 1954 to 1963 illustrates the complexity of memory woven around silences and unanswered questions. These questions are the fractures left in the aftermath of a repressive authoritarian regime that has parallels throughout Latin America. In this way, the story of the Tavárez Mirabal family is germane to broader conversations about trauma, healing and memory in post-dictatorial societies. Most significantly, it is the gripping, universally human story of a family that finds strength, courage and life in the ties that unite them. It invites us to reflect upon the essential, life-giving role of interpersonal relationships in the face of seemingly unbearable terror. By revealing Minerva and Manolo as flesh-and-blood human beings with faults, shortcomings and fears, the personal letters and memoir in this volume make their courage more accessible to readers who may be asking how one manages to resist in the midst of suffocating repression.

Minerva Mirabal and Manolo Tavárez

Dominican-American novelist Julia Álvarez introduced Minerva Mirabal and her three sisters, Patria, Dedé, and María Teresa, to a broad English-speaking public with her 1994 novel *In the Time of the Butterflies*. The novel has inspired book club readings across the country, appears on course syllabi from middle school through college, and was the basis for Mariano Barroso's 2001 film and Caridad Svich's 2011 theatrical adaptation with the same title. The word "Butterflies" / "*Mariposas*" refers to the sisters' codenames in the underground. (Minerva was *Mariposa 1*.) While they have raised awareness about the Mirabal sisters and have captured the public's imagination about "the Butterflies," the novel and its adaptations, along with other literary works such as Mario Vargas Llosa's *The Feast of the Goat / La fiesta del chivo* (2000) and Junot Díaz's *The Brief Wondrous Life of Oscar Wao* (2007) have helped form the myth surrounding Minerva's persona, while overlooking Manolo's integral role as her partner in all things.[1] In fact, the English-language bibliography on Manolo Tavárez is scant. As Minou argues, in order to understand her parents and their activism, it is essential to understand how deeply connected they were to each other on many levels: emotionally, intellectually, philosophically, and politically. Their personal correspondence reveals these deep bonds.

But who were they? Who was the Minerva behind the image of the "Butterfly," the "Mami" who is etched in Minou's memory? Who was the person whose idealized image appears in murals, busts and on national currency? Who was Manolo, "Papi," that strong, reassuring presence who, after Minerva's death, kept her memory alive through bedtime stories and songs? Who was the husband and father behind the charismatic revolutionary, whose words, leadership, and activism form part of the Dominican historical narrative?

María Argentina Minerva Mirabal Reyes de Tavárez was born on March 13, 1926, in Ojo de Agua to Enrique Mirabal Fernández and Mercedes (Chea) Reyes Camilo. Her father was a merchant, and the family owned agricultural land. Her primary education began at the community's rural school. Beginning in the fourth grade, she attended Immaculate Conception, a private

---

[1] These are the primary works in English. Films include Cecilia Domeyko's documentary *Code Name: Butterflies,* Accent Media, 2008, and Juan Delancer's feature film *Trópico de sangre,* Maya Entertainment, 2010. The Spanish-language bibliography on the Mirabal sisters is much more extensive.

boarding school in La Vega. She would graduate with a diploma in philosophy and letters in 1946. It was during these years that she developed the political awareness that cemented her opposition to the dictatorship, largely through friendships with members of a clandestine opposition movement called the Juventud Democrática (Democratic Youth). Minou tells us that from an early age, her mother "stood out for her intelligence, curiosity, social awareness, rebellious nature, and her deep love of reading and studying."[2] Minerva's sister Dedé describes her in her 2009 memoir *Vivas en su jardín. La verdadera historia de las hermanas Mirabal y su lucha por la libertad* (*Alive in Their Garden: The True Story of the Mirabal Sisters and Their Struggle for Freedom*). She writes that their father, Enrique Mirabal, "who knew well and feared [Minerva's] ideas," forced her to suspend her studies and come home between 1944 and 1945, when the Democratic Youth was being formed.[3] (Minerva would graduate in 1946.) During that time, Minerva frequented a bookstore in the nearby town of San Francisco de Macorís whose owner was known to be in opposition to Trujillo, and she obtained a wide variety of books and other literature from friends including Violeta Martínez and Brunilda Soñé. She exchanged ideas with them and other friends who were involved in the Democratic Youth.[4] Soñé, Minerva's schoolmate, led a branch of that group in La Vega. Biographer William Galván relates that she brought back political literature from her frequent trips to the capital and shared it with Minerva. Through this connection, Minerva became a remote supporter of this political organization and similar ones in the capital.[5] In 1949 anti-Trujillo activist Pericles Franco, also a member of the Democratic Youth, heard about Minerva, undoubtedly from their web of mutual acquaintances, and wanted to meet her. By several accounts, they shared a deep friendship and mutual admiration, though not as romantic as some suggest. Friend Emma Rodríguez recalls frequent conversations with Minerva and Pericles about many topics, including politics.[6] Pericles was a known *antitrujillista* (person in opposition to Trujillo), and this friendship, along with Minerva's frequent critical remarks about Trujillo, placed her on the regime's watchlist. She drew increas-

---

2   Minou Tavárez Mirabal, *Mañana te escribiré otra vez. Minerva y Manolo. Cartas.* (Santo Domingo: Editorial Santillana, 2014), 290. My translation.
3   Dedé Mirabal, *Vivas en su jardín. La verdadera historia de las hermanas Mirabal y su lucha por la libertad.* (New York: Vintage Español, Random House, 2009), 63.
4   William Galván, *Minerva Mirabal. Historia de una heroína* (Santo Domingo: Comisión Permanente de Efemérides Patrias, 2011), 113 and 139; Mirabal, *Vivas,* 67.
5   Galván, *Minerva,* 113.
6   Mirabal, *Vivas,* 67; Galván, *Minerva,* 151–52.

ing suspicion when she resisted Trujillo's overtures to meet her personally at a series of parties between July and October, 1949. This is particularly true of her now legendary confrontation with Trujillo at a dance in San Cristóbal on October 12 of that year. This confrontation confirmed her unwavering opposition to the regime.[7]

Most popular accounts of Minerva's life suggest that her trouble with the regime began when she rejected Trujillo while dancing with him at this event. The typical narrative is that she met the dictator's sexual advances with a slap in the face and subsequently became a "political opponent" that Trujillo felt "a relentless need to humiliate."[8] In interviews for Cecilia Domeyko's 2008 documentary *Code Name: Butterflies,* both Minou and her aunt Dedé explain that Minerva's "slap in the face" toward Trujillo was not a physical affront, but rather a verbal rejection, an assertion of her own dignity and agency.[9] Many see Trujillo's subsequent pursuit of the Mirabal family as retaliation for this affront to his vanity and manhood. Some narratives sensationalize the episode for its sexual implications. While this public affront to his image was undoubtedly embarrassing for Trujillo, it does not explain the relentlessness with which he pursued Minerva and her family for the next eleven years. By taking a wider look at Minerva's political awakening and activism, within the broader context of anti-Trujillo resistance movements and gender norms at the time, we can more fully appreciate the threat that she posed to his regime and why the October 1949 confrontation was significant but was only part of a much larger dynamic. In short, it allows us to see Minerva's agency more clearly.

Ample evidence suggests that by October 1949, Minerva was already under surveillance for her personal associations with members of the Democratic Youth and that she had come under scrutiny on previous occasions.[10] According to the accounts of several relatives and friends, her conversation with Trujillo during that dance was political. Galván relates that at one point they discussed Pericles Franco. The accounts of that conversation vary slightly regarding the specifics, but they concur that the dictator asked Minerva about her interest in politics—or perhaps his politics—to which she expressed ei-

---

7   Galván, *Minerva,* 133–37; 148; 151–52.
8   Nancy Robinson, "Women's Political Participation in the Dominican Republic: The Case of the Mirabal Sisters," *Caribbean Quarterly,* 52, nos. 2–1 (2006): 177.
9   *Code Name: Butterflies / Nombre secreto: Mariposas,* directed, written, and produced by Cecilia Domeyko. Accent Media (2008), minutes 21:35–22:17 .
10 Galvan 139, based on testimony from Minerva's friend at the time, Emma Rodríguez.

ther disinterest or disapproval. Trujillo asked what would happen if he sent his young supporters to "conquer" her, using the word *conquistar,* which has clear sexual connotations but could also mean to win her over and subjugate her politically. She reportedly responded, "And what if I conquer them?"[11] This was the verbal slap in the face that has become legendary and that has been recast in fictional accounts as a physical slap in the face in response to sexual advances. The significance of the confrontation in San Cristóbal was not simply that Minerva rejected Trujillo's seductive suggestions, but that, in whatever words she used when she stopped dancing and confronted him in the middle of the dance floor, she confirmed her political opposition and demonstrated that she would not acquiesce to him. This was a time when women of diverse political inclinations had become increasingly active in politics, education, and public life, but they generally showed deference in line with patriarchal norms. Now it was clear that this intelligent, widely admired young woman from an important family in Salcedo was part of the opposition and was intent on standing her ground.

This confrontation prompted her father's arrest two days later. He and subsequently Minerva were accused of plotting against the regime. Enrique Mirabal would never fully recover from the injuries sustained while in prison and would die less than three years later at their home in Ojo de Agua. During the search of the Mirabal home, authorities found at least one letter from Pericles Franco. They arrested Minerva, Violeta Martínez, Emma Rodríguez, and Brunilda Soñé. All were interrogated separately at Fortaleza Ozuma in the capital and were asked about Minerva, her relationship with Pericles, and her reported displays of anti-Trujillo sentiment, such as refusing to toast to his health.[12] Minou tells us that Minerva refused to meet with Trujillo or to write him a letter of apology for the October 12 incident.[13] Minerva was placed under house arrest. She was later detained at a hotel in the capital, since women were not typically imprisoned for political reasons during that time. Her mother insisted on accompanying her. She and her parents were detained again in 1951 for a period of some weeks.

William Galván recounts that Pericles had written to Minerva from exile, asking her to join him, but that she refused to receive the letter out of

---

11 See Mirabal, *Vivas,* 99–101; Galván, *Minerva,* 147–48; Rafael Taveras, "Entrevista con Rafael (Fafa) Taveras, Comunicador," *El día.* YouTube. Nov. 23, 2018. www.youtube.com/watch?v=4JgUzNtSMYg.
12 Galván, *Minerva,* 150–151.
13 Tavárez Mirabal, *Mañana,* 291.

suspicion regarding the individual who was to deliver it. He points to this as the end of their relationship.[14] Regardless, it is abundantly clear that the Minerva who publicly rejected Trujillo's advances in 1949 was not only a source of public embarrassment, but also a canary in a mine shaft, one of many young people in a growing resistance that Trujillo rightfully perceived as a threat.

Minerva's opposition to Trujillo solidified through her study of law at the university and her intimate relationship with fellow law student Manolo Tavárez. The following passage from Minou's biographical glossary summarizes these significant moments in her mother's adult life. I provide supplementary details in brackets:

> In 1952 [Minerva] began studying Law at the University of Santo Domingo after having convinced her parents, who had opposed the idea. However, she was blocked from registering for classes the following year. She was forced to write to the dictator and ask for his permission to enroll. She [met Manuel Aurelio Tavárez Justo while on vacation in Jarabacoa in 1952], and they married in 1955. [Minerva would graduate *summa cum laude* in 1957 but would be denied a license to practice law because of her opposition to the regime.] The couple had two children: Minou and Manolo Tavárez Mirabal. Minerva and Manolo conceived of the idea to form the nation's largest anti-Trujillo resistance movement, which they then directed. Minerva suggested the organization's name, the Movimiento Revolucionario 14 de Junio (14 of June Revolutionary Movement), in honor of the martyrs of the revolutionary expedition of June 14, 1959.[15] The movement was discovered, and she was twice more arrested, sentenced, and released from prison as part of the plot to ultimately kill her. Trujillo went so far as to state publicly that the only two problems facing his regime were the Catholic Church and Minerva and her family. On November 25, 1960, on the way back from visiting her husband Manolo in prison in Puerto Plata, she was abducted and beaten to death along with her sisters Patria and María Teresa, and the driver that was with them, Rufino de la Cruz.

The biographical glossary that Minou provides in *Mañana te escribiré otra vez* also contains a substantial entry for her father. I provide the entry in full with supplementary details in brackets:

---

14 Galván, *Minerva*, 152.
15 For information about the failed June 14, 1959, expedition, see the second paragraph in the section titled "Resistance and the 14 of June Movement" in this introduction.

Manuel Aurelio (Manolo) Tavárez Justo (Jan. 2, 1931–Dec. 21, 1963)—Attorney, leader and revolutionary. Together with his wife Minerva Mirabal, he established the 14 of June Movement, which he led. [Manolo was the eldest of five children born to Manuel F. Tavárez Ramos and Josefa Justo Rousseau.] He completed his primary education in Montecristi and high school in Santo Domingo, graduating from the Escuela Normal de Santo Domingo. From an early age, he opposed the dictatorial regime oppressing the Dominican Republic. In the late 1940s his increasing awareness led to his involvement in opposition groups stemming from the Democratic Youth. He finished law school in 1954 but for family-related reasons was unable to graduate with his class. He graduated on February 27, 1955. He was imprisoned from January 14, 1960 until July 26, 1961. His courage and bravery in the face of the horrific tortures endured during those months in La 40 and La Victoria[16] helped strengthen his political leadership. As soon as he was released from prison following the tyrant's execution, he launched an intense political campaign that spoke to the masses. As head of the [14 of June] Movement, he decided to form the political party named the Agrupación Política 14 de Junio (14 of June Political Association). The overthrow of Juan Bosch, the first democratically elected president in over three decades, compelled him to lead an armed uprising in the Central Mountain Range on November 28, 1963, demanding the return to constitutional rule. Three weeks later, trusting in the de facto government's promise to spare his life and the lives of his companions in arms, they decided to turn themselves in. They were viciously shot dead in the mountains known as Las Manaclas in the early morning hours of December 21. This event prompted the resignation of one of the three members of the government council known as the Triumvirate. Manolo's political speeches have been transcribed in various publications. As was his will, his remains rest alongside Minerva's. They are buried in the garden of the Mirabal Sisters House Museum [in Conuco].

---

16   La 40 ("La Cuarenta") was a clandestine torture center near Santo Domingo, then Trujillo City. The hundreds of collaborators (called *catorcistas*) arrested during the January 1960 crackdown on the 14 of June Revolutionary Movement were tortured and interrogated there before being sent to La Victoria National Penitentiary, also in Santo Domingo/Trujillo City to serve their long sentences.

The Geography of Minerva and Manolo's Lives

The Dominican Republic occupies the eastern 60 percent of the Caribbean island that the Spanish called Hispaniola. Haiti occupies the western 40 percent. The events described in this book took place in three primary locations within the Dominican Republic. Both families lived in the country's northern Cibao region, which begins at the Central Mountain Range (Cordillera Central), extends north into the fertile agricultural lands of the Cibao Valley (along the Yaque del Norte and Yuna Rivers), and rises again into the Septentrional Mountain Range (Cordillera Septentrional) before meeting the Atlantic Ocean. The Tavárez Justo family lived in the northwesternmost corner of this region, in the coastal city of Montecristi. The Mirabal Reyes family lived a little more than one hundred miles southeast of Montecristi in the Cibao Valley, in Ojo de Agua, just east of Salcedo. They had substantial agricultural holdings; produced coffee, cacao and other crops; and Minerva's father was a successful merchant and a well-respected member of the community. Minerva and Manolo's letters often reference visits to one another's family homes, a trip made by car in a few hours. Both Minerva and Manolo studied

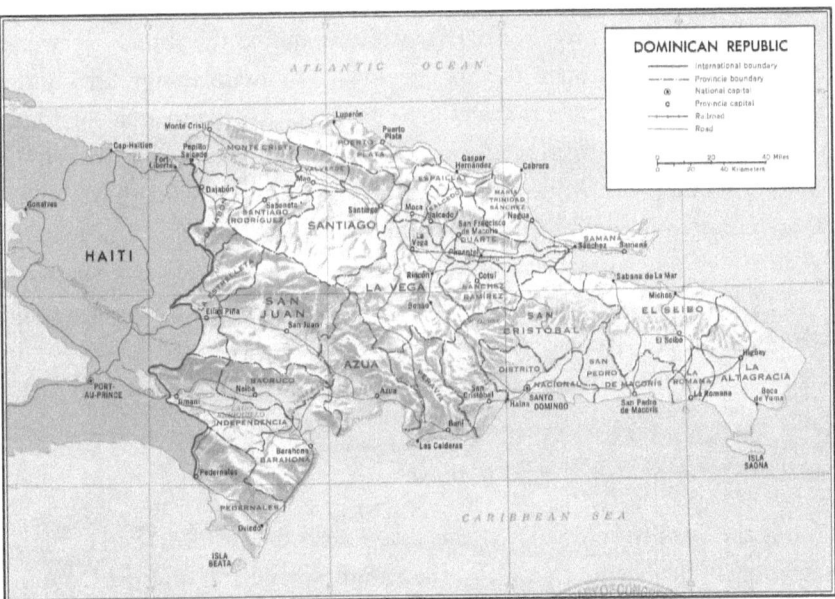

Figure 0.6. Map of the Dominican Republic. United States Central Intelligence Agency. *Dominican Republic*. [Washington, D.C.: Central Intelligence Agency, 1970] Map. https://www.loc.gov/item/2011586142/.

law at the University of Santo Domingo in the nation's capital, which is situated in the center of the country's southern, Caribbean coast, approximately 170 miles from Montecristi and eighty-five miles from Conuco. The capital city was called Ciudad Trujillo (Trujillo City) at the time, in honor of the dictator. After graduating with his law degree, Manolo set up his practice in Montecristi, and Minerva joined him there once they were married. Minerva moved between her home with Manolo in Montecristi, her mother's home in Conuco, and rented rooms in Santo Domingo as she finished her law degree while also having their two children and suffering tremendous stress from living under constant surveillance by the regime. In January 1960, Minerva, Manolo, and hundreds of other collaborators in the 14 of June Revolutionary Movement were imprisoned and tortured in and near Santo Domingo, first at the clandestine torture center called La 40 and later at La Victoria National Penitentiary. Once Minerva and María Teresa were released from prison, they and their sisters Patria and Dedé often traveled the eighty-five miles from their mother's home in Conuco to visit their husbands (including Patria's husband, Pedro) in prison. These circumstances took a foreboding turn in November 1960 when Manolo and María Teresa's husband Leandro were abruptly transferred from La Victoria to a prison in Puerto Plata, on the north central Atlantic coast. The transfer required the sisters to traverse the winding roads through the Septentrional Mountain Range, setting the stage for the brutal murder that would be portrayed as an auto accident. Once Manolo was released from prison in 1961, he lived in a rented apartment in Santo Domingo with Minou and other family members, though his political activism required him to travel, including to New York City. In 1963, he led an armed resistance that was captured and assassinated in Las Manaclas, in the Central Mountain Range. Today, the remains of both Minerva and Manolo lie at the Mirabal Sisters House Museum in Conuco (Salcedo), in what is now called Mirabal Sisters Province (Provincia Hermanas Mirabal).

SETTING THE STAGE FOR TRUJILLO

During the Spanish colonial period (1492–1822 and 1861–1865) and until the beginning of the twentieth century, the economy in what is now the Dominican Republic was based largely on ranching, subsistence farming, and some limited exports. There was a widespread practice of communal land tenure in the interior, particularly in the Cibao. Feudal-like haciendas under the control of regional strong-arm leaders called *caudillos* dominated the southeast.

Spanish colonial rule was followed by a brutal military occupation when Haiti seized control from 1822 until the War for Dominican Independence in 1844. The emerging nation suffered a brief relapse into Spanish colonial rule and decades of power struggles among military caudillos and short-lived authoritarian regimes, whose self-serving economic schemes impoverished masses of small-scale farmers and laborers and bankrupted the government. Their authoritarian rule was often justified as protection against another Haitian invasion. During the period of the Second Republic (1865–1916), the national government was in a constant state of flux, with a dizzying number of military uprisings, civil wars, revolutions, and fighting among regional caudillos, armed with their own militias. The country lacked the necessary infrastructure and political stability to develop a stable and integrated national economy.[17]

During the final decades of the nineteenth century, U.S. investment began trickling into the island nation, as it did throughout other parts of Latin America. Through the "dollar diplomacy" of Theodore Roosevelt, and in line with the Roosevelt Corollary to the Monroe Doctrine, the U.S. assumed control over the Dominican Customs Service in 1904 and during the subsequent years shifted the island nation's foreign debt from European to U.S. investors.[18] Amid continued political instability and in the context of World War I, the U.S. Marines first occupied the Dominican Republic from 1916 until 1924[19] with the purpose of protecting U.S. investments and citizens on the island, and keeping Germany from establishing bases there. As Eric Roorda explains, the occupation government carried out reforms aimed at modernizing the country, reforms that transformed the Dominican economy, institutions, armed forces, education, public health, and society.[20] These modernizing reforms required centralized control over towns and rural areas alike, which was realized through the outlawing of gun ownership by private citizens, mili-

---

17 For an in-depth discussion of the economic situation during this period see Richard Lee Turits, *Foundations of Despotism: Peasants, the Trujillo Regime, and Modernity in Dominican History* (Stanford: Stanford University Press, 2003), 25–64.
18 Eric Paul Roorda, *The Dictator Next Door: The Good Neighbor Policy and the Trujillo Regime in the Dominican Republic, 1930–1945* (Durham, NC: Duke University Press, 1998), 13–14.
19 The second occupation was in 1965.
20 Roorda, *Dictator*, 17. See also Ellen D. Tillman, *Dollar Diplomacy by Force: Nation-Building and Resistance in the Dominican Republic* (Durham, NC: Duke University Press, 2016); and Micah Wright, "Building an Occupation: Puerto Rican Laborers in the Dominican Republic, 1916–1924," *Labor: Studies in Working-Class History of the Americas*, 13, no. 3 (2016): 83–103.

tary patrols of cities and towns, the confiscation of peasant land, the killing of resisters, surveillance by military intelligence officers, and censorship of speech and the press.[21] These mechanisms of repression would continue and flourish under the Trujillo dictatorship.

The occupation also transformed gender relations. Girls had unprecedented access to education. Women entered public life in new ways as educators and workers in areas such as public assistance and became increasingly active in political, pro-sovereignty campaigns. The most significant organization of women in the public sphere was the Acción Feminista Dominicana (Dominican Feminist Action), whose work and public engagement "provided the foundation from which the Trujillo regime [would later involve] women in the politics of the dictatorship through the rhetoric of maternalism and appropriate modernity," explains Elizabeth Manley.[22] This mobilization of women impacted domestic life and challenged patriarchal ideals surrounding family dynamics and authority. Maja Horn finds that Dominican nationalists wrestled with ideas about masculinity and femininity in response to these and other destabilizing changes. They constructed a vision of modern Dominican nationhood that rejected certain Anglo notions of secular modernity in favor of patriarchal ideals.[23]

The U.S. occupation segued into the provisional presidency of Juan Bautista Vicini Burgos in 1922, followed by the election of Horacio Vásquez Lajara in 1924. President Vásquez's perceived ineffectiveness and unconstitutional move to extend the presidential term, amid an economic crisis brought by the fall in sugar prices, provoked a rebellion in 1930. Leading the rebellion was politician and lawyer Rafael Estrella Ureña, who conspired with Rafael Trujillo, then leading commander of the armed forces, to seize control of the government. Though Estrella was initially declared acting president, Trujillo would win the 1930 election, thus beginning three decades of authoritarian

---

21 Roorda, *Dictator*, 17.
22 Elizabeth Manley, *The Paradox of Paternalism: Women and the Politics of Authoritarianism in the Dominican Republic* (Gainesville: University Press of Florida, 2017), 23–24.
23 Maja Horn, *Masculinity after Trujillo: The Politics of Gender in Dominican Literature* (Gainesville: University Press of Florida, 2014), 27–28. Manley explains that "many of the Dominican lettered class—men and women—sought both an assertion of national sovereignty and a return to more traditional gender divisions of labor that extended to a critique of women's expanding social roles beyond the home" (*Paradox*, 34). See also Manley 30–31. For an in-depth discussion of the intersection of gender, race, and national identity, see April Mayes, *The Mulatto Republic: Class, Race and Dominican National Identity* (Gainesville: University Press of Florida, 2014), 122–124.

rule known as the Trujillato, the Era of Trujillo. He would build a repressive state with the compliance of a generation of Dominicans in the context of rising Dominican nationalism.

The Era of Trujillo

Born in 1892 to a lower-middle-class family of Spanish, Cuban, and Haitian descent, Rafael Leónidas Trujillo Molina grew up in San Cristóbal, just west of Santo Domingo. He received an elementary education before working as a telephone operator and then supervisor on a sugar plantation. In 1918, during the first U.S. occupation, he joined the Dominican National Guard and was trained by U.S. Marines. In spite of accusations of criminal misconduct, he quickly rose through the ranks and was named general in 1927 and subsequently chief of the National Police and later commander of the armed forces. In 1930 he conspired to withhold military support from President Horacio Vásquez, permitting the coup that would overtake the government. He was elected president in 1930.

During Trujillo's first year in power, Hurricane San Zenón decimated Santo Domingo. This would prove to be what Lauren Derby calls "a seminal moment [. . .] in the foundational myth of the Era of Trujillo."[24] The grand avenues, modern infrastructure, and impressive buildings that Trujillo ordered for the reconstruction of the capital recast the oldest city in the New World as, in Trujillo's words, the "clean, magnificent, and modern"[25] capital of a nation emerging onto the international stage. In 1936, the Dominican National Congress renamed the capital Ciudad Trujillo (Trujillo City). The hurricane's aftermath and reconstruction altered public expectations for the exercise of state authority.[26] Until Trujillo's assassination in 1961, he maintained unrivaled authority in the Dominican Republic, albeit periodically behind the facade of puppet presidents. Among his many titles were "El Jefe" ("the Chief" or "the Boss"), "The Benefactor," and "Father of the New Nation."

The thirty-one-year "Era of Trujillo" (1930–1961) was among the most

---

24 Lauren Derby, *The Dictator's Seduction: Politics and the Popular Imagination in the Era of Trujillo* (Durham: Duke University Press, 2009), 69.
25 Trujillo, quoted by Hector Minaya in "Dictador llegó al colmo de cambiar el nombre de la capital por Ciudad Trujillo," *El Nacional*, May 26, 2016. Web. https://elnacional.com.do/dictador-llego-al-colmo-de-cambiar-el-nombre-de-la-capital-por-ciudad-trujillo.
26 Derby, *Dictator's Seduction*, 81–82.

ruthless twentieth-century dictatorships in Latin America. In many ways the Trujillato fit the pattern of U.S.-backed military dictatorships in the region, but its grip on the island country was particularly transformative, pervasive, and terrifying. Recent scholarship seeks to understand the regime's rise and longevity as the result of "informed consent and exchange [with the Dominican public] rather than simply coercion and violence."[27] Lauren Derby argues that the theatrical nature of Trujillo's exercise of authority, show of "caring paternalism" and promise of upward mobility for the previously disenfranchised allowed him to secure power and rule "with an iron fist."[28] Under Trujillo, consolidated state power reached into the Dominican countryside and into the lives of its rural majority. As Richard Lee Turits finds, the promise of modernization and progress went hand-in-hand with the promotion of "a new Dominican identity based on anti-Haitianism and in line with traditional urban and elite notions."[29] A critical moment in this campaign was the 1937 massacre of Haitians and Haitian-Dominicans living in the Dajabón region, on the Dominican shores of the Masacre River forming the border with Haiti. The area was a fluid borderland characterized by social, economic, and cultural intermixing. The massacre was an assertion of Dominican authority to enforce a border agreement between Trujillo and Haitian President Sténio Vincent. It was also a rejection of Afro-Haitian culture and blackness in favor of a white-centered, Hispanic national identity.[30] While the extent of the massacre is unknown, and Trujillo supporters cite numbers in the hundreds, recent estimates place the carnage at more than twelve thousand lives during the first week, with likely thousands more during subsequent months.[31] In spite of international condemnation, the regime went unpunished, and Trujillo managed to justify the slaughter as an act of national defense against "the penetration, pacific but permanent and stubborn, of the worst Haitian element into our territory."[32] His supporters justified the massacre as the long overdue establishment of Dominican sovereignty, an "unfortunate"[33] incident necessary for national progress.

---

27 Elizabeth Manley, "Intimate Violations: Women and the *Ajusticiamiento* of Dictator Rafael Trujillo, 1944–1961." *The Americas* 69.1 (2012): 65, n. 10.
28 Derby, *Dictator's Seduction*, 92, 257–60.
29 Turits, *Foundations*, 178.
30 Roorda, *Dictator*, 129.
31 Turits, *Foundations*, 162.
32 Turits, *Foundations*, 168. Turits cites José Israel Cuello, ed. *Documentos del conflicto dominico-haitiano de 1937* (Santo Domingo: Taller, 1985), 456, 466.
33 Salomón Sanz, Jr., in the documentary film *Trujillo: 31 años de historia perdida*. Fundación

It is worth noting that Trujillo announced his intention to eliminate Haitians from Dominican territory at a party given in his honor by Isabel Mayer Tavárez, first wife of Manolo Tavárez's father. Mayer was a close friend and supporter of Trujillo. Years later, U.S. news media reported rumors that Mayer was among those who encouraged the action, complaining that Haitians were stealing cattle from her land in the border region.[34] Whether or not this rumor is true, Mayer was likely aware of Trujillo's plan.[35] A few years later, she would become president of the Comisión Nacional de la Frontera (National Border Commission), whose purpose was to promote "progress" and white Dominican culture in the region.

Trujillo was the mythical father of this national project. With the border clearly defined, he began "taming the countryside," as Turits describes, establishing state control over rural areas and legitimating his regime through various projects, programs, and regulations. On the one hand, land distribution and other public assistance programs improved the rural economy. On the other hand, they were accompanied by increased state surveillance, intervention, and direct control through mechanisms such as "[f]ixed plots, known addresses, surveyed lands, nucleation of dispersed people, the linkage of settlements to national systems of transportation and communication, and expanding rural services, schools, and bureaucracy."[36] Turits explains that supporters (*trujillistas*) accepted this trade-off, crediting state consolidation with ending the volatile period of caudillo rule, establishing public order, and building critical infrastructure in both urban and rural areas, leading to economic development, national autonomy, and the elimination of foreign debt.

Trujillo's paternalistic state reached deep into Dominican homes, providing material assistance, access to education and healthcare, moral guidance, and apparent protection from "menacing" outside threats, including Haitians, neocolonialism, and communists. Manley finds that the regime complemented its paternalistic authority by promoting active participation among women in ways that reflected their traditional familial roles as caretakers. It capitalized on their recent deployment in the public sphere through

---

Rafael Leónidas Trujillo Molina. (Unicaribe of Florida, 2010), 1:00:20–1:00:37.
34 Emilia Peyrera, "Auge y caída de Isabel Mayer, la incondicional de Trujillo." *Diario Libre*, Dec. 13, 2018. Web. https://www.diariolibre.com/revista/cultura/auge-y-caida-de-isabel-mayer-la-incondicional-de-trujillo-JM11596618. Peyrera draws extensively from the book *Hombres y mujeres de Trujillo. Isabel Mayer*, by José Abigail Cruz Infante (Santo Domingo: Argos, 2013).
35 Manley, *Paradox*, 51.
36 Turits, *Foundations*, 181–82.

earlier movements such as the Acción Feminista Dominicana, enlisting them to carry out the regime's social and educational programs. Framing women's participation within a discourse of maternalism, the regime further solidified its role as provider and protector of the nation.[37] At the same time, as Turits explains, women gained juridical equality and greater legal protection from abuse and harassment. Men were expected to provide for their children, including those born to mistresses, which was common, and the value placed on outward demonstrations of respect was particularly high in respect to women.[38]

Elizabeth Manley explains that with the advent of women's suffrage in 1942, Dominican women were further "integrated into Trujillo's party machinery as engines of community engagement." Through the new Sección Feminista of the one official political party, the Partido Dominicano, these *feministas trujillistas* held public office; carried out social assistance programs; proclaimed the moral, democratic, and pragmatic virtues of the regime; and testified to those virtues on the international stage. "They promoted the mythic peace, prosperity, and stability of the Trujillo regime," particularly as a bulwark against communism in the midst of the Cold War. But Manley also finds that women's growing political (especially international) engagement paved the way for women who opposed Trujillo to organize protests and denounce the regime from exile in Puerto Rico, Cuba, New York, and elsewhere.[39]

Trujillo was omnipresent in Dominican life. Streets, communities, plazas, and organizations were renamed in his honor and that of his family. Monuments and busts throughout the country honored the Benefactor, the Father of the New Nation. His image watched over daily life in many Dominican homes through an all but obligatory placard that reminded families that in their homes "God and Trujillo" ruled. The regime controlled the media. School children were taught to celebrate the wondrous accomplishments of the Father of the New Nation and to laud him for his dedication to the Dominican people and for ushering in a new era in Dominican history.

Moreover, Trujillo deeply pervaded Dominican life through a masterfully leveraged political economy of favors and a culture of patronage. The Benefactor fostered a general sense of indebtedness and encouraged compliance by

---

37 Manley, *Paradox*, 31. For a thorough discussion of this dynamic as it evolved over the decades of the Trujillato, see *Paradox*, Chapters 2 and 3.
38 Turits, *Foundations*, 221–22.
39 Manley, *Paradox*, 62–63.

giving seemingly generous gifts to the public, to families, and to individuals.[40] Meanwhile, he unethically accumulated vast personal wealth for himself and for his family, nearly as much as the nation's GDP, including abundant liquid assets, effective control over 75 percent of Dominican industrial production, and "estates [constituting] approximately 9 percent of the nation's occupied land."[41]

The terrifying underbelly of the modern Dominican state was a shadow state that became the eyes and ears of the regime. With roots in the first U.S. occupation, this web of intelligence expanded until it seemed omnipresent and almost supernatural.[42] Multiple state entities, particularly the armed forces, grew their ranks of spies and intelligence agents, whom Trujillo consolidated into the Servicio de Inteligencia Militar (SIM, or Military Intelligence Service) in the mid-1950s. The SIM patrolled the streets in Volkswagen Beetles popularly known as *cepillos*, which "swept" the populace clean of opposition. The Beetles would come to symbolize the regime's nefarious overreach. The constant threat of denunciation coerced Dominicans into compliance, and the state controlled individuals' personal lives through the issuance or refusal of identity cards, professional licenses, passports, and permission to enroll in university. It was a society in which accusations of anti-Trujillo sentiment could and did result in loss of employment, public shaming, social marginalization, loss of property, financial ruin, denial of the right to travel abroad or enroll in university, incarceration, torture, and death (not uncommonly under "mysterious" or "accidental" circumstances). Would-be opposers were often deterred by the threat that their punishment would extend to their families.[43] The regime-controlled newspaper *El Caribe* (*The Caribbean*) featured a "Foro Público" ("Public Forum") in which individuals (even longtime trujillistas) were denounced for real or fabricated offenses.[44] These denunciations often led to loss of employment, financial ruin, and social marginaliza-

---

40 Derby, *Dictator's Seduction*, 259.
41 Turits, *Foundations*, 5.
42 For a more in-depth discussion, see Derby, *Dictator's Seduction*, 209–11.
43 One of many examples is the family of Carmen Natalia Martínez Bonilla, who was instrumental in supporting the activities of the Juventud Democrática. Her father and siblings were unjustly fired, one brother was expelled from school, she was denied a passport, and the family was forced into exile. See Manley, *Paradox*, 98–99 and p. 267, n. 14.
44 Former editor of *El Caribe* Germán E. Ornes provides a detailed, insider's look at the Trujillo regime and its many methods for coercing Dominicans into compliance. He devotes an entire chapter to the press. See Germán E. Ornes, *Trujillo: Little Caesar of the Caribbean* (New York: Thomas Nelson & Sons, 1958).

tion. The Mirabal and Tavárez families suffered all of these forms of repression and reprisal.

In sum, Dominicans lived in a state of constant tension. On the one hand, they enjoyed benefits from new infrastructure and public services, hope for upward mobility, greater economic security (unless one fell out of favor with the regime), some sense of protection from civilian crime, "tranquility," and public order.[45] But hanging in the balance was the real and constant threat of loss and physical harm, including for one's family, friends, and even acquaintances. It is frequently stated that, by the late 1950s, nearly every Dominican family had suffered some loss (or knew someone who had) at the hands of the regime. One's ability to lead a relatively peaceful life hinged on his or her compliance or apparent compliance with the regime, as carefully monitored by the omnipresent eyes of the Chief. That being said, cells of resistance did emerge and evolved in various parts of the country and among Dominicans in exile.

Resistance and the 14 of June Movement

The global political climate of the 1940s fostered several opposition movements on the island and among Dominicans in exile, but the regime managed to truncate them or hold them at bay. In 1946, under international pressure, Trujillo briefly allowed opposition parties, including the Partido Socialista Popular (Popular Socialist Party), which had initially formed in Cuba, and the Partido Democrático Revolucionario Dominicano (Dominican Revolutionary Democratic Party), a center-left social democratic party that had formed clandestinely in 1944 and whose youth branch, the Juventud Democrática, would grow to outnumber its parent organization. The engagement of young people in opposition parties is not surprising given the expansion of university education, the recent integration of women into national politics, waves of anti-fascism coming out of World War II, and the significant presence of exiles from the Spanish Civil War, a number of whom were professors. This political aperture was brief, and in less than a year, the regime began to violently pursue party leaders. Several went into exile and continued their opposition from abroad.[46]

---

45 Turits, *Foundations*, 223.
46 "La resistencia del Exilio Dominicano. La solidaridad internacional." Museo Memorial de la Resistencia Dominicana. Accessed May 15, 2020. http://www.museodelaresistencia.com/la-resistencia-del-exilio-dominicano-la-solidaridad-internacional. See also

With the advent of the Cold War in 1947, Trujillo and his supporters began labeling his critics as communists and subversives. Two planned military invasions by Dominican exiles and international sympathizers—the Cayo Confites Expedition of 1947 and the Luperón Expedition of 1949—were discovered and quashed, the former with U.S. assistance. Under international pressure, several of the survivors were eventually released from prison and would continue their opposition from exile. Other expeditions and conspiracies in the mid-fifties were also discovered and their members arrested. Some would go on to participate in what would be a turning point in anti-Trujillo resistance: the Expedition of Constanza, Maimón, and Estero Hondo in June 1959.

The rise of leftist governments in the greater Caribbean, and in particular the Cuban Revolution in January 1959, were definitive in mobilizing significant Dominican opposition movements. On January 6, 1959, days after the communist victory in Cuba, Minerva, Manolo, María Teresa, and María Teresa's husband, Leandro Guzmán, were among the guests at a Three Kings' Day luncheon at the home of Josefina Ricart and Yuyo D'Alessandro. As those present at that Three Kings' Day gathering would later recall, it was Minerva who proposed that they immediately organize a resistance movement in the Dominican Republic, stating that if it could be done in Cuba, it could be done in their country too.[47] They began to recruit collaborators and would continue to do so throughout the following year. They would soon merge with parallel resistance movements and plot to overthrow the dictator.

The identities of those who hosted that January 6 gathering are significant, as they illustrate how the opposition had grown to include young people from prominent trujillista families. Josefina Ricart's sister Octavia was the first wife of Ramfis Trujillo, the dictator's son. Yuyo (Guido Emilio) D'Alessandro was Manolo's half nephew. Manolo's father, Manuel F. Tavárez, had previously been married to Isabel Mayer, with whom he had a daughter.[48] After divorcing him, Mayer became a prominent activist, politician and Trujillo supporter. She was the founding member of the Dominican Feminist Action, the

---

Museo Memorial de la Resistencia Dominicana, "Juventud Revolucionaria—Juventud Democrática (J.D.)." http://www.museodelaresistencia.com/juventud-revolucionaria-juventud-democratica-j-d.

47 Mirabal, *Vivas*, 150–51. Leandro Guzmán, *1J4. De espigas y de fuegos. Aportes para la memoria necesaria. Testimonios de un militante* (Santo Domingo: Editora de Colores, 1998), 67–68.

48 Carmen Isabel Tavárez Mayer (1912–1994). She married Guido D'Alessandro on May 17, 1930, the same year that Trujillo assumed the presidency.

first woman senator in the Dominican Republic, governor of Montecristi and Santiago, president of the National Border Commission, and a loyal, prominent trujillista. Isabel Mayer would soon become a persona non grata when it was revealed that her grandson was involved in the opposition. This was a defining characteristic of the growing underground resistance: it grew from within social and political circles close to the regime. Within that web of personal relationships, Manolo and Minerva began to emerge as leaders.

In March 1959, multiple pre-existing opposition movements among the Dominican diaspora in Venezuela, Puerto Rico, Cuba, and New York formed the Movimiento de Liberación Dominicana (Dominican Liberation Movement). Their objective was to topple Trujillo and install a government plan for political, economic, and social reform. With the support of the recently installed Castro regime, the revolutionaries trained in Cuba and from there launched an expedition of 198 freedom fighters scheduled to land on June 14 in three locations in the Dominican Republic: Maimón and Estero Hondo on the northern coast, and Constanza in the Central Mountain Range. A series of tragic circumstances led to their capture and execution. Survivors were interrogated, tortured, and then executed. The political agenda of the MLD would soon be taken up by the 14 of June Movement and political party.[49]

News of the failed expedition rallied clandestine antitrujillistas across the Dominican Republic and by many accounts mobilized them in an unprecedented way. Manolo's sister Emma recalls how Manolo and Minerva, who at the time were living in Montecristi, not far from Maimón and Estero Hondo, immediately began strategizing to make contact with and aid the revolutionaries, a plan that they aborted when the revolutionaries were executed.[50] However, Minerva, Manolo, and numerous other Dominicans, both on the island and abroad, continued to build their respective networks of collaborators and prepare to take action. At a time of economic crisis, high taxes, and high inflation, the political situation had reached its boiling point, and many Dominicans felt a greater sense of urgency. As Minerva's sister Dedé Mirabal recalls in her memoir, a broader, more heterogeneous group of Dominicans,

---

49 Brunilda Soñé, the Democratic Youth section leader who attended school with Minerva and shared political literature with her, participated in this movement. See Galván, *Minerva*, 113, for a description of their relationship.
50 Quoted in Mirabal, *Vivas*, 151. Emma Tavárez Justo's account was published in the December 9, 1974, issue of the magazine *¡Ahora!*.

including many young people and members of the Catholic Church, became actively involved in the resistance between 1959 and 1961.[51]

Several pockets of resistance emerged simultaneously throughout the country. One such group was the Unión de Grupos Independientes, later known as Los Panfleteros de Santiago because of their modus operandi: disseminating *panfletos* (pamphlets) with anti-Trujillo propaganda. The group of lower-middle-class youth was led by twenty-year-old Wenceslao (Wen) Guillen Gómez, known for his "extraordinary political clarity," his intellect, and love of learning, though a number of the panfleteros were minimally educated. The group aimed to destabilize the dictatorship through intensive opposition propaganda and by sabotaging official political events. Almost all members of the group were arrested, tortured in La 40, and hanged on January 29, 1960.[52]

Simultaneously, in July 1959, in Salcedo, Conuco, and Tenares, a small group of university students and seminarians began organizing a movement called Acción Clero Cultural. The founding members, Rafael (Fafa) Taveras, Antonio Ezequiel González, and Francisco Aníbal (Pachico) González had close ties to the Mirabal Reyes family. Antonio Ezequiel González Reyes was a first cousin on their mother's side. His mother was Chea's youngest sister, Lalía. His father was Ezequiel González Cruz, brother of Pedro González Cruz, Patria's husband. Francisco Aníbel (Pachico) González was another one of Pedro's nephews. Fafa Taveras was a close friend. He knew the Mirabal sisters from interactions among the families and neighbors. The group initially recruited collaborators among seminarians, university students, and local farmers to organize an assault on Trujillo under the guise of planning an event to thank the dictator for his leadership. Fafa Taveras explains that the false pretense was intended to divert attention away from the group's mobilization and outreach across the region and across the country. The movement grew substantially.

Several members of the González Mirabal and Mirabal Reyes families collaborated in the activities of Acción Clero Cultural. Patria and Pedro's home in Conuco was one site where collaborators made explosives and stored weapons. Patria's daughter Noris recalls that she and other family members helped

---

51 Mirabal, *Vivas,* 149. Regarding the growing sense of urgency see p. 152.
52 "Los Panfleteros de Santiago." Museo Memorial de la Resistencia Dominicana. Accessed May 15, 2020. http://www.museodelaresistencia.com/los-panfleteros-de-santiago.

assemble explosives in the family home.⁵³ Patria's teenaged son Nelson also collaborated, as did María Teresa. Fafa Taveras recalls that Minerva's involvement and leadership was significant. She recruited collaborators, coordinated communication, and leveraged her relative mobility to circulate information and materials. As one of few Dominican women who could drive, she transported weapons and materials for making explosives with the idea that a woman would be less suspect than a man.⁵⁴ The fact that she, a known enemy of Trujillo, operated under this assumption reveals how deeply ingrained gender roles were at the time.

Acción Clero Cultural mobilized individuals throughout the Cibao and in other parts of the country, becoming a significant cell of resistance.⁵⁵ During this time, Minerva and Manolo connected with other antitrujillistas across the country, coordinated the gathering of information, and developed a network that would allow them to consolidate efforts under one parent organization. Under their leadership, Acción Clero Cultural and other cells would merge to form the largest clandestine opposition movement thus far. Leaders of the merged resistance cells met on January 9, 1960, at Patria and Pedro's home in Conuco. Present at the meeting were men from various regions throughout the country, and two women: Minerva and Dulce Tejada, who had been active in Acción Clero Cultural.⁵⁶ During a second meeting in Mao on the following day, Minerva suggested they name the movement the Movimiento Revolucionario 14 de Junio (14 of June Revolutionary Movement) in honor of the failed June 1959 expedition that had inspired so many of them. Manolo was named president, Rafael (Pipe) Faxas Canto was general secretary, and Leandro Guzmán, treasurer. However, several accounts credit Minerva for taking a leadership role in the organization, and Fafa Taveras, in retrospect, points to her as the true leader of the movement, although gender norms at the time kept her from being formally recognized as such.⁵⁷ The goals of the 14 of June Movement were to remove Trujillo, hold free

---

53 "Entrevista con Rafael (Fafa) Taveras, Comunicador." *El día*. Nov. 23, 2018. YouTube. https://www.youtube.com/watch?v=4JgUzNtSMYg. See also Galván, 258–59, and Pedro Camilo, "La Acción Clero Cultural, una organización de la resistencia antitrujillista." *Movimiento Revolucionario 14 de Junio*. Aug. 9, 2009. https://unojotacuatro.blogspot.com/2009/08/la-accion-clero-cultural-una.html.
54 Galvan, *Minerva*, 258–59.
55 Taveras, "Entrevista."
56 Mirabal, *Vivas*, 151. Though not mentioned in this account of the meeting, we know that María Teresa was also actively involved in the movement.
57 Taveras, "Entrevista."

elections, implement the platform of the Dominican Liberation Movement, including agrarian reform, and bring about constitutional reform through a constitutional assembly.[58]

This movement was unlike previous ones in significant ways. As a reminder, we recall who was present at that pivotal January 6 meeting at the beginning of 1959: relatives of fervent trujillistas, of the social and political elite. Nancy Robinson explains that the movement became the most significant internal threat facing the regime. "[It] was particularly disconcerting to Trujillo because of its size and the identity of the participants. The list of those arrested [when the movement was discovered] read like a Dominican Who's Who. Most were sons and daughters of middle- and upper-class families, many from prominent Trujillista homes."[59]

Within a few days, the newly named 14 of June Movement was revealed, and hundreds of *catorcistas* (individuals who had collaborated with the movement) were arrested, imprisoned, and tortured. Manolo was one of the first. He was arrested on January 14, 1960;[60] Leandro on January 19; and María Teresa on the 20th initially and then definitively on the 21st. Minerva was also arrested on the 21st. Patria's husband Pedro and their nineteen-year-old son Nelson went into hiding, but Nelson was soon arrested at his grandmother's home in Conuco, and Pedro turned himself in to authorities when he realized how far the SIM would go to terrorize the family and destroy their homes while he was in hiding.[61]

The fact that Patria was not arrested, in spite of her significant role in the movement, illustrates the extent to which patriarchal notions of gender obscured women as real political operatives. This is not to minimize Patria's punishment: her family was arrested, their home and belongings destroyed, and their property confiscated, but at the time she retained a limited mobility that would later allow her to smuggle information into and out of the prison where her sisters, husband, and brothers-in-law would be held in the coming months.[62] It is also noteworthy that Minerva, who by all accounts played

---

58 Mirabal, *Vivas*, 152–53.
59 Nancy Robinson, "Women's Political Participation in the Dominican Republic: The Case of the Mirabal Sisters," *Caribbean Quarterly*, 52.2–3 (2006): 178. Robinson cites Bernard Diederich, *Trujillo: The Death of the Goat* (Boston: Little Brown, 1978), 35. See also Mirabal, *Vivas*, 152.
60 According to some accounts, Manolo was arrested on January 13. Mirabal, *Vivas*, 331.
61 Mirabal, *Vivas*, 150.
62 For more on Patria's role in the resistance see Mercedes Alonso Romero, *Su nombre es Patria* (Santo Domingo: Editora Búho, 2011).

a key leadership role from the movement's inception, was not arrested until over a week into the crackdown. The SIM had been watching her for years. They knew where to find her. Yet it was a week before they arrested her, María Teresa, Dulce Tejada, Tomasina Cabral, Fe Violeta Ortega, Asela Morel, and Miriam Morales, the seven women imprisoned as part of the crackdown on the 14 of June Movement. The arrests of these women would spark outrage both within the Dominican Republic and in the international community.

From mid- to late January, the SIM seized hundreds of known or suspected catorcistas across the country and brought them to the clandestine torture center La 40, near Santo Domingo. The interrogations were brutal and relentless. Survivors describe maiming, excessive beatings, the use of electric prods, and several other horrific abuses, including a generalized use of the electric chair. The men were forced to witness the torture of women prisoners (their spouses, relatives, and friends) and vice versa. After a period in La 40, prisoners were put on trial and were generally sentenced to excessive fines and long prison terms. Thirty years was common, even for those whose participation in the movement was minimal. Most were transferred to La Victoria National Penitentiary to serve their sentences.

As we learn in Part III of this volume, the conditions in La Victoria Penitentiary made it possible (though dangerous) for Minerva and Manolo to secretly exchange messages from their respective cells. We have the privilege of reading those messages and witnessing the deep bonds that helped them and their comrades survive those harrowing months. Manolo's letters shed light on the gender-based assumptions that he and many of his comrades made about potential risk for the women conspirators:

> It never occurred to me at the time that you could run the same risks. Had I considered that possibility, I assure you that perhaps we'd be far away from here. [. . .] who can possibly consider themselves morally and spiritually prepared for such trauma, such suffering? The thought that they would do the same to you ladies, give you the same treatment, was such a devastating blow for any man, especially when it comes to his wife and sisters . . . [63]

---

63 Letter from Manolo to Minerva. It is the final letter in Part III of this volume.

THE MURDER OF THE BUTTERFLIES

In mid-1960, under mounting international pressure, especially from the Organization of American States, the Trujillo regime was forced to commute the sentences of many *catorcistas*, particularly of women. Manolo, Leandro, Pedro, and other leaders of the movement remained in prison. Minerva, however, was under house arrest. Her being on the outside presented a real problem for Trujillo. The paternalism that characterized Dominican society and upon which Trujillo's public persona was built made it politically suicidal for him to subject Minerva—an educated woman and young mother—to the same brutal punishments as male revolutionaries. But her legendary magnetism, intelligence, understanding of law, and deftness at organizing others in resistance made her a real threat to his regime.

As Minou explains, this book is a celebration of her parents' lives. She refuses to recount the gruesome details of November 25, 1960, when her mother, her aunts Patria and María Teresa, and their driver Rufino de la Cruz were beaten, murdered, placed back into their Jeep, and pushed off the mountain road in what was officially reported as an accident. This event has already been retold in numerous literary, cinematic, and historical texts. It made international news. Popular memory and literature on the Trujillo regime often point to the murder as the event that prompted definitive action by other opposition groups in gestation, including the ten conspirators who would assassinate Trujillo on May 30, 1961. As 14 of June leader and María Teresa's widower Leandro Guzmán explains, it "compelled a gestating group of conspirators to say, 'Enough! We can't take any more. That man is killing women too.'" [64] This is corroborated by General Antonio Imbert Barrera, one of the ten conspirators, who in a 2018 interview recalls his reaction upon hearing about the supposed accident: "Where the hell are the men in this country?"[65] The murder of the Mirabal sisters was a direct violation of a kind of pact that the public had made with the regime, accepting its "facade of democracy" in exchange for "the paternalistic protection of homes and families."[66] The po-

---

64 Interview with Leandro Guzmán in Domeyko, *Codename Butterflies*, 55:22–55:31 min. Original text: "... determina que un grupo conspirador que estaba ya en gestación dijera '¡Ya! No se puede más. Este hombre está matando a mujeres también.'"
65 "Entrevista al General Antonio Imbert Barrera, uno de los ajusticadores de Trujillo." YouTube. Uploaded by *El Día RD*, May 31, 2018. 0:57–0:59 min.
66 Manley, *Paradox*, 95.

litical assassination of three educated, upper-middle-class women with young children violated this pact and was an affront to deeply held gender ideals.

Furthermore, the murder shook the nation at time of mounting, widespread resentment toward Trujillo, a resentment that had been swelling for decades. The regime's far reach was felt in homes across the nation, and "[e]very Dominican family had a victim of Trujillo in its closet," as Nancy Robinson states.[67] In fact, the ten conspirators who would assassinate Trujillo on May 30, 1961, were themselves state agents who had suffered the loss of loved ones at the hands of the regime.

Still, Minerva, Patria, and María Teresa, "the Butterflies," became etched in the national and international imaginaries as martyrs for political freedom and, in later years, for the struggle against violence toward women.[68] By emphasizing their horrific murder, the popularized narrative of the Butterflies has obscured our view of Minerva, María Teresa, and Patria as real agents of resistance. In the case of Minerva, the overly simplistic narrative is further skewed by a popular obsession with the October 1949 dance at which she confronted Trujillo. Its sensational allure obscures the real political activism and personal agency that Minerva developed over a decade and a half. The letters and memoir in this volume bring the complexity of her person into view. They reveal a Minerva who was an outspoken, tenacious, educated woman with clear convictions regarding (in)justice and a legendary ability to inspire and persuade others. Such insights into Minerva's character and way of thinking help us to understand the threat she posed to the regime and why in 1960, Trujillo famously stated that his two biggest problems were the Catholic Church and the Mirabal Family of Salcedo.[69] They also help us understand the political dilemma that led to her murder after Trujillo was forced to release her and the other women of the 14 of June Movement.

However, these letters also reveal Minerva in her full humanity, with vulnerabilities and faults, like anyone else. They show that her activism emerged and came to fruition through a web of relationships, of which Manolo formed an integral part. In fact, these letters are a testament to the courage and solidarity of many friends, neighbors, family members, and fellow collaborators

---

67 Robinson, "Women's Political Participation," 174.
68 For an in-depth discussion of the process through which the United Nations came to declare November 25, the anniversary of the Mirabal Sisters' death, as the International Day for the Elimination of Violence against Women see Nancy Robinson, "Origins of the International Day for the Elimination of Violence against Women: The Caribbean Contribution," *Caribbean Studies* 34.2 (2006): 141–61.
69 Minou mentions this in her mother's brief biography. See also Mirabal, *Vivas*, 180.

who also risked their lives to resist the dictatorship, either through active participation in the movement, or by supporting those who actively resisted.

A Window into Gender Dynamics under Trujillo

The popularized narrative of the Butterflies revolves around a gender dichotomy in which Trujillo is the abusive, patriarchal, and *machista* alpha male, and the Mirabal sisters are the innocent female victims. This is an oversimplification. To understand Minerva's leadership and the challenge that she in particular posed to Trujillo, it is essential to view her activism in light of the complex gender dynamics of the time.

The mobilization of women in the public sphere during the U.S. occupation and later during the Trujillo years provoked the intensification of deeply entrenched patriarchal ideals in Dominican society as it simultaneously challenged those ideals. Even when women were employed outside the home, male heads of household typically maintained authority over women's daily lives, including, for example, decisions about their professions and employment.[70] Elizabeth Manley describes this complex dynamic, particularly as it pertained to female politicians, many of whom "adhered to traditional gender norms within the household yet maintained complex careers in multiple levels of the regime's bureaucratic structure of paternal control." She shows that Trujillo cast these women as "acceptably modern precisely because they fused their maternal duties to their commitment to his vision of the democratic (and later anticommunist) Dominican state."[71] A woman could be modern and contribute to progress while still adhering to patriarchal norms within the family.

Trujillo's public image as "Father Trujillo,"[72] was predicated upon very clear gender roles, which he leveraged in oftentimes contradictory ways. While on the one hand he sanctioned women's active engagement in public life and state operations, on the other hand, he was a notorious megalomaniac who fashioned himself as the alpha male, the epitome of vitality and masculine virility. One particularly sinister manifestation of this megalomania was Trujillo's notorious vanity and his employment of underlings to arrange sexual encounters with young women and girls—even school girls—at the

---

70 Turits, *Foundations*, 220.
71 Manley, *Paradox*, 6. In a note she references Lauren Derby, *The Dictator's Seduction* on this topic.
72 To read peasants' recollections about this image, see Turits, *Foundations*, 221.

National Palace and his residence in San Cristóbal. Some families offered their daughters to Trujillo to gain political favor, but many others hid them, knowing that refusal of such an "invitation" would bring about some form of backlash or punishment.

Derby explains that by conquering the daughters of the white elite, Trujillo was making a political statement, vindication for the disdain he had received years earlier as a lower-class, minimally educated youth of partial Haitian descent. His initial outsider status and ability to dissimulate this through an elegant physical appearance were part of his image as *tíguere:* a young man from the margins who becomes a sort of popular hero, earning respect through street smarts, sexual prowess, and a wily ability to operate outside societal norms. Trujillo was the *tiguerazo,* the ultimate tíguere.[73] However, recent research on gender, politics, and the Trujillato make it clear that as tíguere, Trujillo also personified deeply entrenched notions of masculinity and paternalism that reaffirmed his rightful place as the alpha male, the unquestionable head of state through whom Dominicans enjoyed a long-awaited sovereignty.[74]

Many have interpreted Minerva's confrontation with Trujillo at the dance in San Cristóbal in light of this image of Trujillo as tiguerazo. This is a partially appropriate interpretation but is more complex than it initially appears. This is especially true if we view this confrontation as a challenge of leadership, as one of several events over years in which Minerva's actions challenged Trujillo's authority and as she clearly emerged as a leader in the resistance. Maja Horn's observations about gendered discourse in the age of Trujillo sheds light on this conflict. She finds that "the language of masculinity naturalized political leadership as an expression of 'manly' ability."[75] A large part of Trujillo's manliness was intricately linked to his leadership. For that authority to be destabilized by the leadership of a woman was unthinkable.

The protocols for punishing dissidents under Trujillo's regime were geared toward eliminating men. If applied toward women, those violent punishments would fly in the face of deeply rooted patriarchal norms and would cause outrage. This is exactly what happened. Prior to the 1960 arrest of seven women of the 14 of June Movement, including Minerva and María Teresa, women who were accused of opposing or simply not supporting the regime

---

73 Derby, *Dictator's Seduction*, 185–86; 193.
74 For more, see Horn, *Masculinity*, 35.
75 Horn, *Masculinity*, 36.

were frequently denounced but less severely punished than men.[76] They often lost employment, position, and property and were socially marginalized. Suspected subversives were generally placed under house arrest or punished via the arrest of a male family member. This was the precedent in place when the SIM imprisoned and tortured the seven female collaborators of the 14 of June Movement. It was a move that drew international attention. In fact, the regime had used all of the aforementioned forms of punishment against the Mirabal family, but it shook the nation by taking the punishment much further: first with the arrests and then with the assassination of Patria, Minerva, and María Teresa. Again, this was viewed by many as the last straw, as Leandro Guzmán and General Antonio Imbert have testified.[77] The very patriarchal ideals that allowed Trujillo to secure power were a significant—though not exclusive—factor in his downfall.

"The Steep Mountains of Quisqueya"

During a presentation of this book at a 2018 festival in Higüey, Minou Tavárez emphasized the humanity of her now iconic parents. She urged the audience to listen to the voices that speak through their letters (both in this volume and elsewhere) because they remain relevant to contemporary Dominican reality: "Minerva and Manolo were not extraterrestrials. They were not superheroes. We can see this when we read their letters. They were a Dominican man and woman who loved this country, who dreamed and fought to eradicate its enemies and the enemies of democracy. That struggle remains unfinished, and it is essential that we continue moving forward."[78]

At various moments in this book, Minou refers to this "unfinished struggle" as "the steep mountains of Quisqueya," a metaphor employed by her

---

76 As Derby states, women were "not perceived as full and equal participants in the Trujillista project [. . .] though frequently denounced [they] were less frequently penalized." Derby, *Dictator's Seduction*, 166. See also Manley, *Paradox*, 112.

77 Interview with Leandro Guzmán in Domeyko, *Code Name: Butterflies* and "Entrevista al General Antonio Imbert Barrera, uno de los ajusticiadores de Trujillo."

78 Minou Tavárez Mirabal. "Puesta en circulación de *Mañana te escribiré otra vez* de Minou Tavárez Mirabal en Higuey." Discurso 5ta Feria Gastronómica de la Yuca en la Provincia La Altagracia. YouTube. Uploaded by Opción Democrática, Jan. 24, 2018. https://www.youtube.com/watch?v=QAJ8EARb234. (16:36–17:07). Original text: "Minerva y Manolo no eran extraterrestres. No eran superhéroes. Y eso se puede ver cuando se leen sus cartas. Eran un dominicano y una dominicana que amaron este país. Que soñaron y lucharon para erradicar a sus enemigos y a los enemigos de la democracia. Esa sigue siendo una lucha inconclusa, imprescindible para seguir avanzando."

late father at a rally on June 14, 1963, in Santo Domingo. Remembering the freedom fighters of the failed June 1959 expedition, Manolo Tavárez, then head of the 14 of June Political Association, evoked the mountains of Constanza, where part of the expedition had been overtaken. Quisqueya is the pre-Columbian name for the island now shared by the Dominican Republic and Haiti. He proclaimed:

> Listen carefully, men and women of the ultra-right, listen carefully, enemies of the people, enemies of progress: if you make it impossible for the people to fight peacefully, the 14 of June knows very well where the steep mountains of Quisqueya lie, and that's where we'll go, and there we'll preserve the flames of liberty, of justice, the spirit of revolution, because then we will have no alternative but liberty or death.[79]

In her memoir, Minou looks to her parents' words to find the courage and wisdom to continue the political struggle against the lingering impunity, corruption, and clientelism that festers like an open wound in Dominican politics and society, undermining democracy and perpetuating social and economic inequality. She urges Dominicans to recover the voices of the recent past—silenced through decades of repressive dictatorship under Trujillo and then Joaquín Balaguer—in order to hold accountable those responsible for human rights violations and to see more clearly the path toward true democracy. As she proclaimed in 2018: "No nation on Earth has managed to overcome horror and death without justice. No nation. This helps us to understand our present, to understand why we live in a so-called democracy, in a transition that seems never-ending." [80]

Scholars such as Maja Horn, Jonathan Hartlyn, and others have pointed out that this "so-called democracy" in perpetual transition has been marked by paradoxes, the most "readily evident" of which is that the significant

---

79 Translation of quote in Hilarión Isalguéz, "Hoy se cumplen 54 años del fusilamiento de Manolo Tavárez Justo y 28 izquierdistas," *El nuevo diario*. Dec. 21, 2017. Original text: "¡ ... Óiganlo bien, señores de la reacción, óiganlo enemigos del pueblo, enemigos del progreso: si imposibilitan la lucha pacífica del pueblo, el 14 de Junio sabe muy bien donde están las escarpadas montañas de Quisqueya y a ellas iremos, y en ellas mantendremos encendida la antorcha de la libertad, de la justicia, el espíritu de la revolución, porque no nos quedará entonces otra alternativa que la libertad o muerte."

80 Minou Tavárez Mirabal, "Puesta en circulación de *Mañana te escribiré otra vez* de Minou Tavárez Mirabal en Higuey." (6:30–6:59) Original text: "[N]o existe ningún país en este mundo que haya podido superar el horror y la muerte sin justicia. No existe. Eso ayuda a entender nuestro presente, el por qué vivimos en una supuesta democracia, en una transición que parece ya eterna."

economic and social changes that have taken place since the end of the Balaguer regime (1978) have—paradoxically—not been accompanied by "comparable political reconfigurations."[81] Horn seeks to understand the paradoxes that characterize Dominican democracy by interrogating Trujillo-era political discourse, particularly by Trujillo himself and by his puppet president and later successor, Joaquín Balaguer. She shows that the regime's populist discourse, false narrative of national unity, and empty "performances of democratic legitimacy" (sham elections and legislative sessions, a lack of an independent judiciary) reconfigured the political vocabulary of democracy in a way that infused it with ambiguities and—more importantly—contradictions. That Trujillo and Balaguer boasted that their regimes were modern and democratic lay in stark contrast to their repressive, authoritarian actions. Horn points out that the ambiguous meanings of terms such as "democracy," "equality," "progress," "justice," and "liberty" have endured in the present political imaginary, and that this ambiguity makes it difficult for these concepts to "become an 'articulating point' for future popular demands."[82] For example, the false myth of national unity with respect to race and class obscure the real inequities that exist today and thus hinder Dominicans' ability to demand reform.[83] Dominican historian Roberto Cassá also examines this "transition that seems never-ending" in his study of the lasting legacy of the Trujillo regime. Unpacking the increasingly popular expression that "what the country needs now is another Trujillo," he points to a tendency to dismiss the regime's abuses in favor of its achievements, such as the elimination of national debt, increased access to education and healthcare, reduction in civilian crime, and greater economic security. He laments a general amnesia and a lack of a critical lens for reflecting on the country's history.[84]

What Minou calls for, both as political activist and author/editor of this volume, is to polish that critical lens. She implicitly calls for Dominicans to redefine and reclaim these essential political terms, to refuse to accept the contradictions that have been normalized, so as to transform the "so-called democracy" into a "true democracy." This is essential in order for Dominicans to find solutions to significant widespread problems such as staggering

---

81 Maja Horn, "Dictates of Dominican Democracy: Conceptualizing Caribbean Political Modernity," *Small Axe* 18.2 (2014): 18–35.
82 Horn, "Dictates," 33–34.
83 Horn, "Dictates," 33.
84 Roberto Cassá, "Algunos componentes del legado de Trujillo," *Iberoamericana* 1.3 (2001): 113–127. See pp. 123–24.

unemployment and underemployment, income inequality, inadequate education and healthcare, increased civilian crime, and a deficient judicial system, problems that are exacerbated by widespread clientelism, corruption, and impunity at all levels of government and society.[85]

This is the "unfinished struggle" to which Minou refers. By recovering her family's story, and by demystifying her parents, her book shows that, while their iconic status is exceptional, the suffering that they and their families endured was not; it has been the experience of millions of Dominican families for whom the transition toward true democracy continues to this day. What's more, it shows that her parents' political opposition—and that of many other Dominicans—stemmed from a deep love for the Dominican people (and for one another). By listening to their voices, we see through the tainted veneer of trujillista discourse that vilified all dissenters as communists controlled by foreign influence.[86]

In these ways, the story of the Tavárez Mirabal family resonates with the experiences of people across Latin America. In countries such as Chile, Argentina, Uruguay, Brazil, Guatemala, Peru, and El Salvador, today's generations seek the voices of the past as they confront the lingering impunity and amnesia that hinder their struggle for true democracy. They have resurrected these voices in truth and reconciliation commissions, museums and reclaimed public spaces, documentaries, demonstrations, and a growing body of scholarly work. Activists formerly imprisoned and tortured under dictatorships have become heads of state in countries including Chile, Uruguay, and Brazil.[87] Similarly, the Mirabal family, once persecuted as so-called enemies of the state, has since produced two important political leaders: both Minou Tavárez Mirabal and her cousin Jaime David Fernández Mirabal (vice president, 1996–2000). In this volume, Minou the political activist becomes Minou the daughter seeking to understand her parents. She draws our attention to the personal, to the intimate, to the everyday experiences behind the political activism of their generation. This is why Michelle Bachelet describes their story as one "that resonates with any Latin American."

Minou Tavárez Mirabal's *Mañana te escribiré otra vez. Minerva y Manolo. Cartas* lays bare for the reader the deep connections that united these two

---

85 For more, see Horn, *Masculinity*, 1–4.
86 Horn, "Dictates," 32.
87 Chile (Michelle Bachelet 2006–2010, 2014–2018), Uruguay (José Mujica, 2010–2015), and Brazil (Luiz Inácio Lula da Silva, 2003–2010, and Dilma Rousseff, 2011–2016).

iconic revolutionaries, as well as the strong social bonds that surrounded and nurtured them. These relationships enabled them to endure horrific tortures and emerge as leaders during their most trying moments. They inspired action. They were a lifeline at a time when a cancerous culture of denunciation and mistrust had eaten away at Dominican society and was asphyxiating the families of those who had fallen out of grace with the regime. Today, Minou carries on her parents' legacy in her continued efforts to help strengthen democracy in the Dominican Republic. This journey back into her family's lives helps us to better understand that struggle and to recognize—in her life and in our own—the fortitude, courage and sustenance that one can find in the solidarity of those who surround us. It challenges us to question our own complacency and ask where we might find the courage to stand for justice.

Translator's Note

HEATHER HENNES

OVERVIEW

The original editions of this book are titled *Mañana te escribiré otra vez. Minerva y Manolo. Cartas* (*I'll Write Again Tomorrow: The Letters of Minerva and Manolo*). They begin with a foreword by former Chilean president Dr. Michelle Bachelet Jeria, an internationally known human rights activist whose story resonates in many ways with that of Minou Tavárez Mirabal. In the mid-1970s, both Bachelet and her father were victims of torture under Augusto Pinochet, the dictator who came into power through a military coup in 1973 and who ruled Chile until 1990. Her father died as a result of that torture. After four years in exile, Bachelet returned to Chile, completed her medical degree, and found work treating victims of torture. Her public service emerged from that experience. After serving in the Chilean ministries of health and defense, she was twice elected president (2006–2010; 2014–2018) and has since been named the United Nations high commissioner for human rights. Bachelet's foreword points to the story of the Tavárez Mirabal family as one that reflects the experiences of many families throughout the region.

This foreword is followed by Minou Tavárez Mirabal's introduction in the form of a letter to her late parents. The body of the volume consists of 117 letters and telegrams, almost all of them between Minerva and Manolo, organized chronologically, divided into four parts, and framed by a series of introductory essays. In these narratives, Minou contextualizes the letters, explains numerous references, and reflects on her family's experiences. Interspersed throughout the letters and telegrams are facsimiles and photographs of the originals, oftentimes including the envelopes. The original luxury edition contains facsimile reproductions of the letters in envelopes affixed to pages throughout the book. In addition to reading the transcriptions, the reader can experience taking each letter out of its envelope and reading it in Manolo or Minerva's own handwriting. The economy edition contains rich visual displays of the original letters and envelopes along with family photographs and memorabilia from the time, such as newspaper clippings and movie posters. The book also contains several pages dedicated to family photographs and a glossary containing the name of every individual referenced in the letters.

The body of this volume is divided into four sections arranged in chronological order. "Part I: Courtship" is by far the most extensive. It covers Minerva and Manolo's entire courtship, with letters and telegrams from August 1954 through October 1955. The correspondence is arranged chronologically by month, and each month's correspondence is prefaced by Minou's narrative. For reasons that the author explains, the vast majority of letters in this section were written by Minerva to Manolo; only ten are letters from Manolo to Minerva. Through this reading, we come to know Minerva as a young law student, a woman with her own insecurities and shortcomings, but also dreams and ideals. We witness the increasingly close ties between the Tavárez Justo and Mirabal Reyes families. But we also see how the stress of living under constant surveillance and threats by Trujillo's intelligence agents impacted her health. We learn that she found strength in her family, in Manolo, and in the many friends who refused to abandon the family in spite of their having fallen out of grace with the regime. We read anecdotes by family and friends and a handful of cheerful notes to Manolo from Minerva's close friend and classmate, Hortensia.

Minerva and Manolo were married on November 20, 1955. "Part II: Marriage" spans the years 1956 to 1958, beginning with Minou's description of her parents' lives as newlyweds, living in separate cities while Minerva finished law school and Manolo practiced law in Montecristi. She explains how the regime's intervention in the market led to the financial ruin of Manolo's agricultural enterprise, how Minerva's friends helped her with baby Minou as she finished her studies, and how the two families deepened their mutual relationship.

The summary of the year 1957 is bittersweet. The couple finally managed to settle into one home, together with baby Minou, but they—particularly Minerva—continued to endure constant surveillance and defamation. What's more, after years of Minerva's uphill battles to finish her law degree, and in spite of her outstanding academic achievements, Trujillo denied her license to practice law. Tavárez Mirabal relates that her mother nonetheless assisted Manolo in his law practice while caring for her family. She concludes this subsection by describing the national situation as reaching its boiling point at the same time that dictatorial regimes were facing increasing challenges abroad.

The anecdotes that Tavárez Mirabal shares in her summary of 1958 illustrate two primary points. First, the lethally vindictive Trujillo regime and its accomplices continued to retaliate against the Mirabal family as "hostile enemies of the Chief." Second, in spite of tensions related to what she calls "the only stain on my parents' relationship," Minerva and Manolo were united by a deep mutual love, a union that was further solidified by their shared commitment to ending Trujillo's regime.

Although this section spans three years (1956–1958), it contains only two letters from Manolo to Minerva and two annotated poems that Minerva sent to Manolo. She turns to the poetic verses of Porfirio Barba Jacob (Miguel Ángel Osorio) and Shams al-Din Muhammad (Hafiz) as a way to express her heartache. Given the scant correspondence in this section, it is organized by year rather than by month. Minou introduces each year with a commentary.

The deeply poignant "Part III: Letters in Prison" begins with Minou's narrative of the pivotal events of 1959 and 1960. She describes her parents' leadership in organizing the 14 of June Revolutionary Movement and of their commitment in spite of the risks. She recalls images fixed in her childhood memories of those days when the SIM came to arrest her mother and aunt. She shares anecdotes told to her by collaborators in the 14 of June Movement who had been imprisoned and tortured along with her parents. Their voices tell of the courage, dignity, and strength that her parents demonstrated in prison and that are now essential elements of their legends. She explains how they smuggled notes back and forth, often written on scraps of paper, on cigarette wrappers, and in the margins of medication inserts. These are the very notes that you will read in Part III. For reasons that Minou explains, of the twelve notes that survive from Minerva and Manolo's intimate correspondence while in prison, eleven are from Manolo to Minerva and only one is from Minerva to Manolo. This section also contains three letters from Minerva and María Teresa to their family, one from fellow catorcista and inmate Jorge Tejada to Minerva, one from Manolo's cousin and fellow inmate Puro Petit Tavárez, also to Minerva, and a brief greeting from comrade Tomasina

Cabral. Since most of the notes are not dated, they are arranged in the order in which Minou found them, as she explains.

In these letters, we read that Minerva and Manolo garnered hope by catching rare, brief glimpses of one another, and that Manolo suffered from profound grief knowing that Minerva was imprisoned and that he was unable to protect her. As she leads the reader through these events, Minou pauses; she "tries to breathe." This is a pivotal moment in her journey back to her parents.

The content of these letters ranges from uplifting words of encouragement to expressions of deep longing, worry, and even regret. They provide glimpses of a prison economy that allowed for the circulation of materials, albeit under the constant threat of punishment. There are lighthearted moments in which friends appear making jokes and sending their warmest regards. And there are tragic moments, such as when Manolo plans for a future that we know they will never have.

Finally, "Part IV: Life" begins with Minou's final reflection followed by two brief though heartrending notes. The first is from seven-year-old Minou to her father. He carried it with him into the mountains at Las Manaclas when leading the ill-fated armed resistance against the Triumvirate installed by the 1963 military coup. The second note is the message that he wrote to Minou on the shell of a mountain snail while up in Las Manaclas, fully aware that he would be killed. This is the final letter.

Tavárez Mirabal's narrative in this section begins not with the ghastly details of her mother's and aunts' murders, which she refuses to recount, but rather the period of profound grief and uncertainty that followed their deaths. Drawing from what she would learn later on, she reconstructs the experience of her father and uncles, who remained imprisoned for months following their wives' deaths. She describes her father's homecoming eight months later: the heartbreaking acceptance of Minerva's death, the crowd of people who sought his political leadership, and the solace found in a quiet moment of shared grief with his little daughter, Minou.

In this section, Tavárez Mirabal describes life with her father between his release from prison in July 1961 and his departure for Las Manaclas in November 1963. She recalls the whirlwind of political activity that constantly surrounded the apartment they shared with several other family members. She also invites the reader into two very intimate memories: when and how she discovered that her father had been murdered, and the day she fell weeping into a patch of poppies, realizing that she was an orphan. She candidly shares how she internalized these experiences and how they've shaped her character. This is a deeply moving section in which the impressions and experiences of a seven-year-old girl are woven into the reflections of a mature, informed adult woman who is nearing the end of this journey through her parents' correspondence and her own memories. She concludes with a life-affirming tribute to the legacies left to all of us by her parents, legacies embodied in two particular gifts: the butterfly, and the shell of a mountain snail.

The book concludes with a glossary in which Tavárez Mirabal identifies every individual mentioned in the book, as well as a map of those places in the capital where her parents lived and frequented. I have slightly revised the glossary for the sake of clarity and have added some information, which is annotated. I have noted substantive changes in footnotes within the glossary. I have also moved the biographical entries for Minerva and Manolo from the glossary and have incorporated this information into the introduction. I have also added family trees on pages xiii and xiv.

Approach to This Translation

One goal for this translation is for it to be accessible to readers unfamiliar with the Dominican Republic under the Trujillo regime. For this reason, I have added an introduction and numerous footnotes to supplement those originally provided by Minou Tavárez Mirabal. To differentiate between the author's footnotes and those that I have added, I have labeled the translator's notes with the abbreviation "t.n.".

My second objective, as paramount as the first, is to be a conduit for the symphony of voices that inform, question, remember, urge, and explain in these pages. The voice that guides us on this journey is that of Minou Tavárez Mirabal. In her narrative and footnotes we accompany her as she digs deeply into her parents' lives. She is not only the philologist who explains the cultural and literary currents and historical events that shaped her parents' imaginaries, but also the daughter who through this exegesis feels closer to them. She is driven by questions, and we get a sense that this journey back to her parents has given her some answers, or at least it has allowed her to breathe in a way that she had not before.

Minou's narrative and the correspondence that it frames express a deep love that is the central axis of the volume. It is the legacy that lives on in the Tavárez Mirabal family and the human experience to which we, the readers, can most intimately relate. For this reason, I have handled terms of endearment, including common terms such as *mi vida* and *bien mío* with great care. When a close English approximation is available, such as in the case of *mi amor* (my love), I have rendered it in English. However, on the many occasions when there is no equivalent in English, no similar, commonly used term of endearment, the term appears in the original Spanish. One commonly occurring term is *mi vida,* literally "my life," used in direct address, unlike in English. Another frequently used term is *bien mío,* meaning something akin to "that which is good for me" or "the good in my life." *Bien de mi alma* conveys an even deeper level of intimacy: "the good in/for my soul." Indeed, across its many dialects, the Spanish language is rich in lyrical ways to express affection, which the reader can appreciate in this volume.

Another challenge that arose in this translation was the non-normative use of punctuation and the oftentimes complicated syntax. I have aimed to capture the tone, register, and ambiguities of each letter by maintaining the writer's style while at the same time normalizing punctuation as necessary for comprehension.

One additional aspect of this translation that warrants commentary is the handling of epigraphs. Minou introduces each chapter with select verses from Pablo Neruda's poem "La carta en el camino," first published in 1952 in *Los versos del capitán*. I have chosen to cite Donald Devenish Walsh's English translation, "Letter on the Road," published in *The Captain's Verses* in 1972, noting in footnotes where I have slightly altered Walsh's translation. These modifications are limited to occasional words and phrases.

On a final note, I would like to express my deep gratitude toward Minou Tavárez Mirabal and the Fundación Hermanas Mirabal for their trust, for their support of this project, and for granting me the English translation rights. My conversations with Minou over the course of the project have clarified doubts and enriched the final text. I am grateful for her having entrusted me with this translation, and I hope to have honored the voices of her family, who speak through these pages.

THE LETTERS OF
Minerva Mirabal and Manolo Tavárez

Minou Tavárez Mirabal

Foreword

"... There is nothing as obstinate as memory, which persists in keeping memories alive though sometimes they hurt so very much," said Dedé Mirabal a few years ago, when she launched her book *Vivas en su jardín* (*Alive in Their Garden*). I recalled this statement in the presence of this magnificent new book, in which, with pain and immense love, the Dominican congresswoman Minou Tavárez Mirabal makes it possible for us to know her parents more personally and intimately: Minerva and Manuel Aurelio, heroes of Latin American dimensions.

Today, Minerva and Manolo live on in the memory of those of us men and women who believe in a world of justice and solidarity. And this is so thanks to the sustained efforts of their daughter to recover the memory of her parents. In reading Minerva and Manolo's letters, carefully compiled and contextualized by their daughter, we confirm the deep love in which they lived: two people who found one another in political struggle, who shared a love of art and literature, who undoubtedly came to know one another more intimately in their resolve and courage during their nation's darkest hours.

These pages also speak to us about two young people who are timid and naive when it comes to love, who are creating their story, for themselves and for the world, while they discover one another in a story that resonates with any Latin American.

I celebrate the humanity that moves Minou Tavárez Mirabal to seek to mend her life's central wound by means of this book. As that wound closes, the memory of her parents opens up for the world, wresting their heroic deeds from oblivion.

Michelle Bachelet Jeria
Chile, September 2013

To My Parents

Santo Domingo

May 23, 2013

Mami, Papi,

    Yesterday we celebrated the marriage of Minerva Victoria, your first granddaughter, Manolito and Clara's firstborn child, and in some ways my first daughter, given that she was born long before my other two nieces and my children. She looked so beautiful, and she wanted to wear something of yours, Mami. We had to touch up her makeup because when she was almost ready, I arrived with your bracelet, and she began to cry. I think everyone cried, including me. I've become a bit more prone to crying as I've gotten older. Between that celebration and the night lay five decades of your physical absence. But, as always, the pulse of your presence was deeply felt; it filled us, our friends, and the large family that is your legacy.

    We tried to give Minerva Victoria a small token of love, though Manolito got carried away with it: a little house with a window, made of small panels that we distributed among the guests so that they could write on them their best wishes and notes. So, I took inventory of my thoughts, and when I shared them with your eldest granddaughter, dispersed throughout my reflections on what is paramount were Mami's letters, which Papi had so carefully bound together. All the love in the world, which we've come to know through the blood that flows down to us from past generations, was there in that collection of letters, which I shared with Minerva Victoria. And with the heartbeat of a long-guarded secret, she immediately chose your words to place in the center of the house, a complicity for which I will be thankful for the rest of my life. Quotes that define that love are now there. Of all the books that have been written about you, I believe that the little house for Minerva Victoria, in which one can see the wonderful legacy of love through which we were conceived, that little house for your granddaughter, is the one that would please you the most.

For me, this moment of discovering myself in my own thoughts and dreams is a kind of return. But perhaps, Mami, Papi, it is the first time that I can, without pain, revisit that journey that has been life lived since you. Or with a different pain, which is neither the same nor equal. There are moments in which one's entire being steps back from a dense veil with a sense of melancholy. It's my time, dear parents, because I always feared that loving you was something I'd inherited, and now I know how much, how very much and in what ways that affection has been real, lived in flesh and blood.

Your laughter, Mamá, Mami, Mother, your laughter brings back the memory in sepia of your sensual strides down a hallway. It's seeing you feel the weight of what you would become when, with your beret and insurgent's fatigues, thinking God knows what, you stood in front of the mirror, where my memory, as your daughter, captured you, untouched and eternal. I was there.

Your strides, Papá, Father, Papi, the immense stature that I observed as a child, the strength of your voice in a courtroom or in the night, singing me songs that I would later understand. The silhouette of your handsome face at the dawn of death, writing me one last letter from the steep, rugged mountains full (and you knew it) of beasts. All of this reverberates in my soul like the balm of feeling you alive with me all these nearly fifty years. Behind it all, behind the note that I wrote you when you left, asking that you come back for me, was my one wish for what I would have wanted in life: to carry my bed to where you were, for you were my home, to fall asleep resting on you. This has been a longing forged not only in orphanhood, but in the aspiration to emulate you, to emulate both of you as much as possible. Because I was there.

So, over the course of a few days, with your letters spread over the table, I have attempted this return. It is also a journey back into my own life. Needing to return to the present and move forward, I see that to speak with you is to speak with myself. And now you are the ones who are here.

And so, looking through your eyes, the first thing I see is my brother Manolo. Papi, your commitment to freedom, however it began, interrupted the agricultural career that you had planned for the welfare of your young family. He has brought it to fruition, as if guided by your dreams. Now he is a successful entrepreneur with a lovely family: an excellent wife, Clara, who undoubtedly would have been another daughter to both of you; and Minerva, Minou, and Talía, three precious granddaughters who feel like my own because they fill me with the same tenderness that each one of my aunts felt toward her sisters' children. With that same sense of what is truly important, when you went away, you left the two of us surrounded by immensities.

I have chosen a different path. Mami, you planted in me that thirst for knowledge, that love for your books, which I assumed as my own as soon as I began to read. I learned from them, nourished by the many poems that you recited in the garden in Ojo de Agua. After having heard them so often, Mamá Dedé still evokes them. And with the two of you, because of the two of you, I set off on my journey toward political engagement. It has not been easy, however, because I have the bad habit of swimming a little against the current and of assuming myself unscathed even amid growing deceit and ignorance, self-interests, obstacles, and the incessant pain of struggling to breathe amid what hurts: poverty, defenselessness, injustice, and the need to grow this democracy that you and others like you fertilized with blood.

And then there are my children: Camila Minerva and Manuel Aurelio. You can't imagine how often I've seen you in them, there where you live on. Camila with her irreverence, her endless questions, her intelligence and her rebelliousness, with her way of demanding of herself what nobody else is asking, very much embodies the image I have of you, Mami. Manuel Aurelio clearly resembles you, Papi, both physically and in temperament, with his enormous sense of justice and that goodness that everyone who knew you remembers. "Manolo was a good man," "Manolo was a just man," they repeat. Your grandson is the same way.

For many years I hesitated to release this collection of letters, which I considered to be too intimate. I've shared them on a few occasions as a way of enriching with your voices the tributes that others have offered in your memory. Even so, the decision to publish them was not easy, nor was the task of creating a compass to guide readers along paths that in some cases I myself had never traveled. That's what led me to devote myself to fishing for memories, anecdotes, testimonies, yellowed newspapers. It became painfully clear that everything that is missing—Papi's letters during the courtship; letters that both of you wrote during the crisis you experienced; Mami's from prison; documents; poems; letters to other people, to important personalities of the time and even to institutions; and other pieces of you—had been the victims of not only the assassins' time, but also of other, even more bewildering censorships, of other dictatorships, of other equally disgraceful betrayals. This is why I don't have all of them.

Papi, when I arrived in Santo Domingo after finishing my studies at the University of Havana, Aunt Elsa Justo gave me the box of letters that you had so carefully organized in the apartment on Rosa Duarte Street, where I lived with you until 1963. That was almost thirty years ago. Now I realize that you had reread them avidly, just as I would years later, as if by rereading them you were returning to a time with Mami, to her, with her. I also came to understand that you left them there for us, that you knew quite well what was going to happen to them.

Mami, in that little box, bound with a ribbon and organized by month, were all your letters that Papi saved from when you were dating, as well as the telegrams mentioned in them, also in chronological order. In that same order were—and I confess that I couldn't believe it—the receipts from each telegram that Papi sent you. All of that was kept together with a letter you wrote to Mamá Fefita and a series of magazine clippings showing furniture sets for the master bedroom with some of the annotations you made. Since I know you were more disorganized than Papi, I'm sure that the letters he sent you were spread throughout all your books, drawers, nightstands, pockets, and purses. That being so, I found what little I found.

My history with this collection of letters has been intense. How often have I longed to travel back in time to those days? Days in which I already existed, in which I formed part of two lives that with me completed one another, that lived on, but that would abandon me too soon, such that today, when I write, my memory clings to words, instances, silences.

But this precious testimony of love that trembles in my hands, the hands of an atypical reader, of the daughter who in what she reads searches for a truth that lies beyond what is public, beyond the truth that now belongs to everyone, has also allowed me to see you in retrospect through your own eyes. And I realize that the story that emerges in these letters and is yet to be told is even more beautiful than the one that has given rise to your legends in so many imaginaries. Though my memory may not ever fully capture the geography—the planet—that the two of you were, something precious began growing inside me once I read you through those letters. Now I know that those of us who remain are the skin of your lives, through whose pores you continue to breathe. And I give thanks to life for having allowed me to be born to two such extraordinary human beings, for having allowed me to be with you.

The everlasting testimony of your letters, of your conversations, of your close friends who still tell stories, allows me to imagine, to know, to come to understand the importance of those first few years of my life, when you decided to live by example.

Upon reaching the final letters—the ones from prison—and contemplating their brevity and the precariousness of being written on little papers from cigarette boxes or on whatever was available, an infinite sadness inside me becomes a question that is almost like a bell striking my temples again and again: Where on earth are the letters that you wrote during the courtship, Papi? What unscrupulous being could have robbed me—robbed us—of that part of the story, of history? What hands made them disappear, making those letters just like the thousands of cadavers, victims of Trujillo? What malicious censorship, what disloyal and twisted mind created this void? It seems that I will never know the answer to this question, which feels like electric prods shocking my chest. Reading the letters from prison, I know that the missing correspondence from your courtship is a void where your happy, enamored voice should be. Your words would have been a balm for my own heartache, as Mami wanted. But there are many libraries of Alexandria in the history of humanity. Your disappeared documents are one of them.

Moreover, while I was carrying out this task, it made me shiver to think how close we still are to those who gave human form to those hellish years. The unpunished ghosts appear with first and last names. The henchmen, the snitches, the *caliés*,[1] the informants, the fiends, the spokesmen of fear, the killers are still lurking around, doing evil.

For that reason, Papi, to paraphrase you, I tirelessly repeat the question that we as a generation must ask ourselves: Where are today's steep mountains of Quisqueya? What does it mean to climb their summits, here and now? As we continue to climb, we face a long road ahead and carry a heavy backpack. This is what I wrote to you in a letter in 2010, on the fiftieth anniversary of your murder, Mami. And I assume, Papi, that

---

[1] The henchmen of the Servicio de Inteligencia Militar (Military Intelligence Service, or SIM), the agency created by Trujillo under the guise of national security. The SIM repressed and punished opposition to the regime, using terrifying means such as kidnapping, extorsion, torture, and murder (t.n.)

the path that you viewed in the distance is still the same, albeit different: more democracy, more democracy, more democracy. Today it is essential that the path lead us through political reform that improves our democracy, putting it at the service of our country, for which so many men and women have given their lives and for which we should live. This, your legacy, is still an immense challenge for us.

In the meantime, the coffer of memory continues to grow in riches. There is Mamá Dedé's autobiography, *Vivas en su jardín,* a narrative that springs from the very same devastated heart from those days, from those distant lives, of those events long ago. And you live on at the gravesite in the garden of the Mirabal Sisters House Museum, where the two of you bloom alongside Aunt Teté and Nina Patria.[2] There, each year, thousands of children and young people encounter your story—their history. When one has lived careful to not give in to oblivion and indifference, to not allow absence to snatch away from us what will always be the essence of who we are and who we will become, there is no other option but to walk on "through plazas and through streets holding memory in [our] hands."[3] Thus wrote the Argentine poet Juan Gelman, who lost his son and daughter-in-law at the hands of the murderous military junta that scourged his country. We nine men and women—your children and my aunts' children—have had the privilege of having grown up in the same setting from which you parted more than fifty years ago. Fifty years seems like a long time. But nothing is fresher to me, to my siblings, and to our entire family than the immortalized memory of your lives there: yours, Mami, almost palpable, and Papi's, as an extension of yours.

In a magical way, protected in a healing spell imposed by Mamá Chea, and by Mamá Dedé, Tonó, Reyna, Pedro, and all the people who had the fortune of knowing you and loving you, the life you left behind forms part of the landscape there, in Ojo de Agua and in Conuco. It lives on in the greens and purples of the *caimito* and the *samán* trees over the tombs that hold you, as plant and mineral. It lives on in the morning butterflies in a garden that eternalizes footsteps that, almost by accident, made history, and it lives on in the snails that carry their homes and their paths with them. Mami, the little green table on display in the House Museum,

---

2   Tía Teté (Aunt Teté) is María Teresa; "Nina Patria" is a truncated form of Madrina (Godmother) Patria. (t.n.)

3   Juan Gelman, "Ahora," *Poesía reunida (1956–2010),* (Barcelona: Seix Barral, 2012), 494. The translation is mine. (t.n.)

where you used to read in the early morning hours, drinking your boiling hot coffee, was the same one at which I passionately used to read your books during breakfast on hurried early mornings before rushing off to school. The patio where we played and dreamed is the same one that many have come to visit. The path leading from the door that Mamá Chea closed on November 25, 1960, traverses our memories and becomes in a dreamlike way the same path that led you away with Nina Patria and Aunt Teté only to return forty years later to dwell near the stone and the water that, like the example you left us, flows perpetually. Papi, it is the same door that you found closed when you came home from prison.[4]

At this point I can breathe because this story of yours was always about life. Testimony to that fact are these letters that I hand over today to the people for whom you fought and to the world that recognizes you as the heroes that you are. These letters are also a manifesto of resistance, a living testament of love, of commitment and of courage.

Never have you been as present as you are today, in this split second in which fifty years of absence are transformed, when democracy, freedom, and love continue to be, as you understood them, constant movement that yearns to transform the world into a place that is more humane and more just.

You did this, and your sacrifice, Papi, Mami, continues to be our very own present-day challenge. Many thanks, many times over.

Your daughter,
Minou

---

[4] As the author explains in Part II, her grandmother closed the front entrance upon learning of her daughters' deaths and refused to open it until they returned home. This is why Manolo found it closed when he arrived at Mamá Chea's house after being released from prison. (t.n.)

I
Courtship

August 1954–October 1955

Figure 1.1. Telegram from Minerva to Manolo, August 3, 1954. Courtesy of the Fundación Hermanas Mirabal.

Figure 1.2. Minerva with a perm. Letter from Minerva to Manolo, November 1954. Courtesy of the Fundación Hermanas Mirabal.

Figure 1.3. Manolo at age 23. The first photo that Manolo gave Minerva. Letter from Manolo to Minerva, January 18, 1955. Courtesy of the Fundación Hermanas Mirabal.

Figure 1.4. Dedé, Hortensia, Minerva, Patria, and Jaime Enrique in Ojo de Agua, 1955. Courtesy of the Fundación Hermanas Mirabal.

Figure 1.5. Manolo with his cousin Isabelita Justo on the day when he graduated with his law degree, February 25, 1955. Courtesy of the Fundación Hermanas Mirabal.

Figure 1.6. Minerva driving a Jeep, with friends. Courtesy of the Fundación Hermanas Mirabal.

AUGUST 1954

> I found you after
> the storm,
> the rain washed the air
> and in the water
> your precious feet gleamed like fishes.
> —Pablo Neruda, "Letter on the Road"[1]

Three telegrams and one letter document what would be an important month in my parents' lives. Although there was clearly prior correspondence between them, I do not have it in my possession, unfortunately.

The chronologies that have been published until now insist on situating their first encounter in Jarabacoa in the year 1953. In reality, though, my archaeology of Minerva and Manolo's love unearthed the fact that they first met on Holy Thursday 1952 in Jarabacoa, where they were both vacationing. She had just turned twenty-five, and he was twenty-one. I arrived at these facts after delving into careful research into this part of their lives—which they themselves put into ink on paper—and after searching for their voices in the memories of those who had the good fortune of knowing them and interacting with them back then.

Witnesses to that first encounter tell me that Papi was immediately captivated by Mami that day, and that they spent all night talking. They also told me that my father knew very well who Minerva Mirabal was. He knew of the various imprisonments that she had suffered since the infamous ball in San Cristóbal in 1949, when she directly confronted the tyrant, both politically and personally. In other words, Manuel Aurelio Tavárez Justo knew that night that he was conversing with a girl who, more than three years prior, had "fallen into disgrace," with all the weighty implications this had in those days.

Some months later, in September 1952, having overcome political and familial obstacles, Minerva was able to realize her long-awaited dream of being admitted to the university. She was about twenty-five years old.

Life would reunite them at a later time, when they were both law students. It seems that this reencounter took place during Mami's second year at the university, toward the end of 1953, after she was denied readmission to the

---

1   Pablo Neruda, "Letter on the Road" ("La Carta en el Camino"), *The Captain's Verses*, Translated by Donald Devenish Walsh (New York: New Directions, 1972), 143, with slight modification to Devenish Walsh's translation in the last verse. Each section of Minou's narrative begins with an epigraph from the same poem. (t.n.)

university by express order of "the Chief."[2] She was obligated to participate in various meetings, to speak at an event praising the tyrant, and to write a note to the dictator himself in hopes that he would allow her to continue her studies. In a November 1953 letter to my Aunt Teté (María Teresa), Mami tells her that "Manolo Tavárez" lent her a book, and an entry in Aunt Teté's diary from the end of that year or the beginning of the next clearly indicates that my mother had met "someone" whom she was thinking of bringing home.

According to the testimony of Avelina (Lina) Soriano, one of Papi's classmates, he arrived to class one day very elegantly dressed in a formal suit. Both she and Luis Espínola asked him where he was going "wearing a tie and everything." "They arranged a date for me with the most beautiful and cultured girl, the one with the best library in the country," he replied. Lina said to him, "Ah, you're going to meet Minerva," which surprised Papi, who asked her how she knew. "Well," she told him, "I've known her since high school, and no one else in this country fits that description." She also warned him, "Listen to me, there are bodies that are attracted to one another as if by magnetism. You won't be able to separate yourself from that woman," a comment that later inspired Papi to give her the nickname "*Pitonisa*," "Fortune-teller."

Doing the math, I reach the conclusion that my father courted my mother for almost two years, beginning with their first encounter in Jarabacoa. It was surprising to me after all this time to discover how much she made him work in order to court her. Their courtship began on August 15, 1954. In my father's telegram at the start of this collection of letters, he announces his June 14 visit to Ojo de Agua, during which she finally accepted him as her boyfriend.

In order to understand certain names, situations, details, aromas, and sounds that emerge in the letters, in the epistolary lyricism of a man and a woman who took root in one another, with so much life lived and yet to live, it is essential that those of you who want to visit these memories have a guide who leads you by the hand, not only to understand the ONE that the two of them were, but also their era, comprised of tiny instants in which they could truly breathe, of imposed distances, of suffocating daily horror. In this way, we rediscover ourselves a bit amid these evocations, in the history that has made us the country that we have become since then.

That is why I am here, with my sights set on what I, too, have sought throughout this life without them, a life that was imposed upon me: to watch them, to listen to them, to know them beyond their flesh and blood and to

---

2   Trujillo, "el Jefe," meaning "the Chief" or "the Boss." (t.n.)

step inside them, beginning with Lina's premonition and up until a time and a space where they have remained fixed for me and for you.

And so the summaries that you will find at the beginning of each month's correspondence in the first part of the book, and at the beginning of each year in the second part (about their married life and time in prison), are intended to be a voice that accompanies Minerva and Manolo and that expresses them from their own perspectives and a little from my own, since I too am part of their love that endures.

Telegram from Minerva to Manolo. Salcedo, August 3, 1954.[3]

We're postponing the trip. Regards. Minerva.

Telegram from Manolo to Minerva. Montecristi, August 14, 1954.

I'm going tomorrow. Regards. Manolo.

Letter postmarked August 24 in Salcedo. Received in Montecristi on August 25, 1954.

8/23/1954

Manolo,

Yesterday I received your letter. I thought it would never arrive. I was almost rebuking you: Ah, yes, before you used to write me right away, but now you're sure of yourself! I was also mortified at times when I remembered what I said and did. Since you didn't say anything, a voice inside me took it upon itself to torment me, though I'd feel even more remorse were I not sincere with you. I want you to always have good memories of me, or rather, I'd never want to hang my head in shame in front of you. It's a good thing that your letter arrived!

I'm not writing to you now just to tell you all of this. Actually, I've been thinking of writing since you left.

María Teresa had a sore throat, but she's better now. Nobody here sends you regards in return because I didn't consult with them before

---

3   I use this reference at the beginning of the letters since almost none of Minerva's to Manolo are dated, and none of them indicate the place from which she wrote them. Thus, the only way to situate them is by the postmark on the envelope and, in some cases, from the context. All were sent to Montecristi, where Manolo resided. His, on the other hand, were directed indiscriminately to Ojo de Agua or to the capital, which at the time was suffering the offense of being called Ciudad Trujillo [Trujillo City].

writing. Margot, however, did say to me: "Tell Manolo that Raúl and I are going to roast a pig for him sometime."

Don't worry so much about being a bother. No one here has said anything. On the contrary, I think that Mamá is glad that I have a little bit of happiness. Haven't I had enough pain? It's the law of compensation.

I won't read this letter again so as not to condemn it to drinking the hemlock.

Affectionately,
Minerva

Telegram from Manolo to Minerva. August 23, 1954.
Saying hello from afar, with all my affection. Regards. Manolo.

SEPTEMBER 1954

Your love also helps me:
it is a closed flower
that constantly fills me with its aroma
and that opens up suddenly
within me like a great star.[4]

September is an important month in my parents' courtship, as reflected in Mami's letters, and as surmised from certain comments that Papi makes in his. Names that will be repeated throughout the correspondence enter into the epistolary universe, names of their family and friends, especially Hortensia Marcial Silva, Minerva's classmate, who is perhaps the person most frequently mentioned in the letters from these years of courtship. Some letters include their own little notes to Manolo. There are accounts of events relating to my aunts, such as Aunt Teté's throat surgery, Nina Patria's almost mythical garden, and an auto accident that Papi and Uncle Jaime suffered on the highway to Montecristi, among other things.

During this month there is also documentation of when Papi serenaded Mami, a story that he himself used to tell me at bedtime when we lived together after his release from prison in 1961. He used to sit on my bed and reminisce that he had traveled from Montecristi to Salcedo to serenade her with

---

[4] Neruda, "Letter on the Road," 147 and 149, with modification to Devenish Walsh's translation in the fourth verse. (t.n.)

Héctor "Chery" Jiménez, a friend of his who was a composer. Years later, he would be one of the composers of the "Hymn of the June 14th Movement." Given that the roads were so long and rough, the piano that they brought arrived out of tune, which meant he had to sing almost "a cappella." He always used to end the story singing me "Mujer divina," "Muchacha de ojazos negros," and "Yo vendo unos ojos negros,"[5] songs that formed part of the serenade's repertoire and that of their love affair. It moved me to imagine my mother listening to those songs while hiding behind her door, which she did not open that night.

This was the beginning of a relationship that would have to overcome constant geographic separation through letters, telegrams, notes, and messages. The letters from this initial phase of their relationship reveal not only anecdotal situations, but also their characters, especially Minerva's, as she is the one writing. The letters show my mother to be reflective, self-critical, passionate, and at the same time naive. It's astonishing how she spontaneously (as she often notes) opens herself up and wants her boyfriend to do the same. Every relationship that begins comes with doubts, and Minerva was definitely a demanding woman, forced to mature the hard way through reading, thinking, and circumstances, but not through romantic relationships. For that reason, not only would she write to Manolo to tell him about daily events, but she would also allow the intellectual and ideological load that was shaping her to emerge in her letters. Her correspondence was clearly not a banal matter for her; "Letters should contain ideas," she asserted.

Once again, in order to enroll in her third year of university, she had to overcome obstacles that remain unclear. She mentions this in a letter delivered by hand, and she opens up about the anxiety caused by being politically "marked," along with her hope that nothing happen to Papi because of her. We can imagine that this fear was behind Minerva's hesitation to surrender herself to a romantic relationship, so to speak. She was apprehensive about what this relationship could mean for the man with whom she was falling in love.

I have testimonies, and many of them, from people whom she alerted about these dangers. When Luly Caraballo met Aunt Teté and began to study with her at the university, Mami pulled her aside and asked her if she knew who they were and what risks their company entailed. When Luly responded that it didn't matter to her, Mami replied that, though she didn't doubt it, she

---

5   "Divine Woman," "Girl with Big Dark Eyes," and "I Blindfold Dark Eyes." (t.n.)

recommended that Luly consult her parents because she didn't want to put her in situations that could jeopardize her and her family.

As for my father, his girlfriend's letters allude to his habit of writing to her tirelessly before she accepted him, yet she complains that his epistolary intensity waned once he finally managed to win her over. However, their relationship aside, Mami's expectations were that he give of himself all of which she knew he was capable. She insisted that he work on his thesis, that he read, that he not distract himself with writing to her, and that he see her as she was: a woman who, when it came to love, had practically no experience, but who was willing to learn everything by his side.

"That which is inherited does not erode away." I like to think that there is some of that direct voice in me, that way of approaching loved ones with an eloquence for stating even the most unpleasant truths. Minerva Mirabal called things by their names, and when she wrote them down, she could be, and she knew it, truly and sometimes uncomfortably frank.

Postmarked September 9 in Salcedo. Received on September 11.

Sept. 5, 1954

Manolo,

Since you told me that two lines were good enough for you, I thought about writing just that, but I'm unfamiliar with the art of summarizing. The first line would say: "I miss you." But that tormenting voice, that meddling voice says to me, "That's not an idea, that's a feeling. Letters should contain ideas." And now you see, I'm writing you this one, which might end up being long . . . and unpleasant. Your letters say only pleasant things, or things that aspire to be pleasant, (and sometimes they make me smile), but you know that I like to say unpleasant things and, still, you ask me to write to you. I already told you that we'll probably just keep going around and around.

In the first place, I'm protesting your decision to come on the fifteenth. That's really far away. And if you knew it and could tell Dedé, why, when I asked, did you tell me that you didn't know?

I spent the week with Patria tidying up her garden. She really wanted to ask you to come today and to go for a walk. Of course, it remains merely a wish because I wouldn't ask anything of you that could distract you from your work. I'm not going down this path because it's full of spurs, and the voice tells me that it's not good for a letter to be full of protests. But, yes, there is still one more thing: Pedrito told me that you were upset when I tried to dismount by myself in the park. If you had told me so, maybe I would have tried to smooth things out. Forgive me, I was very nervous. Was that what caused your headache? What a shame!

María Teresa is all afraid now because you told her that the operation was painful. In any case, she goes for an exam the day that we pick up Hortensia, which, depending on her, I think will be the tenth. She (Mary)—in short—says a big hello. All those madrigals[6] about my "purity, chastity and innocence" make me blush. I'm tempted to start reading lots of naughty books to find out what it is that I don't know.

If your mother's greetings are true (are they?), I thank her very much. And there is no reason to be sad because some bushes have dried up. There are plenty here, and if they don't take root for you, we'll send them in a planter (how kind!).

This afternoon we're going to Moca or La Vega, where an uncle of mine lives. The trip was going to be to Julia Molina,[7] but I wanted you to be with us, so we decided to leave it for later.

But you must be tired already, or fatigued, or hungry, or have to bathe, or who knows what. I won't tire you any further. Farewell. My innocence doesn't allow me to say goodbye any other way. (Don't laugh! Though—ok—laugh, I'm laughing too).

Minerva

Unstamped.

Sept. 9, '54

Manolo,

"I take my weak pencil (I mean pen),"[8] remember? . . . to tell you that we've canceled our plans to travel to the capital because Hortensia is

---

6 "Complex polyphonic unaccompanied vocal piece on a secular text developed especially in the 16th and 17th centuries" ["Madrigal." Merriam-Webster Dictionary Online. www.merriam-webster.com.] Minerva likens Manolo's serenade to this musical genre. (t.n.)

7 This province, which used to be named after the tyrant's mother, is now called María Trinidad Sánchez.

8 Apparent allusion to a misunderstanding or inside joke stemming from the polysemic nature of the word "lápiz," which in some dialects signifies "pen," though it more commonly refers to a pencil. (t.n.)

unable to come now. Perhaps it will be sometime next week. I'll let you know.

It wasn't until yesterday that I received the letter that you wrote on Sunday. I don't know what happened to it. I'm glad you liked the book, but I don't remember Paula anymore. I'd like to know which attributes of hers you attribute to me. Bring it.

Thank you for the serenade. It was very lovely. I regretted not speaking with you. I would have, had I known it was a quick trip, but at the time I thought that you were in Salcedo.

Do me the favor of thinking about and reading and deciding about your thesis!

Affectionately,
Minerva

Unstamped.

Sept. 12, '54

Manolo,

Surely this letter won't seem strange to you since you've come to know me a little better. (This week I've had a lot of doubts and have been too impatient. But that's nothing new.) You know that I've deprived myself of many things—things that come very naturally for any girl—only because of my character. Although I've made every effort to tame it, it's always extremist at its core: it gives of itself completely and it demands everything. That's why I'm rather guarded about entrusting my friendship and affection. I don't want to assume more than what others feel *spontaneously* toward me. This is why, until now, I have repressed my attraction toward you: because I was afraid that you wouldn't return the intimacy and affection that I have desired for so long. Could you possibly satisfy my soul, my longings? I don't know. But it's essential that we be sincere to avoid later disillusionment. If you were to feel the same, I would be so grateful. I hope that this letter, a reflection of my selfishness and intransigence, teaches you a lesson! But how do I know what you think? You want to keep me guessing, as you made clear the last time we saw each other. But although I may not be very intelligent, I'm also not stupid enough to not know how to stop myself in time, to think you were going to give me more than you were. Why aren't you direct with me? Or am I being unfair to you? Is something the matter? I've reached that conclusion. There was a time when you didn't mind spending hours writing things that I might never read. Later you told me that writing to me became a drag "for you too."

It's clear then that your affection is waning. Now you've gone a week without writing. Very well. Don't think that I'm reprimanding you. I like your attitude, or rather, I like that you're sincere, but I'd like you to be even more so. Only by being wholeheartedly sincere will you have the right to say that you "are satisfied" with your behavior toward me. The truth never hurts me, but I hate insincerity, and it's one of the things that I do not forgive.

Thank you for all of the attention and kindness you have shown me. I will not forget them easily!

Minerva

Letter postmarked September 14 in Salcedo. Received on September 15.

Sept. 13, 1954

(I lost my pen,
 I hope that you don't outdo
 Champollion[9] but that you understand it.)

Manolo,

I'm sorry that you've had so many setbacks these days. If wishes protect and help, hopefully things have already started to go well for you!

I've written you letters in the past few days. I didn't send the first one because... you don't want to know! There was a storm. I decided it would be the last one. I thought that you hadn't written to me all week, that you hadn't replied to me, and it was that the post office was closed for vacation. I wrote the second one "*in mente*" yesterday, upon receiving yours, but I went to Jarabacoa because... well because I wasn't going to stay here waiting for someone who wasn't going to arrive. Now I'm sorry. Today I received your letter. Imagine that: Mamá, Mary, all of us here are so sorry to hear about the accident.

I didn't sleep these past two nights. I was thinking that maybe part of the issue was that you hadn't mentioned wanting to return. I suppose

---

9 Jean-François Champollion, (1790–1832) the French philologist who deciphered the Rosetta Stone. (t.n.)

that you haven't slept either. I'm so sorry! What do you know about the effect that your letters have? Have you received one? No? You've decided to pique my curiosity. I like to know what you think. Don't pay attention to my theories about letters; I don't want to stifle your spontaneity. The fact that they make me blush doesn't change the fact that they've been healthy, stimulating; they have awakened my desire to learn, to remedy my ineptitude. But I'm not going to consult you about the books I read. What nerve! It would be better if you recommend me one. For that matter, it would be even better that you not include me among your female students in plural, or I will find myself in the position, dear Professor, of finding myself other professors, you know? In moments like that, I wish the sofa were as long as the table, so I'd feel miles away from you. I'm glad that you're sincere. Tell your mother that I say hello back.

Were your parents implicit in the serenade? To put it another way, the ones who made you think of it?

We're going to the capital every day, and we keep on going. Tomorrow it will be 9 months since Papá's death. I'll go to Mass and will probably talk with Hortensia. I'll give her your regards. She's not mad at you.

I met Delta B., and it seems that there are a lot of presumptions and conjectures about our feelings out there. Of course, I was quick to deny such a far-fetched thing. Or do you think the opposite? Now I recall that in your letter, you give her my name. I'm still not convinced. I hope this letter doesn't seem too flippant for your mood, but I do hope that it brings peace to your spirit and joy to your soul.

So long,
Minerva

Postmarked September 18 in Salcedo. Received on September 20.

Sept. 17, 1954

Manolo,

I'd rather not have to write to you. Today I don't have any material. But we'll probably go to the capital on Monday. Hortensia's vacation begins that day. I offered to let you know, and I don't know how to say that I've been unable to fulfill a spontaneous promise. I'm glad that your matters are being resolved as well as can be expected. I was very worried for two days awaiting your—why not say it?—the letter I was hoping for.

I thought so many things! Afterward I received your telegram, which didn't seem very spontaneous. "Ah yes," I told myself, "he must have received my letter!" And I stopped feeling impatient about receiving yours. Of course, I'm happy about the news you gave me, but I can't deny my reaction. If instead of "I'll write to you tomorrow," you'd have told me that you wouldn't be able to . . . whatever . . . I'd have worried, I'd have written to you, etc., but I wouldn't have felt disappointed that you forgot your promise until you received my letter (3 days). My God! I feel like I make you dizzy with the word "spontaneity." It's as if it were the only thing that mattered to me. You see, I am in fact one of those women who "overestimate feelings based on trivial things."

By the way, are you using the word "curiosity" ironically? Anyway, it really made me laugh. You'll see that I've called it an "inclination."

If you come on Wednesday we'll definitely go somewhere since I want Hortensia to enjoy herself, and I'm committed to doing whatever I can. So as of now we're inviting you, however, wherever, and whenever it may be.

I'm sending you the letter that you wanted to read. Don't get upset with me if you don't like it. I haven't even opened it because I know that if I reread it, it's bound for destruction. I detest everything I write.

I'd forgotten to return Danilo's regards. Tell him that I'd be pleased to see him around here again.

Hortensia asks what's new. I'll tell her in front of you if we get together. Be prepared!

Goodbye. I pray that everything goes well for you.

Your demanding, intolerant, wary and now not-so-diligent student,

Minerva

Telegram from Minerva to Manolo on the same date.

Impossible to go today. Regards.

Unstamped.

Sept. 30, '54

Manolete,

I received your letter a short while ago. Mary is going to Salcedo, and I want her to bring this to you.

I was so happy to hear from you. I was happy that you are now working on your thesis, that you are working with Díaz Belliard, that you've seen Hortensia. I'm sorry that she's sad, etc., etc. I was rather downcast for two days, due to a number of occurrences. I thought that once again it was going to become difficult for me to continue studying, but perhaps it won't be so bad.

I was thinking of telling the girls to go in the car so that you can come back in it, so I can talk with you, but in any event, I think I'll go on Monday. María Teresa will ask Rafael David about my registration form, so I'll know if it is local or if it has transcended from beyond. Please, Manolete, be careful! For your sake and for mine! I have a lot at stake, and it hinges on your attitude. I think the grief would kill me if I knew that something happened to you because of me. But I don't want you to worry either. The worst part is the uncertainty, and now I think that it's nothing. But I'm telling you this so that you always be careful. Don't say anything to Hortensia.

I still haven't thought of any reading that could be useful to you. If you know of something that you want (for ex. *Courtroom*[10]), tell me in your letter today, which I hope you send with Chiche. They're waiting for the letter. How difficult this makes it to say something loving! But you understand, right? Don't waste time, and work hard on your thesis. Wishing you success!

Mine

OCTOBER 1954

"Who were we? What does it matter?"[11]

Papi spent much of October in the capital, so I don't know whether Mami only sent him one letter, or if only one letter from October survived the tyranny and the malice. In this letter, the couple's more playful spirit emerges:

---

10 The author of this work, Quentin Reynolds (4/11/1902–3/17/1965), had been in the Dominican Republic due to the October 1937 massacre of Haitians. In the January 22, 1938 issue of *Colliers* magazine, he published a condemning article that unleashed the dictator's ire. It's worth noting that Minerva refers to this book in this letter, which was hand-delivered. The copy that is preserved in Minerva's library was published by Editorial Constancia, Mexico 1951.

11 Neruda, "Letter on the Road," trans. Donald Devenish Walsh, 149. (t.n.)

Mami went about her classes with the typical chatter of young love, talking about Papi nonstop with her friend Hortensia, like any other girl in love.

The letters often reveal the affectionate relationships they had with the workers at the Mirabal farms, and of how these individuals became part of the family that employed them. Fello Rojas, for example, was a carpenter from Salcedo who did repairs at the house in Ojo de Agua. Both Mami and Hortensia mention him to Manolo, as if some of the anecdotes from their recent visit to Ojo de Agua had been worth telling. In the very first letter, she mentions other workers whom the Mirabal Reyes family loved deeply and whom Manolo would come to love just as much. Margot, for example, was Margarita Mora, the household cook, who had also been nanny to Nelson, Aunt Patria's eldest son. Raúl, who promised to reserve a roasted pig for Papi, was in charge of one of my grandpa Enrique Mirabal's farms.

The truth is that the cooks, nannies, drivers, employees in the store and on my grandparents' farms, as well as in my aunts' homes, all ran risks. They risked themselves when so many people were pulling back their support, and they often played vital roles in the events that would later be historic for our family and for the country. The loyalty, solidarity, affection, and familiarity between employees and employers was also part of a lesson in humanity for my mother and her sisters.

Now with only Dedé remaining in Conuco and Ojo de Agua, each time that we, the girls' children and grandchildren, visit her there, we continue to enjoy that culture of affection that exists in our countryside.

Postmarked October 11 in San Francisco de Macorís. Received in Trujillo City that same day.

October 10, 1954

Manolo,

Surely, you're now deaf or have an earache, or maybe you have one less syllable in your name, worn out by excessive use. We have mentioned you so often! The poor lady who took your seat in the car insisted on knowing your last name, considering it was the only thing that she didn't know after 160 km of listening to me talk about you. (Sorry).

Hortensia is here looking at the photo album. She wants me to share her joy with you (exact words). She has enjoyed everything and everyone so much, including Fello Rojas, and she regrets not having come sooner.

(There's no "talk of leaving.") That's what it said on the original 2nd page of this letter. I'm replacing it because I gave Hortensia paper to write to you, and she called you "dearest." Oh, no, I want to call you "dearest" too!

Dearest Manolo:

Tell me, are you behaving yourself? I really want to go on Saturday, but I don't think it's possible. Mary has terrible *hives*.

This letter tastes very bland to me, especially compared to Hortensia's, but today more than ever I'm having trouble writing. I don't know what's stifling me, and I have to send it so that you receive it tomorrow, and you don't become impatient. Work hard on your thesis. That way, when I come to visit, I won't study either, and we'll spend a lot of time together.

Mamá and everyone send you their regards.

Affectionately,
Minerva

Dearest Manolo,

Just a few words to tell you how happy, delighted and satisfied I feel while savoring all the good things found in this corner of the world. I want to tell you so much, that I can't find the words. All these kind people have won me over with their affection. How divine, and what personalities they have, beginning with "Fello Rojas" and ending with "Margot." How vivacious!

I'm so grateful for all your efforts during my trip! My stay in this grand "Ojo de Agua" has been so rejuvenating! When I get there, I'll give you details. Minerva is grinning "like a Cheshire cat!" I'm really enjoying seeing her so happy! Everything leads back to talking about you. Can you imagine?

See you later.

Affectionately,
Hortensia

November 1954

> [Y]ou will come with me to fight hand to hand
> because your kisses live in my heart
> like scarlet flags,
> and if I fall, not only
> will earth cover me
> but also this great love that you brought me
> and that lived circulating in my blood.[12]

The complex intimacy of two beings who love one another starts to become clear. Both of them seek in the budding relationship a mutual and intimate understanding that transcends affection, infatuation, and even the glossy photograph of a future that they envision against all odds. It's curious how that relationship comes clearly into view through the veil covering the patina that, over time, has coated my parents' letters and the memories shared by others.

I find that, once and for all, their correspondence discredits all those despicable men and women who survived them (of course) and who even survive their murderers. It discredits those individuals who have tried and who continue trying to convince us that Minerva was nothing more than a beautiful woman with whom the deplorable tyrant had become infatuated, and that Manolo was nothing more than an idealist who, broken-hearted by his wife's murder, chose to sacrifice himself. "Death would have been liberating, though also cowardly," he states in one of his letters from prison, when he confesses to Minerva how difficult it was to endure "that long, cruel and terrible moral torture" of knowing that the women were incarcerated. The living testimony in their correspondence clearly situates us along the path that they followed together, a journey of commitment until their last breath.

And so, it is in November that Minerva's modesty, her commitment to maintain her image as an unblemished woman, which she maintained until her death, was to become clear to the man she loved. My mother used the shield of what she considered to be right and dignified to explain to Manolo the platform of honorability upon which they would establish the ONE that they were and would continue to be. She drew not only from her own convictions, but from the values she internalized at home, in a family for whom

---

12 Neruda, "Letter on the Road," 145, with modifications to Devenish Walsh's translation in the first and third verses. (t.n.)

resolve, dignity, responsibility, loyalty, and courage were not mere words: "I'm grateful to you and love you more because you show that you want to be by my side, but you needed to go work! And you know my position on this: I don't have a mother watching over me, and as you very well know, at this point it reflects very poorly on us to be seen standing or sitting in a corner. It's true, right?"

And precisely for the admirable purpose of building their desired future together, of deserving it, Minerva focuses all of her efforts in her November 1954 letters on encouraging her boyfriend to finish his doctoral thesis and graduate with his law degree. She goes as far as to "preach to him," as she admits.

They were young students, and they were alive and in love. Mami got a perm to please Papi. Papi and his brother-in-law Jaime Ricardo built a seventeen-foot-long boat on which they frequently went fishing. Years later, under the pretext of fishing, they would take that vessel out to the open waters at night to listen to radio transmissions of the Dominican exiles abroad, primarily in Cuba and Venezuela. As colleagues, they shared books about law and literature, films, and even articles published in *Selecciones,* one of the few magazines sold with the regime's consent.

And they talked about what was important to them, because they knew that the life that they sought had to be invented, to be constructed, to be established.

Undated. Postmarked November 11 in Trujillo City.

Beloved Manolo,

Because I told a little fib, I find myself in the following predicament: I urgently need the measurement of your ring finger. In my desire that you graduate soon, I told you that the ring was here, but that is not true. Today when I went with Hortensia to tell them the measurement, there were so many rings to try on, that I felt confused and decided to just ask you for your size. So draw the ring that you have on a piece of paper like this ○ and send it to me right away.

I'm writing this in class, in the one from 6 to 7 (Roman Law), and Hortensia, who is here beside me, is glancing over.

I decided to write you anyway because I enrolled in Amós Sabrás's

Reasoned Arithmetic[13] class, and doing calculations, I found that if I wait to receive your letter, and it takes three days, plus the three that mine takes, and another three for your response, many hours are going to pass without word from you. I hope that right now you are happy with the result of the lawsuit. Hortensia asks how those favorable "criminal proceedings" are going for you.

"Hortensia" sends regards to your mom, Fefita—And as for me?

Manolo, seriously, I'm worried about the outcome of the trial. Will I know tomorrow? Please don't make me wait impatiently. Be courteous and "behave yourself." This morning I received your telegram, but I still didn't know what time you arrived, since it doesn't say when it left Monte Cristy[14], like it does on envelopes. By the way, today in class M. Cristy was mentioned a lot, and Hortensia didn't even take the hint. This letter is so full of nonsense! But I want you to know—if you don't know it already—that I have you on my mind and that I miss you a lot.

Tavares, who by the way is more interesting this year, is going to chew me out, and they've already rung the bell. Goodbye.

Hortensia is going to put this in an envelope and drop it in the mail.

Affectionately,
Minerva

Note from Hortensia:

(I didn't know that Mt. Cristy was going to make such an impact. Today she hasn't paid attention in class.)

Note from Minerva:

During the conversations either—I add.

---

13 Amós Sabrás Gurrea (1890–1976), professor of mathematics and member of the Partido Socialista Obrero Español (Spanish Socialist Workers' Party) who was exiled from Spain at the end of the Spanish Civil War. He spent several years in the Dominican Republic, where he was professor of mathematics and held several other titles at the University of Santo Domingo. He wrote a book titled *Aritmética razonada* (*Reasoned Arithmetic*). ["Amós Sabrás Gurrea," *Diccionario Biográfico de la Real Academia de la Historia.*] (t.n.)

14 One of a few variants on the spelling of Montecristi that appears in the letters.

Postmarked November 15 in Trujillo City. Received on November 16.

Nov. 13, 1954

Manolo Dear, Dear Manolo,

I've missed you so much! But in spite of that, I figure that it's ok, and there's no need "to rage against people who work in justice." You had to go, and the hand of God (don't laugh) made it such that you were unable to work on the case from here. I've thought a lot, which is why I'm speaking to you this way. I'm grateful to you and love you more because you show that you want to be by my side, but you needed to get to work! And you know my position on this: I don't have a mother watching over me, and as you very well know, at this point it reflects very poorly on us to be seen standing or sitting in a corner. It's true, right? Now if you come for a weekend, we'll go to a matinee, etc. Anyhow, we'll go out together three or four days, and that's different because, if you were to work here, I would only see you for a bit on workdays, whether because of my studies or because of my sense of responsibility and work ethic, with which you're very familiar. It wouldn't be possible any other way. Now, when you want and are able to come to my family's place to see me, know that I'll be more than happy to go home! Remember, too, that I'd prefer that you defend your thesis . . . in other words that you put this ahead of me, ahead of everything. Later, if you want, you can put me in that place. I have a feeling that you won't defend it until February. If that's the case, forget what I'm saying, but don't forget that I'm deeply hurt by the fact that you haven't defended it. Not because I still feel responsible; no, *mi vida,* I can't be understanding in that regard. Like your father says, nobody is responsible for what a person does except for that person himself. You are the only one responsible since, if you had put *all* your efforts and undivided attention into it, you would not have it hanging over your head.

But enough with the sermons. My desire to let you know how I see things has led me to become preachy. Forgive me . . . and on to the letter.

I called the salon after you left, ate, and went to get the perm. At three o'clock I was ready at the university. I won't say that it looks good on me, but I'm very comfortable, and I don't have problems combing it. I hope the curls grow quickly so that when we see each other they'll be a little longer.

Oh, Manolete! How embarrassing about your family! How can you go and tell them those things? I for one won't be able to show my face to any of them. Your mom is very attractive in the photo, so youthful! And the precious twins, absolutely adorable. I'm returning it to you so that you can put it back into the family album. Meanwhile, I'm waiting for the ones you'll send for me to keep. (Of course, I don't think that the twins have turned out ugly like "you.")

Today I found the copy of *Selecciones* and good grief, blessed memory! I kept meaning to give it to you so that you could read what you wanted to read. But I never did, and now you're really far away...

Dedé came yesterday. Everyone at home is well.

Regards to your family. And to you, I send that little heart, on loan.

Affectionately,
Minerva

Postmarked November 22, 1954 in Trujillo City.

Nov. 20, 1954

Dear Manolo,

On Tuesday I went to the Dominican Bookstore and was looking at the new edition of *Penal Code*. It's by Abigail Coiscou (1954).[15] With respect to Article 319 there are various Supreme Court rulings that might be of interest to you. I think you should buy it. I was tempted to copy them and send them to you, but the voice said, "Bah, Minervuana, don't do that! Don't you regret the feeling (so abundantly clear) that inspired your letter and that was neither understood nor shared since not even out of politeness were you answered promptly?" And the voice prevailed. In a way, I'm glad because it's... how shall I say?... it's like a liberation. When your letters arrive, they'll be well-received, but I never want to wait impatiently again. Thank God you've given me a lesson that did away with that phase.

Yesterday I went to Internal Revenue to pay the money for the ring. When it arrives, they will send you a receipt so that you can pick it up. What are the plans that you think I'll find objectionable? I suppose you mean that I "will notice" that you devote more enthusiasm and attention to the *long-term* plans for the boat than to the *short-term* plans for your thesis. (I suppose that it's lying at the bottom of a drawer, forgotten.)

---

15 Abigail Coiscou (1897–1983). *Código Penal y leyes que lo modifican y lo complementan* (Santiago: Ed. El Diario), 1945.

You know that doesn't surprise me; I already told you that I had a feeling, better said, that I "knew" that you weren't going to defend it. You mentioned a special graduation ceremony to appease me, but you didn't do anything because, instead, you went back to your hometown to resolve the situation related to your accident.[16] (This is one of the reasons. How many more are going to pop up?) If it weren't for this, you could consider yourself very lucky. Don't we all have our own difficulties? The merit lies in not allowing yourself to be defeated by them. I pray to God that new reasons don't force you to put off graduation until next October. I had resolved to quit harping on this, and here I am again on this same topic. It must be because, as the adage goes, "Out of the abundance of the heart the mouth speaks."

Manolo, if you haven't sent the Criminal Proc.[17] lecture notes, don't worry. Someone here offered them to me. But in any event, give them to me the next time, since you said something about them going to another address. I don't want them to get lost.

I've already started studying Civil L.[18] since they've designated a day for asking questions. So, I've had no choice but to sit down and read it. On the other hand, it's better that way; I don't go out, and to top it all off, I still have the flu.

María T. and Chelito send their regards, Chea sends you her warmest regards and says that she misses you a lot. Today I wrote to Mamá and told her that you send everyone your best.

Many thanks to your mom for her flattery. How kind. (I'm glad you've dotted your i's. I don't deserve them.) A warm hello to everyone. Don't forget don Joaquín.

I'm sorry that your father is ill. My deepest prayers for his health.

Goodbye. Sending you my affection.

Yours always,
Minerva

---

16 The reference is to a trial for an automobile accident that he had had with Jaime Ricardo returning from the farm.
17 Criminal Procedure.
18 Civil Law.

December 1954

> And when the sadness that I hate comes
> to knock at your door,
> tell her that I am waiting for you
> and when loneliness wants you to change
> the ring in which my name is written,
> tell loneliness to talk with me [...][19]

Coming to understand my mother through her letters means entering into the thoughts of a woman who knew herself to be complex. It means unraveling little by little the skein of reflections in which she searches for herself. The final month of 1954 was especially significant in this context: Minerva reveals herself in her words and in her states of mind, apparently needing to be transparent with the man with whom she has fallen in love, even in the pages of her own contradictions.

So, amid the loneliness that she felt in Trujillo City in the days leading up to the first anniversary of my grandfather's death, far away from family and her boyfriend, who lived in Montecristi, she admits to feeling depressed, and her doubts cast a shadow over those afternoons when she awaited his letters. This is a sad December, in which the flowers will be cut from the bougainvilleas to adorn Enrique Mirabal's grave. He never recovered from the physical injury sustained during the brutal imprisonments to which he was subjected as a result of the incident between Minerva and "the Chief" in San Cristóbal in 1949 and in subsequent years.

It is a shame that we don't have my father's letters from those days. I would have liked to read those "tender" missives in which he responded to the concerns of a woman whose feelings were particularly intense and who expressed herself through those feelings: her sadness, her doubts, her day-to-day concerns, without losing the fortitude to keep her sense of humor alive. I'm told that she never lost her sense of humor, even during the worst of times, when she felt threatened by the dark shadows that pursued her relentlessly until they ultimately took her life.

She makes us smile when she tells of her distractions, her "good pencil," her studies, particularly in the anecdote about her exam with Professor Virgilio Díaz Ordóñez, a well-known Dominican politician and writer who served as provost of the University of Santo Domingo. Her intelligence and wit emerge

---

19 Neruda, "Letter on the Road," trans. Donald Devenish Walsh, 145–47. (t.n.)

in the way she tells it: "I finally took Díaz Ordóñez's exam, or rather, he took the exam, and it turns out we couldn't have agreed more."

These letters from December have a more introspective tone. Amid the various anecdotes, certain individuals from her surroundings continue making an appearance, individuals who by then were familiar to Papi. Among them is Ana Antonia Rosario, better known as "Tonó," who grew up with the Mirabal Reyes family, lived almost her entire life in their home, and was like a third mother to all of us. These letters also reveal Mami's taste in films and music, which she developed along with an interest in literature, painting, sculpting, photography, embroidery, landscape design, gardening, sewing, and architecture. She was an intrinsically free, profound, and perceptive spirit who, as she herself said, would sustain herself with an idealism that would later lead to political action and resistance of the most defiant sort.

And with regards to Papi . . . I can't help but draw a connection between two images: the one that Mami evokes of him on their "dear corner," standing there with one foot on the wall, and the terrible photograph that was taken of him after he was released from prison, in which he appears looking over the site where my mother and aunts had been killed. It is the same image that Dedé recalls from her last conversation with Papi, of him on the veranda at the house in Ojo de Agua, in the same position, while with absolute conviction and serenity he said to her, "Dedé, my death is imminent." And it was.

Not postmarked. Received in Montecristi on December 6, 1954.

December 3, 1954

Dear Manolo,

Tonight, when I got back from the University, I found your letter. It made me so happy. I wasn't expecting it. I'm sorry you won't receive my letter today since I mailed it this morning. You could have received one, but don't you remember that bit about "sow and you shall reap?" You inhibited my spontaneity! You know something? When I read this letter of yours, which "aspires to be a loving one," you can imagine what I felt: a certain uneasiness, a certain suspicion . . . "Will it end up sounding forced?" said the voice, etc., etc. But anyhow, you deserve a prize just like a good boy who's done his homework. That's why I'm responding right away.

I finally took Díaz Ordóñez's exam, or rather, he took the exam, and it turns out we couldn't have agreed more. The topic was "The Middle Ages," and we came back to that famous discussion about whether or not it's dark, "the night" of the Middle Ages. We talked about the Crusades, Peter the Hermit, etc. I learned a lot.

You'll notice that I'm writing to you in pencil, but I'm not in the habit of being careful, and my pen is constantly lost. My patience for searching for lost objects is also lost, and this pencil is a good pencil; it's always on hand. By the way, your letter went out this morning because I spent the entire night and morning looking for a little piece of paper on which Antonia wrote to me saying that Mamá complains about you because you're not going to turn out to be a good guy like Pedrito. You haven't written to her. I was thinking about sending it to you, but like I said, it disappeared at the last minute.

I'll leave on Monday at 3 p.m. I'm laughing right now thinking that if you follow my demands precisely, I'll find a ton of letters there waiting to be answered, right?

I love you,
Minerva

Postmarked December 5 in Trujillo City. Received on December 6.

December 5, 1954

My beloved Manolete (says Isaura),

Today at 12 I received your letter. I also became worried, but I don't think there's anything particularly the matter with me. And don't say that I don't give you much detail. Don't you, perhaps, give even less? Better yet, let's flip a coin. You know what? I thought you weren't going to catch the plane, and I called your house to ask how you had traveled, and they told me by car. Later Olga told me that you arrived before she left. I'm happy to know that you got there all right.

I'm also happy with the portrait of the twins. They really do resemble you, don't they? What sweet faces they have. Give them my thanks and tell them that I hope to have the opportunity to meet them personally.

I went to the doctor, and he told me that I have only a slight infection in the right sinus, and he prescribed aureomycin. I'm taking and applying it. Tomorrow I have to go back for a check-up.

Anyway, and that bit about "I was at the office?" Had you told me that you have an office, or is that a new development? Poor don Joaquín, the butt of all the jokes ... but "blessed are the poor in spirit ..." What an old wise guy!

I'm reading Beethoven.[20] Tomorrow, God willing, if I'm not overcome by fear, I'll take the History of Culture exam. I'll write to you from the Commerce Department. (period) Machado is watching me.

How I wish I were in Ojo de Agua. I don't know why I'm depressed. Last night on my way back from the university, I was thinking about that. (Then, on the corner, "on your dear corner," I saw someone standing there with one foot on the wall, the way you used to stand back in the day. For a moment I had an illusion. I felt a longing for it to be you. It was probably Nanando.[21] Anyway, the issue is that I don't study, read, nor have any desire to listen to lectures, and I'm wasting a dreadful amount of time. I'll feel better with Mamá, so I'm leaving for Ojo de Agua on Monday.

I haven't seen Hortensia. She has the flu. I'm not good at riddles, but if it starts with an F and ends in leas, maybe your head is full of them. Oh joy!

Mine

Postmarked December 14 in Salcedo. Received on December 15.[22]

Dear Manolo,

On Thursday I received your letter. Since you'd told me in the capital that you might come this weekend, and you didn't mention anything, I didn't go ahead and write to you. Then on Friday I received the other one. So, I decided to call you on the telephone since, in addition, Carlos and Esperanza came that day and I wasn't able to write to you. But according to what the telephone operator told me, you were 4 km away on the beach at Club Ramfis, and it wasn't possible to contact you. On Saturday I learned that you had canceled your trip to Danilo's, and I thought there was no way you'd receive it ... Or maybe I didn't write to you because this

---

20 Apparent reference to *The Life of Beethoven* by Romain Rolland (1866–1944), which she mentions again in a subsequent letter. Another biography of the musician, Stefan Zweig's *The Mystery of Artistic Creation,* survived the ransacking of Minerva's library.
21 The name is barely legible.
22 Inside there is a memento from the Mass commemorating the first anniversary of Enrique Mirabal Fernández's death.

week marks the one-year anniversary of Papá's death. I'm not exactly in a happy mood, and I don't like to write mournful letters.

Mamá also received your letter. What an obligation, right? But I meant it as a joke. You weren't under any obligation to write to her, and much less speak to her about us. That was not my intention; I was referring to the time that she spent alone.

Nor is it my intention to ask you to not go out. That would be asking you to lie to me. I put myself in your place; if I weren't in mourning, I'd hop from one dance to the next. Don't you think?

Look, Manolete, stop calling me a gossip and a schemer. You know that I'm not. It's all in your imagination. And who knows? Maybe I'm ahead of the game. Look, I went back and read your first letters. They seemed spontaneous, sincere, affectionate. I wanted to send you that love song: "What is happening? What are we. . .," etc. etc.

It's possible that there is a discrepancy between the ideal and reality, and I can't help being an incurable idealist. When I try to conform to reality, I resemble one of those rivers whose murky waters hide its bed from view. It's possible that you and I will never really understand one another. By that I don't mean to say that you are not an idealist. You simply take life as it comes, as it should be. I can't be like that. This is my tragedy. Forgive me if I'm not explaining myself clearly, don't try to understand me. I don't understand myself. I think I lost my train of thought; I don't remember what I was going to say.

I'm sorry that you won't be able to see the bougainvillea blossoms. We're going to cut them for Papá's grave.

Manolo, haven't you seen the ad for *We Are All Murderers?*[23] I'd really like for you to see this film. I'm guessing it will remind you of your thesis topic, and it's good for you to think about it. You know what? I'm writing to you from bed, with achy bones all over because I spent the day washing the stones in the patio. I really enjoy doing that to distract myself.

María Teresa, Mamá, Patria, and Dedé all say hi. My regards to your family. Thank you for the kind invitation to visit your home. You know it's very difficult, but I really appreciate it.

I anticipate and hope that by now you're enjoying the holidays. Forget

---

23 *Nous sommes tous des assassins.* This 1952 French film makes a plea against the death penalty and in favor of abolition. It caused quite a worldwide stir due to the novel perspective with which it addresses the topic. Manolo's thesis deals with the rights of people deprived of their freedom and those in penitentiary systems.

about this *pelúa*[24] as much as you want, and have fun. Truly, I want you to enjoy yourself.

I love you always,
Mine

Postmarked in Salcedo on December 14, 1954.

Dear Manolete,

I was so, so, so happy to receive your letter. I was very sad for several reasons, among them because yesterday I wrote to you and, as I'm accustomed, I wrote many unpleasant things, and the voice told me, "Manolo is going to dump you."

Today I'm writing just a quick note to thank you for such a tender, affectionate letter and so that you forget a little bit about what a smart aleck I am. I'll take it to the post office myself so that it reaches you even sooner. I have a thousand things to do today and, to top it all off, we have visitors. My pen is useless.

Goodbye, *mi vida*. Come soon. Wishing you great success with your first trial.

Yours,
Mine

Postmarked December 30 in La Vega. Received on December 31.[25]

December 30, 1954

Dear Manolo,

If you come on Saturday, I doubt that you'll receive this beforehand since the mail is slow these days, but I'm keeping the promise that I just made to you on the phone. After I spoke with you, I called Hortensia and we talked for a long time. I'm really glad to have spoken with her . . . and with you. They're being a real pain here; they say that they had to fix the Monte Cristy line before I could talk with you, and it seems to have been the case, because I tried for three days to call you. I imagine that they'll

---

24 An affectionate nickname that Manolo had for Minerva, in reference to her hair. (t.n.)
25 It includes five National Lottery tickets.

come from home to pick me up on Saturday, but if you go early and pick up the girls, they'll come earlier with the car to pick me up.[26]

In any event, I want to do it this way because my aunt and uncle want to meet you, and they say that this is the only way. I'm sending you the tickets that I forgot. Manolete, forgive me for this choppy letter; I'm a bit scatterbrained as usual or maybe even a little bit more. Have you ever felt like after talking on the phone, it's like you're in another world? I think that's what it is.

I can barely walk because my foot has gotten worse.

It makes me so happy to think that I'm going to receive two letters from you. If it weren't for this blessed foot of mine, I'd go to the post office to ask what time the mail arrives. I, too, miss my dear *muchachito* very much.

Affectionately,
Minerva

January 1955

My love, it is night.
The black water, the sleeping
world surround me.
Soon dawn will come,
and meanwhile I write you
to tell you, 'I love you.'[27]

Of the letters that Papi wrote during their courtship, the earliest one in my possession is from January 18, 1955. I found it when I was an adolescent attempting to read all of the books in Mami's library in the order in which they were arranged. There were several letters and poems prior to that date, from a time when he was still pursuing her, but I have found only one of those: an envelope postmarked January 1954, which I discovered tucked inside a book. The January 18, 1955, letter shows that my parents were growing closer through their mutual interests, among them poetry. Federico García Lorca was one author whom they both enjoyed quite a bit. Lorca was fortunate; of the many books mentioned in the letters, his was one of the few that survived

---

26 She was spending a few vacation days in La Vega and is probably referring to her Uncle Simeón (Mon) and Aunt Ozema, who lived there.
27 Neruda, "Letter on the Road," trans. Donald Devenish Walsh, 149. (t.n.)

the repression and the raids. What remains of Mami's enormous library forms part of the exhibit at the Mirabal Sisters House Museum in Conuco, where the girls returned to live when their own houses were ransacked and destroyed.

Papi notified Mami—who had insisted repeatedly that he finish his thesis—that he would finally go to Santo Domingo to defend it. He had been unable to graduate with his class due to the fact that my grandfather, Papá Manuel, suffered a cerebral hemorrhage in mid-1954. That event forced him to interrupt his studies and was the reason for his return to Montecristi.

The names he had for her—Mamy, Darling, Chiqui—appear along with her pet names for him—Manolete, Nolo, "*mi muchachito*"[28]—and the affectionate way in which Papi called María Teresa "Mary." There is reference to the fact that Mami will meet Uncle Jaime, who at the time was Aunt Ángela Tavárez Justo's boyfriend and future husband. He would be shot dead along with my father in Las Manaclas in 1963.

As for Mami, I think it's important to draw attention to the misgivings and unease that filled her life with respect to her living situation. She and Aunt Teté were forced to move frequently due to persecution and harassment. Mami would not allow herself to complicate the lives of family and friends. Each time she met someone, she would ask them, "Do you know who I am?" She made it very clear that her being a persona non grata in the eyes of the regime could affect those in contact with her and put them at risk of being blacklisted as enemies of Trujillo.

And so she had to move from the residence of the Carmelite Sisters to the home of Mercedes Conde de Isa (doña Chelito in the letters). She lived there for over a year, as did María Teresa for three months, beginning in October 1954, when she began her studies in engineering. They were forced to change residence because General Miguel Rodríguez Reyes moved in next door. In spite of being a close relative on Mamá Chea's side, he created a very tense and threatening situation for doña Chelito for "having two hostile dissidents living in her house." The general took it upon himself to report anyone in the neighborhood who dared come close to them. Today, as unbelievable as it may seem, the appalling impunity that plagues us allows for a street and a neighborhood in Arroyo Hondo to carry his name, in honor of this scheming accomplice's loyalty and service to the despot.

---

28 "My darling boy" or "my dear boy," a term of endearment that in Caribbean Spanish does not sound as condescending as it might in English. (t.n.)

Persecution pursued them, even inside their new residence, the home of Evangelista Mues from San Francisco de Macorís, the mother-in-law of Marino Vinicio (Vincho) Castillo. The anguish of living not only watched, but constantly spied upon, in that house becomes palpable in the letters.

Reading Papi's letter alongside Mami's, I recognize the power of conversation in their relationship. Throughout the entire correspondence, Minerva's desire to not base their epistolary relationship on banal or mechanical letters is very clear. Preserved with one of the letters is a bit of paper that appears to have been torn from a notebook. On it, along with her class schedule, is a note in which she articulates, "This bit about writing each week for the sake of answering a letter that comes to satisfy an 'obligation' or service leaves me rather disenchanted and diminishes my interest."

As we will see throughout this collection of letters and in the testimonies that tell us the story of the ONE that was being forged throughout Manolo and Minerva's courtship, Mami wouldn't really have much reason to be worried; intelligent conversation and common ideals were the foundation for the love and strong friendship that existed between them. My parents shared and talked about everything... until death.

Postmarked January 4, 1955 in Salcedo. Received on January 7.

January 3, 1955

My dear Manolo,

As we were saying yesterday... That is, to pick up where we left our conversation last night, there's nothing new to tell you. But, yes, *mi muchachito,* I have things to write to you. I lay awake and thought of several things that I hadn't told you; I reconstructed and reviewed our entire conversation. Remember? You "accused" me of being stubborn about several things, among them giving categorical answers. That's a lie! It was that I had a point in my favor. Don't you remember that I had answered that question that day on the rooftop? "Whenever you can," I told you. Or had you forgotten?

I'll probably go to Macorís tomorrow to speak with Nelsy. Afterward I'll decide when we're going to Trujillo City. If you don't come, it will probably be on the 7th to get our lives back in order again. I see now in the paper that classes start that day. You know, I'm not as sad as you think. María Teresa says that "it's thanks to God that we're coming out of the situation as well as we are," since everything else seems made up. I'll write to you as soon as I know what we decide.

Today I read almost all of "The Dreyfus Trial."[29] I batted a record number of pages. I didn't write to you this morning because I got up late, and there was no one to take it to the post office for me.

María Teresa woke up with a terrible cold. If you decide to come, let me know, because in that case, I won't go on the 7th but rather after you come.

I hate to close since I believe I have several other things to tell you, but I'll try to remember them for my next letter. Give my best to your family.

I'm very sad without you and am sending you my affection,

Minerva

What is it that you wanted me to say to you in my letters? Ah! . . . yes, yes, "I think of you all often, always!"

There were various small pieces of paper inside the envelope of the previous letter. They appear to be notes from a class notebook.

Sociology—Thursday from 4 to 5, Wednesday and Friday 6 to 7
  Theory of Knowledge—Tuesday, Thursday and Saturday—6 to 7
  History of America—Tuesday, Thursday and Saturday—5 to 6
  Antillean Prehistory—4 to 5

In my next letter I'm thinking of telling Manolo outright that I'm finding this correspondence rather boring. This bit about writing each week for the sake of answering a letter that comes to satisfy an "obligation" or service leaves me rather disenchanted and diminishes my interest, which apparently, he doesn't wish to keep given that, although he should have realized it a long time ago, since I've insinuated it to him, and I've even taken the initiative, he hasn't wanted or hasn't known how to understand. He can't possibly be unaware that I'm rather unpredictable and fickle and that monotony will be his undoing!

We'll talk on the way out, but clarify something for me: Is it almost 6:00 or 7:00?

---

29 The only text dealing with the Dreyfus case remaining in Minerva's library is "J'accuse" by Emile Zola.

Are you truly worried? If it has to do with me, there's no reason to be. Just one thing: I have to form my opinion of you just as you are, not as you'd like me to imagine you. Sincerity is essential for you to be my friend. Do you want me to think that you don't do something if in reality you do? Understand that the sin—if there were one—would be in committing the act, not in my knowing about it.

My Dear Manolo,
I'm so very sorry that you were upset this morning. I know that it wasn't your fault, but ours, that we were the ones who provoked it. I didn't even remember what Ureña had talked about, but now I understand that you were right.

I love you very much,
Minerva

Postmarked January 9 in Salcedo. Received on January 10.

January 8, 1955

Dear Manolo,

I'm not going to the capital until Monday. After we talked, I decided to leave the trip for that date without an alternative plan, in spite of what we discussed. I'd almost say as a result of what we discussed. I don't like uncertainty, and I didn't want the trip to hinge on a telegram that might arrive late. I didn't send anyone to the post office to pick it up this morning. I don't know; maybe I was giving it time. I was thinking, "If Manolo didn't send me a telegram, and he were to surprise me, I'd be so happy!" But as you can see, at noon I went to run an errand with Mamá and still didn't know anything. I found out tonight when I got back. Manolete, what a shame you're not coming. Tonight, like one other night, I heard a car pass by and for an instant felt a thrill thinking it was you! You know, I'm feeling very sad and have no desire to prepare my suitcase, nor read, nor do anything since I learned that you aren't coming. The address is 15 Felix Mariano Lluberes Street, and you're useless! You wrote me no more than one letter this week.

Manolo, before I forget, I've thought about telling you a thousand times (maybe I've told you): Have you given any more thought to your thesis? You promised me that you'd type a copy. Have you done it during this vacation? Look, if it's true that you're going to "Trujillo City,"[30] why don't you bring Professor Ramos the draft? At one point you were thinking of doing that. Don't put off until tomorrow what you can do today. Don't even think that I'm going to accept you without an argument if you don't do it to please me, knucklehead!

Margot is fervently entreating me to say hi for her (reading and writing) and Mary says "Me too!" In short, everyone says hi, and I ... Get a load of this! ... It seems that writing to you has cheered me up.

Goodbye, my love. Think of me.

Mine
Regards to your family.

Postmarked January 11 in Trujillo City. Received on January 12.

January 11, 1955

My Dear Manolo,

Yesterday I wanted to write to you, but I ended up waiting all night for Parra, who had promised to bring me your letter. He appeared this morning deeply apologetic. Of course, he's already received dispensation because the "insults" had already fallen like rain.

I so wanted to be with you last night, you know? The voice is acting like its regular self. The Dr. and his wife were here with I don't know who else. Everyone was talking. I was listening, being attentive, but the voice was saying, "Manolo, if only I were with you! My hands in your hands!" And I kept thinking about that day when I told you that the dress wasn't scrunched up.

Please know that we're doing very well, so don't worry. We feel like we're with family. The lady of the house and the girls are kind and always smiling. You'll see when you come.

You've made me look bad, as I see that you *are* good for something since you wrote to me more than once last week. Well done! But don't let me grow too accustomed to those sweet, affectionate letters because, if one day for whatever reason you don't come through, don't complain

---

30   Interestingly, Minerva wrote "Trujillo City" in English. (t.n.)

if I think the world is ending and I board a flying saucer headed for the moon.

Hilda says that if I don't put the letter out now, they won't pick it up, and it won't go out. So maybe you'd like to receive it sooner, though it not be any longer than this, right?

I'm glad we have lots to talk about when you come since I, too, am eager to talk with you, that is, to fill you in on my new life, which is rather okay. Besides, it seems that now I'll feel much less awkward receiving you here.

The most loving of goodbyes from your
Mine

Postmarked January 14 in Trujillo City. Received on January 17.

January 14, 1955

Dear Manolo,

I received your two letters just a moment ago. It turns out that the address is #19 and not No. 15 like I told you in one of my letters and forgot to rectify in the other. Hortensia told me that she had spoken with the mailman. I thought that you didn't have time to write to me, but if there's the slightest error in the address, they return them. Thank goodness the mailman knows me by now since I was the one who went out to let him in. But it's very late, and I can't write more than a few lines if I want to send this off, so I'll do whatever possible to write to you tonight or tomorrow, I mean, because if you're coming on Tuesday, you might not receive it in time.

I wrote to Mamá the day I arrived. Mary Teresa, very happy and grateful, says hello back to you. We mention you a lot here. Hortensia is doing well. She says hello. We come home together on the bus since now we don't live as close. The street is between Danae and Pasteur Streets, parallel to them. If you come by way of Independence Ave. and turn toward the Malecón, it is the second house, that is, almost on the corner of Independence. For sure, here we're close to everything, and in certain respects we're far away from everything.

You know what? I've started going out on the town. I went with Hortensia to see *Magnificent Obsession*,[31] a lovely film. I'd have loved for

---

31 A 1954 film starring Jane Wyman and Rock Hudson. Wyman plays a widow who becomes

you to have seen it. Today I only have an hour of class since they changed my schedule, and I have two lectures with Guerrero, who won't be there, so maybe I'll go with Hortensia to see *Adorable Creatures,*[32] which they're showing at the Elite. It's French and supposedly quite lovely. Tomorrow I'm planning to study with Milagros, who said she was coming, since she lives close by. She's going to come study on a regular basis. Unlike what we did last year, the house here is very spacious, and we have more than enough room.

I'm glad that you're going to drive the tractor; that way you'll become nice and tan. Does that mean that I'll finally meet Jaime? I'm glad, but I'll feel embarrassed.

I won't write to you like I said at the beginning because I've poured all my material into this letter, and I thought it was going to be brief. It's your fault if this doesn't arrive on time. You're always going around complaining that my letters are brief, whereas you write me these tiny little things that I read in the blink of a rooster's eye, in a flash.

I don't know if I told you that Antonia is here. She came in the car with us. She's spending a few days with her sister, and she is the one who fixed up the room for us and helped us settle in. It turned out very chic.

Manolete, how long since I last saw you! Tell your family and Joaquín that I say hello.

Yours,
Mine

Letter without an envelope

Monte Cristy

January 18, 1955

Miss Minerva Mirabal
Trujillo City

My Darling,

Ten days have passed, and in all that time, I've received only two letters from you.

What is it? Why haven't you written to me more often? Have you

---

blind. This film is also mentioned in the February 2 letter.
32 A 1952 French and Italian film directed by Christian Jaque and starring Daniel Gelin, Danielle Darraux, and Antonella Lualdi.

forgotten about me a little? Your last letter didn't seem as spontaneous as the previous ones. Perhaps it's my thirst for tenderness that makes me so demanding, as you have often pointed out to me.

Do you truly think that I deserve to be characterized that way? I've been like an orphan lacking affection for a long while, my love! Only you, Mamy, have known how to quench my thirst for love. You've filled my loneliness. Oh, *bien mío,* how I cherish those moments we spend together! You are so loving, so adorable. You bring me the warmth, the impetus, the divine stimulus that my life has been missing. Maybe that's why I can't help but become restless when one of your letters "isn't as lovey-dovey," as you call it. Yesterday I wrote to you and explained the difficulties that forced me to postpone my trip to a later date.

Darling, since I've always respected what Mamá Chea might think about your trips to Salcedo when we're able to meet up, I was asking you where you thought it would be better that I go: to the capital or to your house.

To me it's all the same, except for the fact that we're more comfortable at your house, and I have the pleasure of being with your family again. Whenever you write to them, always remember to give them my regards. I'm hopeful that maybe we'll be able to spend this weekend together. In any event, I'll let you know ahead of time. But don't let that stop you from writing to me. Your letters can wait for me. Understood?

Here my days are rather boring. I barely do anything but read and study, and that with very little interest. I finished reading *The Red and the Black*[33] and a scholarly article about Federico García Lorca.[34] This poet has some marvelous works. Whenever you go to a bookstore, look for these works of his for me: *Yerma, Mariana Pineda; The Shoemaker's Prodigious Wife,* and *Blood Wedding.*[35] I'll bring you the article about Lorca so we can read it together. It's a magnificent study.

Tell me about you. How has your mood been at the University? I've decided to go at the beginning of February to take care of my graduation ceremony, degree, and other matters.

---

33 *Le Rouge et le Noir* by the French realist writer known by his pseudonym Stendhal, one of Minerva's favorite writers.
34 In what remains of Minerva's library there are various plays and the complete poetic works of this famous Spanish poet assassinated by the Franco dictatorship in 1936.
35 *Yerma, Mariana Pineda, La zapatera prodigiosa,* and *Bodas de sangre.* (t.n.)

Now I'm wondering, might you be the real motive? You tell me, my doll.

Regards to Mery and to Hortensia.

Yours,
Manolo

Postmarked January 26 in Trujillo City. Received on January 27.

January 25, 1955

Manolo, my darling Boyfriend,

How was your return home? Tell me, did you stay in Salcedo? I imagine that if so, you've seen the tractor. My trip went rather well. I arrived at 4 p.m. and talked with the girls until 6 and went to bed right after supper. This morning I went to see Milagros since she didn't know I was here. We studied Civil Procedures and made good use of the time, except for those moments when I lost track. I arrived back just a moment ago, ate and am about to bathe before going to the University. But I want this letter to reach you today, or at least that it be sent today. You told me that you didn't mind if I wrote briefly, as long as I do it frequently, right?

When I arrived, I had the pleasure of reading your letter and the displeasure of having given you reason to quarrel, so I hope that you write to me so often that I never again go past 10/2 (in other words, 2 letters over the course of ten days). There are only 20 days left before I see you, but I hope they pass quickly and that maybe you come a day early on the 14th, which is Valentine's Day. Are you in love? Do you know? I believe I am! I say a lot of crazy things. I miss you so, so very much, and I think about you so much that I dedicate way too little time to my studies. Don't be offended, but I'm thinking of forgetting you a little so that I can study more. That way I don't have to crack open the books while you're here.

Today I'm thinking of buying Volume III–IV of Procedure at Economato with the money that Mamá gave me. With the money from the Public I.L.[36] book that I sold, I'm going to purchase the volumes that I still need of Planiol.[37] What detail! I'm making you dizzy, right? Mary

---

36 Public International Law.
37 Marcel Planiol and Georges Ripert, authors of *Traité élémentaire de Droit civil* (*Elementary Treatise of Civil Law*) (1901).

sends her regards. Everyone here says hi. Relay my affection to your mom and to your whole family.

Goodbye, Love. Study and work hard. Think a little about your thesis and a lot about your

Mine

Postmarked January 31 in Trujillo City. Received on February 11.

Dear Manolo,

Yesterday I received your second letter. I started to write to you, ran out of ink, had to go to the doctor since I had a sore throat again, had to do a million things. The thing is that I didn't write to you. I didn't do it on Friday when I received the first letter because I was annoyed. You don't say why you went four days without writing to me, nor do you tell me why you arrived in Monte Cristy on Tuesday night. (Learn to count the first and last days of the contract term.) You're going out too much! I spent the week studying Procedural Law. I thought I would finish the first volume on Friday, but Dedé came, and I went out with her. We went to the zoo and to some stores. She was here when I received your letter, and we applauded several of your stories. I didn't study yesterday either (Saturday) because, as I told you, I wasn't well and had a lot to do. I didn't go to the university either.

Today (Sunday), Hortensia was supposedly going to come over to study, but she hasn't come. Mary went to a movie with Hilda. It's pouring rain here, and . . . You know what? . . . I'm thinking about you a lot! I'm glad you saw the film, but you didn't tell me that you wanted to be with me. At least things are going well for you. What I want is for you to be successful with everything and that you come soon, very soon. You'll have to study with me since I'm not planning on taking a break from my studies. Plus, you remember what don Isidro used to say about how useful you could be to us since you could explain some things to us. Ha ha! I hope that what you've told me about your thesis is not just to put my mind at ease.

Manolo, you can't imagine what I was thinking when you didn't write to me before receiving my letter: "Ah, men are all alike. They want to seduce a woman and get whatever they want, without conceding anything.

That's it! I'm going eight days without writing to him." And as you can see, you're my weakness.

It would be better if you took some tips from *Carteles*[38] on the rules and theories of romance. Maybe that way you won't neglect those small details that are so important when it comes to love, details to which your girlfriend pays close attention. Besides, you were so amused reading about kisses and that piece about lifting legs in ecstasy. I'll write to you tomorrow when I receive the corresponding letter, and I'll write to you as long as you do the same. I'm grateful that your family speaks of me with affection. Give them my best, always.

Will my *muchachito* like this little note? Perhaps not. But you told me that you knew how to add details to my letters. Do so if you wish. I give you permission, I love you.

Mine

February 1955

To tell you 'I love you,' care for
clean, lift up
defend
our love, my darling.
I leave it with you as if I were leaving
a handful of earth with seeds.[39]

Excessive and idealist are two characteristics that my mother readily attributed to herself. Throughout my life, I have often mirrored these qualities and have seen them as all too close, all too true both in her case and in mine. Indeed, excess translates to feeling, and idealism in its purest sense translates to one's heart beating to the rhythm of ideas. For Minerva Mirabal, love is also understanding, knowing, acting with drive and intensity. From what I intuit based on Papi's letters, and from what little I lived with him and continue to

---

38 This Cuban variety magazine was popular in the region and was one of the few foreign publications in circulation in the Dominican Republic during those years. It contained pieces by some important Cuban intellectuals such as Alejo Carpentier and Emilio Roig de Leucshering.

39 Neruda, "Letter on the Road," 149, with modification to Devenish Walsh's translation in the fifth verse. (t.n.)

live in his memory, I conclude that for him too, that was living. They were made for one another, I say to myself.

These letters bring us closer to their protagonists' human souls, perhaps because in them—beyond the truths—they leave nothing hidden. This mother that I had and that I have, this father that I had and that I have, transcend the mythical subjectivity with which the world approaches their stories. The extraordinary thing about this collection of letters is that it brings them closer to us; it makes them all too human, all too close, all too alive. Minerva Mirabal doubted. Manolo Tavárez sailed. Mami had a sore throat and limped on an injured foot. Papi suffered from terrible migraines and took a long time to defend his thesis. Heroes breathe too. They forget the occasional accent mark and cross out what they wrote, until their lives are taken away. In some of the places where Mami crossed out text, we can even see her fingerprint.

The February letters feel more intimate, and Mami allows herself to be a loving girlfriend, like when she tells my father that she feels weak to the bone with the need to rest her head on his shoulder. In these letters, she sounds as much in love as any woman in love: "every nook and corner spoke to me of you, and in the midst of it all, I repeated your name: Manolo."

New names of acquaintances, films, and characters from their readings appear in these letters. In one of them, Mami compares herself to Poppaea: "I'm more vulnerable than I appear, and not nearly as good as you think (Poppaea)." Poppaea Sabina was the wife of the Roman Emperor Nero. This is a noteworthy exaggeration since according to the Roman writer Tacitus, "That woman had it all, except for honesty." This seems to be in reference to Claudio Monteverdi's opera *The Coronation of Poppaea,* given that Minerva had developed an interest in this musical genre while at Hortensia's home.

Isaura Ventura, who was mentioned in a previous letter, was a student and a friend of Mami and Aunt Teté. She lived with them at the home of Chelito Conde. Silverita Trujillo, a close relative of the dictator, was their classmate at the school in La Vega, and Mamá Dedé recalls that they later ran into her once in the capital. When she mentions Elba, my mother seems to be referring to the sister of Dr. Ignacio Rodríguez Chiappini, one of Papi's close friends.

We Are All Murderers, a 1952 film that Mami mentions more than once, caused quite a stir by making a strong case for abolishing the death penalty. In another letter, she compares herself to Jane Wyman, who co-starred with Rock Hudson in *Magnificent Obsession* (1954). Wyman plays the role of a widow who has been left blind. Mami refers to this character several times in light of a problem with her foot, and given the coincidence with her limping.

What's more, there are several short phrases that are left unexplained for fear that the letters might fall into the wrong hands. From them one can discern the obstacles, problems, discrimination, persecution and threats that my parents received on a daily basis. So, it's not difficult to imagine that when Mami writes, "... I bathed in time to leave by 2 o'clock to go to Hortensia's with María Teresa, to take care of an errand of hers that has me very worried," this was not about some simple, everyday problem.

Tranquility was not exactly something that my parents, nor my aunts, nor my entire family would experience in their lives. Growing up amid all of this was a challenge, and achieving "normalcy" was something that forever seemed unimaginable.

Postmarked February 2 in Trujillo City. Received on February 4.

February 2, 1955

Dear Manolo,

It's been several days since you last wrote to me. I'm thinking that perhaps you never received my letter from Sunday (on Monday) because of a problem with the mail. Or have you forgotten me? You tell me to write to you, but you don't take the initiative. Is it out of pride? That doesn't align with your theory about achieving love through work, about intellectual love. On multiple occasions, I have been the one who has taken the initiative. Otherwise, just look, this makes the third letter I've written to you, and you've only written twice. I've wanted to see if it would be spontaneous like you say, but I'm convinced that you only do it when you have a letter from me to respond to. Don't tell me that's not the case; I keep close count.

However, for one last time (let it be noted) I'm forgiving you and writing to you, as if nothing had happened. But please, don't deceive me. I'm more vulnerable than I appear, and not nearly as good as you think (Poppaea).

You know what? All this time I wanted to write to you, but I waited to see whether I'd receive so much as a few sentences from you. I see that I don't deserve them. You know why else I didn't write to you? Well, because what I'm feeling these days isn't something you write down, it's a desire to be with you, a longing... I don't know... things not worth writing in words that mean nothing. I want to be with you! I just need some herbal tea and... as I grow accustomed to you being my boyfriend, you see how I don't know how to express myself? I'll give you an example: this letter. I don't know if you'll understand this, if you can interpret what I'm very unsuccessfully trying to tell you.

Mary is saying that the letter won't go out if I don't send it now. This comes as a blow to my inspiration. I don't know whether or not I should explain to you that this letter is written in pencil because it came out that way. In other words, the tip of the pencil didn't spew out ink. Get it? Yes? How clever! You deserve a prize. Claim it however you like.

I love you very much,
Minerva

Postmarked February 4 in Trujillo City. Received on February 5.

(I don't recall the date)

My Dear Manolo,

Just now (7 p.m.) on my way back from the university, I was laughing to myself. I was thinking "I'm going to write to Manolo, and I'm going to put: 'I'm writing to you because I'm happy. I've laughed so much! So much that tears have filled my eyes,'" etc. The thing is that I was going to write to you even though I had already written this afternoon, but I had a lot to tell you, and as I was telling you before, I was laughing to myself on the way back, and a young fellow who is here at the house said to me, "But, Miss, you've come back rather happy, laughing to yourself." It's that on the way back, I was thinking of you, and, you know what? What a pleasant surprise: two letters from you! Your two letters, which I received together this afternoon, by which point I wasn't expecting them.

Among other things, I wanted to tell you that last night I dreamed that we had bought a lottery ticket for the "32," and I saw your desk, a very lovely desk, and when I asked you why you hadn't told me that you had purchased it, you replied, "but it was with the money we won in the 32." That's why I was thinking, and am still thinking about sending you a lottery ticket. But if by chance I don't find one, and thus don't send you one, buy one if you see one! (It probably won't be a winner.)

Now I'll tell you about my life. It's raining a bit here too. To avoid getting wet, I rarely go out. I read, study . . . a little bit of everything. Of course, I don't know how a person as excessive as me adapts to such small dimensions . . . to so little. To tell the truth, I don't feel like going out. I haven't been back to the movies. On Sunday (in the afternoon) I went to study with Hortensia. I ate supper there, and we studied until nine o'clock.

I'm limping again, with one infirm foot. I have what they call a "ganglion cyst." Do you know what that is? If only you had seen me today: *juuust* like Jane Wyman, using my parasol as a cane, just like in the movie, feeling out the terrain. I looked just like her.

Manolete, *mi vida,* what a joy to receive your two letters. I put this one on hold to have supper, and I was there in limbo, with that cumulus of feelings that still makes me act as if I were in a different world . . . And how unfair I am! I'm so sorry that *mi muchachito* hasn't been well these past few days! And he wasn't receiving letters from me! Sweetheart, by now you must be better, but this letter will make up for all the whining from the past few days. Besides, you'll come soon, and I think I'll be good to you from now on.

Although you haven't mentioned anything to me, I might call Joaquín at the hotel to say hello (if it's the same one where he was staying). I think highly of him, and I'm overlooking his indifference, as I do when it comes to certain people.

Chea and Isaura came to see me recently one night. They found me in bed. (I go to bed like that every night: eating supper and going to bed). I cheered up being with them. Look, by the way, Mary's classmate is here studying and tells me that the lady where she lives (neighbor) says a lot of flattering things about me and asked her why I hadn't visited them, that they had invited me. She added, "I told her that you tended to stay in your room." You see? Is it out of habit that I don't go out? Or because *I love you too much,* and I'm looking out for you?

My love, I must tell you once again that it seems this pen is damaged; it doesn't want to spit out any ink. I'm sorry. I always pick what's easiest and what I have on hand. Say a special hello to the twins for me, and give my warm regards to everyone at your house.

With all my affection,
Minerva

Postmarked February 5 in Trujillo City. Received on February 7.

My dear Manolo,

Today my heart calls you by a thousand different names. The affectionate synonyms are stirring up inside me. *Mi vida,* I'm contrite, remorseful. During the past few days (before yesterday) I wrote you a letter that may have made you suffer. How it pains me!

This afternoon I went to the university. I left at 6 since I wasn't able to go to the office (that was because I hear someone talking about an office) Philosophy. I'm still imitating Jane Wyman with the cane and the shaky steps because of the limping caused by the little blister on one toe because of a burn that the Merthiolate caused me (one thing caused by another and causing another, etc., etc.) Well, back to my story, I arrived here at 7 because the bus situation is a serious matter—I ate supper and went out (in Hilda's boyfriend's car. He is here.). I went out on an errand that, as an aside, might not please you, although I hope you like it. But don't ask me about it because it's a surprise. After the errand they brought me to the Malecón. The breeze was very pleasant, and I was thinking of you. We were watching them work on the Festival, and then casually they mentioned that you had written to me. Imagine my desperation. I didn't dare ask that we go back. My anxiety was caused not so much by a desire to see your letter, which I knew would last a matter of minutes, but by the thought that today you'd receive my letter, which is so pretentious and ugly, as you say. (Manolete, are you going to dump me for picking fights?)

I'm trying to study. Last night your letters wouldn't let me. They filled me with a sweetness that, as it turns out, was incompatible with Commercial Law and territorial competency. I've become wed to Procedural Law, and up until now it is my only favorite.

Manolete, my love, I've been able to style my hair the way you like it. Hopefully I can have it like this when you come, to please you.

Bring me the copy of Accioli's *Public International Law*[40] that you lent me last year; I need some information from it, and as you know, I sold the other copy. I also sold *Penal Code* in order to buy the new edition, but I spent the money.

I'm not sending you the "32" because I didn't manage to buy one.

---

40 Hildebrando Accioli (1888–1962), author of *Traité de Droit International Public* (1946).

Milagros told me to be sure to tell you hi for her and that she's very concerned about your visit. Everyone says hello.

I think I'm suffering from calcium deficiency. (Don't be alarmed.) My longing to rest upon your shoulder has left me weak to the bone.

Yours,
Mine

Postmarked February 7 in Trujillo City. Received on February 8.

February 6, 1955

My dear Manolo,

I'm writing to you from Hortensia's house. I came to study and stayed to eat, so I've decided to write during the time set aside for digestion. I was thinking of doing it yesterday, but I went to Silverita's birthday and had some cocktails that put me to sleep by 7. You can't imagine how I thought of you at Elba's. Every nook and corner spoke to me of you, and in the midst of it all, I repeated your name: Manolo. (Hear it as it should sound: lovingly.) Hortensia is talking to me here in bed and is almost keeping me from connecting my thoughts. She says I've mentioned you too often and that I want to tell her for the hundredth time the anecdotes that she already knows by heart.

I'm so very sorry that my letters didn't reach you in time and that there were all those misunderstandings. As soon as I received your telegram, I telephoned you because I wasn't able to do it on Saturday morning. Hortensia says no, that I should tell the truth, that it was because I was overcome by desperation to talk with you. Manolo, I don't believe that they charged you $3.40 for the call, since we barely uttered half a word. If I'd imagined that, I wouldn't have told them to charge the call to you, but I didn't have any money.

Yesterday I received the letter that you wrote me telling me about the trial. I've already responded to all the other ones. I suppose you haven't received them because, since they were written in pencil, they thought that they weren't important, and they left them for last.

Manolo, I'm going to write to you tomorrow, Monday and Tuesday, and then I won't write you again, since if they take 4 days, then perhaps they won't reach you, and when they arrive, you'll be on your way to T.C. (God bless you, my son.) Since you'll be there for several days, it's best not to send them, though that depends... Maybe I'll write to you on Wednesday. Goodbye, my love.

Sending regards from Hortensia and loving affection from
Mine

Manolete,

When you come, we're going to see *We Are All Murderers,* which they're going to show at the Capitolio for $0.25. Besides, there are several good films being advertised at the Capitolio.

I'm sorry that you got scalped, you should have done so with a barber and not with a gambling slip. I insinuated the 32 to you, and I thank you for taking it so literally. Hortensia is going to respond to your three letters in the following paragraph, but she'll have to use another sheet of paper:

Note from Hortensia:

Manolo,

This is impossible; this girl is incorrigible. This paper was for me, but she wanted to keep telling you more. A moment ago, she was telling me how she'd had her fill of that. Then I was thinking that you're going to get a kick out of this because when she overloads, she explodes, and you know that those missiles are long range. So much for the 3-mile limit for territorial sea, so be careful. I'll write when there's more paper.

H.

The postmark is illegible. Received on February 8.

February 7, 1955

Dear Manolo,

I just received your letter, which I suppose was written yesterday, Sunday. I don't know about the dates. I was so happy to receive it, though I was hoping for 3 or 4. The best thing to do is to count all the ones I've received to see if they add up to eight or ten like you say. I wrote to you yesterday too, and I hope you've received it. I forgot to tell you that for now I have faith, *mi muchachito.* I just worry that some obstacle will emerge, and you won't be able to come. I beg God that doesn't happen. I feel a frailty, a weakness in my bones, a terrible longing to rest upon your chest, but if for some reason you can't come on the day you said, don't worry about it. Let me know. I'll understand. How I laughed imagining the swarm of lottery ticket vendors running after you! Don't pay any attention to me from now on.

I'm studying a lot. My foot has healed. I'll write to you tomorrow. Regards to your family. Is there anything you could add to this letter?

Yours always,
Mine

Postmarked February 10 in Trujillo City. Received on February 11.

Dear Manolo,

Just a quick note on the run, since Milagros left at 12 p.m. after studying. I bathed right away in order to leave before 2 for Hortensia's with María Teresa to run an errand of hers that has me rather worried, but I wanted to make sure to write to you beforehand so that this goes out today. I hope all is well with you, that everything is going splendidly, that this letter arrives before you leave, and that it brings you a light-year of affection. I haven't received a letter from you today. Have we reached the end of the 10 or 12 that you wrote? Right now, I'm trying in vain to remember the things that I thought about last night to write to you today.

Receive a caress from
Your Mine

MARCH 1955

They will touch this fire
and the fire, my sweet, will say your simple name
and mine, the name
that only you knew, because you alone
upon Earth know
who I am, and because nobody knew me like one,
like just one of your hands,
because nobody
knew how or when
my heart was burning;
only

your large brown eyes knew,
your wide mouth,
your skin, your breasts,
your belly, your insides,
and your soul that I awoke
so that it would go on
singing until the end of life.[41]

Although Mami dated the first letter "March 6, 1954," the postmarks on the envelope indicating the date sent and the date received show that it was actually March 6, 1955. The context and the reference to my grandfather's visit—having gone to the capital with part of the family for Papi's graduation on February 25—point to Mami's mental lapse when writing the year. There are two other letters from around that time that say 1954.

It seems paradoxical that Manolo, who only a few years later would suffer the regime's tortures more than anyone, would choose as a topic for his thesis, under the direction of Professor Leoncio Ramos: *Justice and Punishment: Considerations Regarding the Historic Evolution of Penal Systems* and that among his conclusions, he would propose that the penitentiary system move toward improving the prisoners' living conditions and that the treatment they receive be humane and moral.

My father spent about three weeks in the capital between mid-February and early March. Afterward, they write little between the two of them about what they did, but thanks to what Minerva writes to her family, we know that Manolo went back to the capital on March 11 or 12 and stayed until the 22nd.

The second letter includes a note from Nina Patria, reminding Papi that he could always spend the night at her house when he was in Ojo de Agua.

"Love," "*mi vida*"[42] are terms of endearment that Mami had started to use more frequently with Papi, which shows that her affection, familiarity, and trust had overcome little by little all the questions, restraint, doubts, and distance of the first months of courtship. By this time, my parents found themselves deeply in love. "Goodbye, Love, I'm sending you a farewell as tender as the one you gave me (but, please, not in public)," she writes.

On March 8, Mami refers to a visit by Mamá Dedé and her husband at the time, Jaime Fernández Camilo (Uncle Jaimito), accompanied by his sisters.

---

41 Neruda, "Letter on the Road," 149–51, with modifications to Devenish Walsh's translation in the fifth, seventh, and twelfth verses. (t.n.)
42 "My life." (t.n.)

One can imagine that with such a small circle of friends who weren't afraid to spend time with the Mirabal sisters in Trujillo City, the visits arriving from Salcedo were a treat that they thoroughly enjoyed.

Throughout the correspondence, we catch glimpses of what my parents were reading, which I personally find fascinating. In the long letter dated March 8, Mami expresses her delight at the fact that Papi has enjoyed one of her favorite writers from the 1940s, Romain Rolland, a French activist and pacifist. The only book currently found in her library is Volume II of *John Christopher*, which she had lent him, and to which she apparently refers. In the same paragraph, she mentions Beethoven's biography along with Rolland.

In this letter we also see Mami's typical epistolary style of producing content that is not only anecdotal, but that also reflects the ethical, existential, and social concerns that they shared. She relates that Hortensia had received a letter from her boyfriend, Wadi, breaking up with her because he was going to respect his mother's decision and marry an Arab woman. Hortensia reacted by wanting to become a nun and by closing her heart to love. This letter is a testament to my mother's understanding of true friendship. It is evident that by this time, my parents shared everything; even without reading his responses, we surmise that Papi was involved with his girlfriend's family and friends to the point that Mami asked him to write Hortensia a letter advising and consoling her.

There is also reference to the surveillance and harassment by the *caliés* with whom she was living at the home of Evangelista Mues: "In regard to how I'm doing, I'll say that in many ways the atmosphere has improved, so rest assured."

In the subsequent letter, we realize that she is indeed looking to move to a different house and that she does not even want to tell my grandmother, so as not to upset her. She accepts Papi's advice and prepares to move out quietly and without prior notice: "I won't leave this house until I leave during Holy Week. At that time, I'll tell doña Evangelista, either that I've satisfied my attendance requirement, and I'm not planning on returning to the university, or that if I return, it will be to study with a classmate at her place and that María Teresa is faced with the same problem. If I don't tell her this way, I'll write to her from home just like you told me," she writes.

I imagine how immensely defenseless my mother felt, unable to trust anyone, not even the people with whom she lived. Much to the contrary, she felt terrorized there. She was losing weight, becoming ill, and suffering from insomnia. She would sleep with Hortensia and spend all day at the university in order to avoid going back to that house. A paragraph from the March 25 letter clearly reveals the horror surrounding her:

> ... yesterday I paid the owner the monthly rent to convince myself of my decision to wait until Holy Week, but I think that has worsened my condition. How awful! Is my spirit quickly aging? I sleep with Hortensia almost every night. I go to the university in the afternoon, but still, I understand what prisoners with temporary release must feel when they are allowed to leave during the day.

Nonetheless, while she eagerly awaited Holy Week, Mami continued trying to live with some kind of normalcy, which she was never permitted because she had defied the regime. She attended French classes at the French Alliance, exercised, and enrolled in extracurricular courses in philosophy. What character! Papi continued to be the shoulder upon which she rested her tormented head: her accomplice, her friend, her boyfriend, her colleague, her companion, her comrade, her territory.

Postmarked Trujillo City. Only 1955 is legible. Received on March 8, 1955.

March 6, 1954

Dear Manolo,

Do I need to tell you how very much I've missed you? You know. You're so good to me, my love. Since the moment you left, I thought of writing to you so that you'd receive this letter tomorrow or Tuesday at the latest. I came directly here from the airfield and studied. I did not go to the movies at 10 like I told you. I didn't feel like it. Your loving farewell lingers on my cheek, as if palpable. Sometimes it seems that if I turn my head, I'll see you there. I feel you so close!

I didn't go to the university this afternoon. It was Milagros's birthday, and she begged me not to go. We met up with Hortensia, bought pudding "by the pound," sang Happy Birthday and had a condensed milk cocktail. If my spirits hadn't been so low, I'd say that we had fun.

Today, Sunday, (5 p.m.) I haven't gone out. I exercised on the machine and slept a little while. I might go to Hortensia's now to bring her some eggs that Mamá sent her. (I wrote to Mamá.)

Oh, Chiqui, don't worry about how I am. I'm fine. With regards to what we discussed, in a subsequent conversation I became convinced that it was Rosita like I'd told you. The lady told me that she hadn't taken that into account and that she didn't detect anything bad about her. That's why she didn't say anything to me, until she called her attention to that particular thing, in the end. Maybe they're right; each person has her own way of being.

Tell me how everyone is at your house, if your father got back ok. The girls loved him. On the way back, they were telling me about a poem that he had recited for them. What a nice man! Tell your mom that I'm very glad that she takes care of you, that although you say you don't need it, it's good that she snubs all those girls who want to bother us.

I had done most of the French exercise to send to you, but late yesterday someone used the typewriter and threw it away, so I'll have to redo it, although I won't send it to you until you have the code. I'm writing to you on the paper that you gave me, *mi vida*. Look how it's come in handy.

Goodbye, Love, I'm sending you a farewell as tender as the one you gave me (but please, not in public).

Your Mine

Postmarked March 8 in Trujillo City. Received on March 9.

March 8, 1955

My dear Manolo,

Last night when I got back from the university (from French) I found your letter. It did me such good! However, while thinking about flirting with the girls on the corner, you forget that you miss me, that is, to tell me that you miss me. Dedé came yesterday with Jaimito and his sisters. She insisted like crazy that I tell her whether I'd met your father, etc. I was taken aback, and you know what she said to me? That it was so she could tell Mamá since it was something that had her concerned. I wouldn't have imagined. I didn't think about everyone else because, in that regard, I personally prefer to let things run their course. Your father told me that it was best to go with the flow. I hope that you turn into a current that's at least convincing if not overwhelming and that you carry some of them to our house so that they can meet.

Mi vida, thank you for saying all those comforting words and for mentioning Rolland. I'm glad you liked it. I suppose it's difficult to obtain the complete works. You probably remember what the man told us about the Beethoven set: that it included 20 illustrated volumes in an expensive edition, which is hard to come by here. I'm telling you because you know how much it interests me, and I've been looking for it forever, but in any event, I'll run the errand.

I went to the photographer's, and he told me that the photos will be ready on the 25th. You look really good.

Milagros just left. I started writing to you while she was getting ready. She told me not to forget to tell you how much we missed you at 10 when we were eating cold eggs. They were tasty, with a little bit of salt so that they do some damage.

I'm glad I didn't write to you yesterday. I was very depressed and didn't want to worry you, but I'll tell you: on Sunday I went to take your letter and the one from Mamá to Hortensia so she could drop it in the mail for me. She was on retreat, and she decided to become a nun. Coincidentally, that same day a letter arrived from Wadi, informing her "so that she not learn it from someone else" that he was going to get married before returning "to please my mother, who has wanted me to marry an Arab woman." Imagine how the events unfolded. At her house (Hortensia's) they didn't know anything about her decision, so they interpreted the best they could the fact that we were both crying our eyes out. I still can't hold back the tears when I think of those moments. You know how much I love her and that in her I've found my ideal of friendship based on understanding and selflessness. Yesterday I was telling her that I couldn't even study with her because I couldn't encourage her, nor do it naturally when we didn't share common ideals.

As you can understand, that came as a relief to her and was done on purpose. I told her that I was thinking about writing and telling you, that I am as convinced as you are that she is bringing this upon herself by insisting that she'll never love again like she has loved, and that it seemed to me that she only knew "the decorations" of love—the flowers—because true love is understanding, and she can find a man who is better and who makes her happier than he did. He doesn't deserve her when, knowing her and seeing her for who she is, he stomped all over her feelings that way. But she told me that she doesn't want to love again. No, I told her, what you want is to hold on to that illusion, to put it on a pedestal. It's just like how common sense tells us that a gambler wants to win, but deep down inside he has an uncontrolled desire to lose it all. "One day you'll be convinced," I told her. "Ah! If I could promise you that we'd work together when we finish, I'm sure that with Manolo and me, you wouldn't feel so alone." I accomplished one thing: I got her to postpone her decision. I understand that I've been selfish, but it hurts so much to lose someone you love, and we'd lose her. Right, my love? Worst of all is the uncertainty that this would make her happy.

Be understanding with her, my love, write her a letter like the other ones you sent, which I'm sure were a real comfort to her. I'm going to her house to study now. From there I'll call Eva to see what's happening with your exequatur[43] and to ask them to let me know as soon as it arrives at the attorney general's office. I hope that your work is going well. Tomorrow is a holiday, and I'll probably spend the day studying at Milagros's house.

Today I haven't even exercised. I'll do it tonight.

I'm sending you this little fragment of Patria's letter. Give my best to everyone at your house.

I love you very much. I count on you for everything; you are like my crutch, my old shoe, my love. It's a terrible feeling, so weak to the bone and not having your beloved shoulder nearby.

Hugs,
Your Mine

Fragment of a letter that Patria sent to María Teresa and Minerva:

Kisses to Minerva. Have her tell Manolo that he has a place here with us when he comes back. With much love from your sister, Patria.

Postmarked March 11 in Trujillo City and stamped "received" twice: on March 12 and on March 15.

March 10, 1955

My dear Manolo,

I just received your most recent letter. I received the other one yesterday. As you'd anticipated, I spent the day studying with Milagros. I came back at six, like in the good old days, remember? And when I arrived, tired and with an irritated throat, I found your letter, which I needed. I was

---

43 Official permission required to practice law under the Trujillo regime (t.n.)

going to respond right away, but I got to changing my clothes to go to the Alianza, and by the time I ate supper, I'd run out of time. I arrived at eight to do my exercise, and when I plopped into bed, it was because I was worn out. As an aside, all of this really helps me to sleep well. But going back to your letter, I lament that mine have been delayed. (It seems I've lost track of what I was going to tell you because they called me to eat, and I had to set this aside.)

I've called Eva twice but haven't been able to reach her, so I still can't tell you anything about your exequatur.

They already sold the Ganaux,[44] so that's the reason I didn't buy it. They bound the Public International book for me, and it turned out really nice. The three volumes cost me $5.00. What do you think?

I'm about to go to Hortensia's to go to the university together. I've gone every single day since Sunday. Graciela says that if it weren't for me accompanying her, she'd be dead. Be sure to write to her. She knows that I've asked you to write, and she might be awaiting a few lines from you. They will lift her spirits.

Love, you are so good and understanding. I cried when I received your letter. I think I'm too sentimental.

In regard to how I am, I'll say that in many respects the atmosphere has improved, so rest assured. It seems that in a way, they've understood that I'm very sad, and although they don't know why, they try to be understanding with me. I really appreciate that.

They returned *Broad and Alien Is the World*.[45] You can take it when you come.

I don't know if I told you that they put A. Óscar Pacheco as our Procedure[46] professor. Tavares remains unchanged. They also put don Pachi in Roman.[47] On the one hand the schedule is lightened up because now I have class every day from 3:00 to 4:00, and I don't have as much overlap between the classes from 6:00 to 7:00 and Philosophy. I'm making prog-

---

44 The name is unclear but is possibly a reference to René and Pierre Garraud, two canonical authors of French criminal law. The reference also appears in Minerva's letter postmarked Sept. 22, 1955.
45 A distinguished novel of Latin American Indigenist literature by the Peruvian Ciro Alegría (1909–1967). Mami's library contained the first edition from 1941.
46 Civil Procedure. (t.n.)
47 Roman Law. (t.n.)

ress on the machine. What agility! If I continue like this, you'll be amazed when you see me.

I think I've written you enough foolishness.

Tell all your family that I say hello, and tell your father many thanks for his kindness. As you know, I, too, liked him a lot. Write to me long, frequent letters. Think of me.

Your Mine

Postmarked March 22 in Trujillo City. Received on March 23.

March 22, 1955

My dear Manolo,

I thought of writing to you yesterday, but Jaimito came, and I had to run an errand for Dedé, so time got away from me. I've missed you a lot. Last night after leaving French, I went to Hortensia's, and we studied until 12. I just got back from there. It's 8 in the morning. You know what? *"More,"* you're very demanding. What a quarrel that was on Sunday. I'll have to put you on a diet, because the more you get, the more of a glutton you become. Chiqui dear, I hope you've had a good trip and that you're working a lot and studying more.

Yesterday I asked Herrera Billini about the copies issued by the notaries, and he told me that a judge's authorization is required for their issuance in all cases. So, then I pointed out to him what you'd told me, and he promised me an answer by today. He said he was going to see what precedent has been established.

Love, I had so much to tell you! But now I don't remember. They were sweet nothings. I'm sorry for not having gone to the airfield to say goodbye to you, or at least having telephoned, but since doña Emma moved, I no longer have a phone nearby that I can use.

I still haven't figured out how I'm going to go about leaving. I'm thinking about going with Hortensia to look at a house today, but imagine, I'm trying to think of how to tell Mamá in such a way that she doesn't worry.

Manolete, I don't want you to worry at all about me. I'm not doing so poorly. It's just that I miss you immensely, and I'm feeling very whiny, and so I can no longer count tolerance among my few qualities. But we'll see each other soon, and we'll be relaxing at home together. I still haven't looked at the calendar, but I hope Holy Week is right around the corner.

I'll write to you tomorrow to tell you the professor's response. Write me a lot and always think about your girlfriend, who loves you very much.

Mine

Postmarked March 23, 1955. Received on March 24, 1955.[48]

My dear Manolo,

Just a few lines to send you my affection. I offered to write to you today to let you know about your question, but I wasn't able to see Herrera Billini.

My love, I've decided what I'm going to do, just as you suggested. I won't leave this house until I leave during Holy Week. At that time, I'll tell doña Evangelista, either that I've satisfied my attendance requirement, and I'm not planning on returning to the university, or that if I return, it will be to study with a classmate at her place and that María Teresa is faced with the same problem. If I don't tell her this way, I'll write to her from home just like you told me.

Manolete, my pain is gone. I've slept well these nights at Hortensia's, and Graciela has treated me with some cupping glasses, which healed me. Man! I liked them way too much. Hortensia laughs at how much I enjoyed it. I'm also taking some vitamins that Dr. Melgen told me to take. I'll try not to lose any more weight so I don't scare Mamá when she sees me.

I'll write to Mamá now. I'm going to leave this letter "half baked" until twelve to see if I receive one from you.

I just received your letter. I'm so sorry that you're sad. I'm sorry about the priest who was killed,[49] about your mother. In short, I hope that upon receiving this you are in better spirits.

Love, I'm writing to you from my room. The smoker is here interrupting me with her visual chatter. I prefer not to continue writing to you so that I don't end up writing something atrocious. The second trimester of

---

48 The letter itself is dated 1954, but the context suggests that this is an error, as in the previous case.
49 Father Vicente Yabal or Llavaly, a young priest and friend of the Tavárez family, very well known for his social work in Montecristi and Villa Vázquez. He died in a traffic accident.

classes ends on Thursday of next week. I'll very likely leave on Friday at 6 with El Rubio.

Say hello to your mom, your dad, the twins, Ángela, Díaz Belliard and to [?] Jaime. Study hard, Love, I'm with you at all times.

I love you,
Minerva

Postmarked March 26, 1955 in Trujillo City. Received on March 28, 1955

March 25, 1954

My dear, cherished Boyfriend,

Did you tell me that it seemed like a century has passed since we parted, or is it a unilateral daydream on my part? In my loneliness, the minutes seem like hours; that's how time passes for me. I want to have patience. I look at the ceiling a hundred times to convince myself that it's not falling on top of me. It's useless. Yesterday I paid the owner the monthly rent to convince myself of my decision to wait until Holy Week, but I think that has worsened my condition. How awful! Is my spirit quickly aging? I sleep with Hortensia almost every night. I go to the university in the afternoon, but still, I understand what prisoners on temporary release must feel when they are allowed to leave during the day. But, my love, I don't want to worry you; forgive me for telling you these things, but right now I don't have time to think about what I'm going to tell you (I'm always writing you in a rush), and it seems that this anxiety is spinning out of control.

I received your letter yesterday afternoon. How it cheered me up! I'm sorry that you don't have as much work as you'd like, but it will come. All in good time. Today I finished studying Commercial. I know nothing. Tomorrow we start studying Roman, which I hope to finish before I leave. That way, all I'll have left is International, and I'll be caught up (in theory).

I'm finishing this letter at Hortensia's. I'm going to send it to the post office with Graciela. Hopefully you've received my letter relating the professor's opinion with regards to the copies: you always need to request court authorization, because this is a special provision for the applicants, who are the only ones who can request them. You know what? I too think a lot about our last moments together. *Mi vida,* cheer up. We're united in spite of everything, in spite of the distance. I love you.

Yours,
Minerva

Note from Hortensia:

P.S. Manolo, no one, not Mary nor I have gotten anywhere begging this animal to . . . to go to the Dr. Don't look at me if you find her in the hospital.

Note from Minerva:

P.S. Don't pay attention to the evil tongues that try to worry you.

Kisses.

Postmarked March 27 in Trujillo City. Received on March 29.

Dear Manolo,

Since Friday the 25th when I picked up the portraits, I've been meaning to send them and write to you, but I kept waiting for a letter from you. Then, since there was no way they were going to be sent out, I didn't worry about doing it. How strange that you complain about my letters. Last week I wrote to you every day, and you only 3 times. Besides, maybe they're a reflection of your letters. By any chance do you write to me at the last minute when the mail is going out in order to fulfill an obligation? And as you can see, I don't complain.

There's nothing wrong with me. I just feel tired when I finish studying. In the 1st place, because I study a lot, and in second place, because I feel very weak.

María Teresa had a bad case of the flu. She got up today but didn't go to the university. She cheered up quite a bit when your letter arrived. What does Manolo say? Not I; I felt disheartened. It seemed to me that the bit about you missing me is just an easy way to fill paper. Hilda's boyfriend asked me about you fondly and sends you warm regards.

I haven't talked with Hortensia about going for Holy Week. I'll tell her today, although I doubt that she'll go. Manolete, I think that if you don't go for Holy Week, I'll scream my head off. When you tell me that you might be able to go but not for the whole week, I get the impression that you doubt whether or not you can even go. Oh, no, noooo! Am I going to have to wait so long to see you? Do you see? This is why I wanted you to economize, but apparently a couple of spendthrifts like us will never be able to do that.

Mi vida, I'm glad that you study and that you aspire. At least our common ambition links us, in addition to our great love.

Love, you have to get used to the fact that some days I'll write more or less than others, so . . . And on exam days? Oh, my love, how slowly the time passes and how unproductive it is for me to study. When will the day come when we can relax without having to think about exams?

I'm very tired, *mi muchachito.* That's why I'm writing a shorter letter. Today I've suddenly forgotten a thousand things that I wanted to tell you. I kept the two photos. Say hello to everyone at your house for me. Thank you for having written to Mamá.

Hug me, my love. I'm hugging you back across the distance.

With all my soul,
Your Mine

Postmarked March 30 in Trujillo City. Received on March 31.

March 30

Manolo, my Beloved,

Just a few lines to tell you that I received your two letters. The first one last night at Hortensia's, when I went to study, and the other one just a few minutes ago. I was on my way back from Milagros's house. By the way, she has a stomach bug. I was studying with her and doña Ana, and on the way back, I was thinking about you, about the last letter that I wrote to you, which was so pessimistic. My love, forgive me for all those cold letters that I've written to you lately. You are the best thing in the world.

Don't write to me here anymore since I'm leaving on Friday morning. I hope to find one from you there.

I saw César and was chatting with him. You know what, *mi vida?* Perhaps the exhaustion isn't from working so much, but rather because I'm a bit weakened, and the constant coming and going, back and forth to

Hortensia's, in short, everything all together. I'm a bit tired again today; I haven't even had the energy to delight in others' misfortunes.

How embarrassing! Your letters are always so lovely, and mine seem like rough drafts. It should be the other way around... But they make you happy, right, *mi muchachito?* You know what? Today your words didn't sound empty to me; they resonated deep within me. I miss you too and desire with all my soul to see you soon.

You see? I have really, really enjoyed this letter. I think this is the first time you've responded to everything I've said in one of mine, and you haven't left me hanging. I forgot to tell you that I held on to one additional photo that wouldn't fit in the envelope. I've it set aside for you.

Goodbye, Love. I have to mail this right away.

I'll talk with Hortensia right away. It's doubtful she wants to go.

Yours,
Mine

APRIL 1955

You will come with me,
at that hour I will wait for you,
at that hour and at every hour,
at every hour I will wait for you.[50]

My mother spent Holy Week of '55 in Ojo de Agua, just as she had planned. The months of academic pressure and extreme vigilance had taken their toll, both on her and on Aunt Teté, which is clear in Mamá Chea's reaction upon seeing them arrive: "I wasn't prepared for a wake." They were gaunt and exhausted, both physically and mentally. The family home and the care of loved ones were precisely the balm that they needed. That's how she portrays it to Papi, who as we see in Mami's letters, was clearly worried.

It's incredible how Mami found the fortitude to recount even the most unfortunate events in an amusing way. What's more, it seems as though telling them to Papi enabled her to see them from a distance, as if she were not the one involved. But those of us who read these writings and know what Minerva may have feared deeply but did not express, understand the gravity of

---

50 Neruda, "Letter on the Road," p. 145, with modifications to Devenish Walsh's translation in the second and fourth verses. (t.n.)

those apparently trivial anecdotes that reveal, for example, the circumstances under which she had to move out of Evangelista Mues's house.

In spite of the fact that the other residents in the house took siestas ("the little beasts were napping"), and the owner, "by happy coincidence," was in San Francisco de Macorís, the move still presented various problems when they returned from vacation. How does it feel to be under perpetual surveillance and observation, in the very eye of the hurricane? Tragic, I suppose. It has been fifty years since my parents' murders were part of the reason that Dominicans live in a country that is not our own. It is like the world that Ciro Alegría describes in his novel, which my parents had read. At least now, one can fill her lungs with air. The following paragraph, written at a later time, when Mami was staying with Hortensia, reveals more about the hell they experienced in that house than any detailed description: "You speak to me today of moving. I am ever so thankful to God that I did it. I still feel vertigo from the danger, like someone who is still not sure that she is free from it."

Written in full awareness that there was no privacy under the dictatorship, the letters are labyrinths into which we must enter if we are to encounter the horrifying reality of Manolo and Minerva's lives. In these somewhat coded conversations, one can clearly perceive the deep mutual understanding between them. Manolo knew that Minerva was in danger. Minerva knew that everyone around her was in constant peril. This is why I realize each day that my parents' mere existence required many acts of heroism. All the men and women who were close to them approached the edge of the abyss by simply being so. The friends, associates, neighbors, and workers who never left their sides and who never wavered in being there to protect them were heroes.

Postmarked April 7 in Salcedo. There is no stamp of receipt.

April 5, 1955

My dear Manolete,

It's terrible that you're not coming. Do you know what it's like to feel disheartened? On the other hand, I'm glad to know that you've found a location for your office.

Oh, my love, what a letdown to write to you! I had it in my mind that as long as I wasn't doing that, the hope that you would come was still alive. And I don't want to believe that it's dead! This is going to be a sad Good Friday indeed, just like the one in the song.[51]

You know, I think you've forgotten about me a little. I'm jealous. You went off to the casino on the beach (with a lowercase "b") and spent all your money on friends. Don Manuel will tell me! But I don't want to believe that about you. You've escaped a sermon. I just got back from Santiago. I stopped by the post office, and your letter wasn't there. I just now received it. You want me to write you long letters, but there are so many things that I have to tell you that they could only be summarized in the "song without words."[52] That is, all I want is for us to be lulled to sleep by the music of a long silence, together, my love! My thoughts are a vicious circle in which the question about whether or not you will come becomes all tangled up. What restlessness, what desperation to see you, *mi vida*. You have me really spoiled. But I'll tell you something, my love, I'll try to be understanding. If you don't come, I'll resign myself to the idea and will write to you again as always. I'll try to tell you everything by mail as if I hadn't hoped to tell it to you in person (and the worst part is that I don't want to show that I'm sad).

I'll tell you about my trip home. I spent two days packing suitcases. When the girls saw that I was packing everything up, they asked me if I wasn't coming back, and I replied with a yes and the most plausible reason. That's when Jaimito arrived, and we left. You see how it all seems so simple when I tell it this way? But I have some stories that will make you roar with laughter, most of all when we brought out part of the luggage and sent it "racing" to Hortensia's with María Teresa while the little beasts were napping. The cook's little boy was going to cry, since she left him to go carry a suitcase for us, and (go ahead and laugh) I picked him up so that he wouldn't wake them, and I left with one arm full of packages. It broke Mary's heart because she thought I was becoming motherly in the midst of the attack. There were a number of mishaps like this until finally we left amid hugs and expressions of thanks that have culminated in a letter that I have just finished writing to doña Evangelista, who by happy coincidence was in San Francisco and who is the "faithful bearer" of my

---

51 Reference to a song by Puerto Rican composer Rafael Hernández, made popular by Fernandito Alvarez and his Trío Vegabajeño. Its inspiration was a 1952 aviation tragedy.
52 Famous lyrical pieces for piano and organ by the German composer Felix Mendelssohn (1809–1847).

gratitude for all of the kindness that they bestowed upon us (literally). Don't tell me I waste too much paper. It's the best act of diplomacy that I could've made, since on Monday I'll have to go pick up my bed and the rest of my stuff.

When we arrived, Mamá, in her colorful language, lamented that she wasn't prepared for a "wake." That's how emaciated we were! But a good rest and this tranquility of spirit have restored our healthy appearances. As for me, at least, they tell me that I look refreshed and healthy. Mamá says that if you saw this girl with the long, disheveled hair, you wouldn't think it was the same skeleton of a critter that arrived on Friday. Of course, she doesn't know that you call me "*pelúa.*"

Do you remember how sad this letter began? But it ended up making you laugh, didn't it? When the girls called me to dinner, I told them, "I'm going to write a letter to Manolo that will make even the rocks cry." But even I ended up laughing. You see, my love? All I want is to liven you up. Don't mind my poor taste. Keep in mind that I love you and . . . that I, too, experience that thing that you asked me about in your letter.

I just now read your first letter (from Saturday). It's possible that the dream that you're telling me about is a premonition that you won't be coming. I've dreamed about your house twice, so get your things in order over there.

Sending my love,
Your Minerva

Postmarked April 12 in Salcedo. Received on April 13.[53]

April 10, 1955

Dear Manolo,

As soon as I closed my last letter, I thought of a million things that I still wanted to tell you. I was going to write again right away, which would have been helpful since now I'll have to make a mental effort to recall them—or better yet—forget the older things and begin with the newer ones. I blame my not writing on the fact that your trip fell through. In any event, half of what I had to say will have to wait.

I was so thrilled to hear you yesterday! You sounded downcast, almost

---

53 The envelope contains a typewritten letter signed by Manolo, requesting bail for a Mr. Bernardo A. Alemán, "for having committed the crime of abducting a minor."

silent, my dear Nolo! But what you said struck me as very sweet, perhaps because it seemed unusual, uncharacteristic, and spontaneous over such a distance. And how brief those moments are! I laughed when you told me how good I was. I admit that I'm rather egotistical; my goodness doesn't go beyond "impatience of the heart,"[54] concerned less about sparing someone else from pain than about sparing myself. I called you yesterday because "I" couldn't stand the thought that you were sad and lonely. Oh, Chiqui, last night when I got back, I started telling Mamá that I'd spoken with you: "Ugh! I forgot to ask him about my letter" . . . and, "He was in bed." You can't imagine my thoughts then: "I forgot to suggest that he go back to bed. If he cheered up, and with all those Holy Saturday parties, waaatch ouuut! Any other woman would send a telegram telling him to go back to bed!"

Chiqui, I'm sorry that you've had a setback in your career, but I urge you not to worry. I know it's difficult, but you must practice self-restraint. Papá used to say:

> Having a clean conscience
> is the primary imperative.
> As for the rest, may *each one*
> resolve matters as best he knows how.

You have to let a lot of things go because tolerance is the cornerstone of harmony and tranquility. But when tolerance is impossible (as long as indifference doesn't harm us more than anger does) it's worth it to practice self-restraint until we internalize the adage that "there is no greater disdain than indifference." Oh my, what a sermon. I hope you take something away from all this racket.

Listen, Manolete, every time you ask me if I'm still leaving tomorrow, it makes me want to stay here until you're able to come. I have another week without classes, but it's because of the move and Mary, and I don't get any studying done here. I told you that if you wanted to come here, I will happily come back. Remember how you asked me at the last minute if everyone else wasn't bothering me? Here we will be with Mamá, relaxed, not having to worry about being a bother. So it doesn't matter. I'll come back even if it's next week unless—listen carefully, knucklehead—unless there's something you have to take care of there. I know

---

54   Citing the title of the novel by Stefan Zweig (1881–1942).

very well, you brute, that you haven't followed through with obtaining a notary commission, so I'm going to spur you on with a stick. And don't think that you'll ever see me again, or that I'll love you at all. If you don't have a notarial notification, all my affection packs up and leaves, my love, my sweet love! Do you realize that I've spent my vacation reading your letters? They say so many nice things. I was thinking about organizing them chronologically, but one thing led to another, and I haven't done it. I'm telling you this because I'm writing to you over a full box. I took one out thinking it was the most recent, and it turns out to be the reply to a complaint that I filed on February 1. I've laughed to myself thinking "and that was while he didn't know the rest," that is, that the complaint was based on the fact that you had written that speech for Emma I.[55]

Look, Manolete, I really want a small portrait of you, one that shows you the way you are, without a graduation gown or anything like that. I've told you this a hundred times. I'll have to drag you to Atilano.[56] I gave the portrait to Patria. It made her very happy, and she says thank you. I was dying from remorse remembering Hortensia, who told me that you had offered her one, and I never gave it to her. I put mine in a little frame to place on my nightstand.

Everyone here has been teasing me because you haven't come. Regardless, Jaimito wanted us to leave in time to get there by this afternoon, supposedly to steal a... How do you call those things that people over there often use to hang things on wires? In the end he wound up arguing because, apparently, I didn't want to go, and he wasn't going to invite me again, and he wouldn't go even if I invited him (wink wink).

Margot says to give you her best, that I'm writing this here in the kitchen, and that she has left me in peace without bothering me. She says she's ticked off because you didn't come ... with her cabbage and everything to make stuffed cabbage rolls; in short, a bunch of things.

Why in your letter do you tell me, "when you come, if that's how it works out"? Are you doubting because of me, because of you, or because of both of us? I'm not sure if I'm explaining myself clearly. You explain it to me: because of me, if I decide to go, because of you, if you decide

---

55 My aunt Emma Tavárez Justo was queen in a beauty pageant, and Papi wrote the words to her salutation.

56 Atilano Sánchez attained considerable fame as a portrait photographer in the 1940s and '50s, according to *Historia de la fotografía dominicana, Volume I,* of the Colección Centenario by the León Jimenes Group, 2010.

to take me; because of both of us, if we find a better option. Clarify this point for me. But I warn you about one thing: you don't have to reply to this letter all at once; it's worth three (go by the number of words, not pages). Not only that, it makes up for the days that I quit writing to you and for the ones that I spent not doing it. *Mi muchachito,* I'm still leaving tomorrow. I really need to! Don't listen to me about coming here. I'll be fine with whatever you do. I'll be happy, and H. will kill me if she finds out. She wants to see you there.

Yours forever,
Mine

Postmarked April 12 in Trujillo City. Received on April 13.

April '55

My dear Manolo,

Yesterday, as soon as I arrived, I received your letter, and today I received the other one.

As a result, they've left me with a happy thought: I imagine that you've already received the one from me, the one that I sent you from Salcedo.

It went really well for us just now, of course not without grief related to the move, but thank God we've come out of that quagmire all right. Mary feels very at ease here, and we're not even settled in yet. I don't know if I told you that Graciela left. She happened upon a magnificent opportunity: the wife of the Pres. of Helmurs,[57] whom she met at the post office, after having her request permission to spend a few days at their house, offered her the same salary but with all expenses paid if she stayed to live with them. Anyway, all this to tell you (although, I think you'll also be happy to know) that Mary has moved into Graciela's room. She put her desk and everything there, and this way we don't bother her when we're studying. As you might imagine, I sleep in Hortensia's room with her. Bitín sleeps next to Mary's room.

I haven't gone to the university. We don't have Law classes because of comprehensive exams. But I'm thinking of going to Philosophy this afternoon because my attendance in that class is abysmal. I, too, have often thought about the twins, but most of all these past few days when I was thinking that if you were coming, I'd send them a little memento. By the

---

57 Apparent reference to Elmhurst, a U.S. construction company.

way, Mary and I were talking about them yesterday. I also often think of your dad and mom.

I was just telling Hortensia, who just got back from the office, what you said about her letter, and she came at me with a thousand things: that I tell you that she'll write to you tomorrow, etc. I replied that I'm not going to tell you anything, that she not mock me, and that I won't give you her regards (how drastic).

Love, I'm going to close now to sleep a bit. Do you want to? I'll definitely write to you tomorrow. I think about you often, and your extremely affectionate letters make me very happy.

I love you very much,
Mine

Postmarked April 13 in Trujillo City. Received on April 14.

April 13, 1955

My dear Manolo,

I was hoping to receive your letter today. It worries me to think that maybe they haven't sent you the one that I wrote you from home on Sunday. Please, if you haven't received it, wait for it before thinking that I'm writing very little these days, as the letter in question is a marathon letter, and I didn't say anything to you yesterday thinking that you would receive it and that today I would have your response.

Chiqui, do you know how many times I've read your last letter? I love you more than anything.

Isaura came this morning and sends you her best regards. Hortensia just got back from the office, and I asked her, "so what was it that I said I had to tell Manolo?" And the servant said: "Oh, that you all study a lot at night." So, there you have it, that is my life: study and . . . thinking about you. Love of my life, you need to buy your graduation gown so you don't have that hanging over your head, and you know that if you don't set money aside for that, there won't be enough. I hope your financial situation has improved so that you're able to buy it.

When you come, I want you to bring the two volumes of Planiol[58] so we can bring them to be bound, since Mamá asked me what I had done with the money that she gave me to bind them, and I told her that I had

---

58 Previously cited French lawyer.

done it. I don't want to look bad even if it means having those bound, since she was going to bring one of Josserand's[59] books that's at home and that I forgot, and until I go, I won't etc. (basically I lost my train of thought). This is poorly planned (I'm referring to the letter). I'm feeling down because I was hoping for a letter from you, and I'm loving you too much.

Mary is doing very well, and she sends you her affection every time I write to you.

Yours,
Mine

Postmarked April 15 in Trujillo City. Received on April 16.

April 14, '54

Dear Manolo,

This morning I received your letter and felt so very badly that you still haven't received one from me. As I was telling you yesterday, I wrote you from home on Sunday, but I left the letter for them to drop in the mail, and I see that they haven't done so. I'm so sorry!

Mi vida, tell me what "f.... a" means. I'm such a brute that I don't understand it. However, I have had the pleasure of seeing that analogous thoughts are crossing paths in our letters. If you have finally received my letter from Sunday, you'll realize that we've coincided in framing our respective portraits and in talking about it, as if we were thinking the same thing. Oh, Chiqui, how very sorry I am that you have gone these past few days without letters from me. Just yesterday I was saying to Hortensia: "Manolo believes that I'm understanding but he's wrong. I'm feeling desperate because he hasn't written to me today." Hortensia says those are "matters of the heart." I'm sorry I don't have a penal code on hand to study articles 309 and 311 with you. I hope that it comes out well in your letter.

You speak to me today of moving. I am ever so thankful to God that I did it, and I still feel vertigo from the danger, like someone who is still not sure that she is free from it. The first few days, especially the first day with Patria, she and Hortensia were laughing at me because I was explaining to

---

59 Louis Josserand (1868–1941), French lawyer and author of *Civil Law* (Ed. Bosch and Cía, 1950).

them that they had planted crazy ideas in my head about being persecuted. But now I realize how right they were. I mean, all the boys went away, they left the house empty, and you can imagine what a state those beasts are in. The last thing they did was get Luly (poor Luly) in trouble with doña Emma. But thanks to God and to that very warm letter that I wrote to her, they couldn't harbor any ill will toward me.

I'm going to end for now since Hortensia is waiting for me to study. I'm sending my unwavering and sincere regards soaked in affection.

Your Mine

Last night I left this little piece blank to send you a bit of affection today. I lay awake thinking that you hadn't received my letters. Hortensia is very busy. Forgive her.

May 1955

> Farewell, but you will be
> with me, you will go within
> a drop of blood circulating in my veins
> or outside, a kiss that burns my face
> or a belt of fire at my waist.
> My sweet, accept
> the great love that emerged from my life
> and that in you found no territory
> like the explorer lost
> in the isles of bread and honey.[60]

The correspondence from May was scant, and it was rough. The first letter whose content suggests that it was written this month is not dated, and the postmark from the "Trujillo City" post office is illegible save for the number 21 and the letter "M," which leads me to think that it corresponds to the month of May. My mother gave it her best effort and managed to obtain Papi's exequatur in what seems to be record time. Judging from the exchange of telegrams, we can imagine that he came to pick it up and took advantage of the opportunity to spend a few days visiting her, but she was already one step ahead: going through the process of procuring a notary commission for him.

---

60 Neruda, "Letter on the Road," p. 143, with modification to Devenish Walsh's translation in the seventh verse. (t.n.)

In texts prior to and following May, Mami insists ad nauseum on the importance of Papi obtaining a notary commission. The fact is that the law stipulated a minimum age of 25, which he had not yet reached. Mamá Dedé explains it well in a paragraph of her memoirs, *Alive in Their Garden:*

> Minerva insisted that Manolo become a notary. He dragged his feet without telling her the reason: he didn't meet the minimum age requirement. He hid his age from Minerva because he was younger than her. When Minerva became aware of the age difference, she dug in her heels. "I'm not getting married," she said, and she broke up with him. But because she was so in love, she allowed herself to be convinced, and they were married on November 20, 1955.

Since Mami was disillusioned without knowing the real reason for Papi's reluctance to obtain the commission, one of her May letters contains a paragraph so radical that, today when I read it, it hurts me perhaps as much as it must have hurt him when he received it:

> That is why I didn't study this morning. That is why I didn't sleep last night. I know how much this will hurt me when exams come around, but I have a pressing need to be sincere. I don't want you to think that I'm trying to impose my opinion on you. If you know me even a little, you'll know that I have given up many things because I love you, because I thought that we were going to struggle together . . .

Maybe two people who withstood so much should not have suffered over such petty, worldly things, I tell myself. But they did. They, my father and mother, were human beings, young like my children and nieces, like today's young Dominican men and women, like young people in any corner of the world.

Telegram from Minerva to Manolo, May 11.

Exequatur ready. Come. Minerva

Telegram from Minerva to Manolo, May 12.

We're leaving in the afternoon. Notify me here if your trip impossible. With affection, Minerva

Postmarked "M" (illegible) 21 in Trujillo City. Without stamp of receipt.

My dear Manolo,

Since I don't date my letters, I'll have to number them. This is the fourth. I imagine you'll receive them together tomorrow, all of them. Manolete, I'm so happy after having spoken with the professor. You know that I felt rather shy, but once I mentioned your name and told him that you had sent me (this is so nice, it will make you laugh) he told me that of course he remembered you, asked if you were in Monte Cristy, etc. He told me that he'd be happy to take care of those things for you, that you should send your documents, that if the law wasn't providing enough information that you write to him or to the secretary asking for reports. He mentioned which ones, but I've forgotten the names. I only remember that you are to send the number of the *Official Gazette* containing the announcement of your exequatur so that you don't have to send the diploma. Anyway, even if you don't need the reports, I hope that you write to him right away to thank him for his attention. You don't know how much I love him for his kindness and how grateful I am to him. On Monday they're going to operate on the cyst that he has beside his ear, and he is going to spend 3 days in the clinic. So, we will go see him. *Amore,* take care of all of this right away (the criminal record certificate and other documents) and send them so that they are here by Monday, and if you are missing anything, let me know.

Love, I'm going to drop this in the mail so that it goes out tonight. I hope you care as much as I do.

Kisses from your
Mine

Written on Tuesday, May 24. Postmarked May 25 in Trujillo City. Received on May 26.

Dear Manolete,

I just got back from buying a few things for María, and I was very disappointed when I found that I hadn't received a letter from you. All along the way I was thinking about what joy it would bring me to receive a little letter from you that said, "In this very package, I'm sending a certificate with all the necessary information and my application for the notarial commission." It seems that I am not going to have the pleasure of seeing you as interested in this as I am.

Yesterday I received your letter, which made me very happy, and I'm not going to respond to all of it because I have to write to my beloved mother and to yours so that Hortensia can send them certified tomorrow at the post office. But I want this to go out today. If I were to learn that you have sent the information, I would give it to the professor. They did not operate today as I had informed you. I haven't studied for three days. Let's see if my throat rests. I hope that it's better in three days.

Goodbye, Love. I can't bear the thought of you forgetting me even for a day.

Mine

Postmarked May 26 in Trujillo City. Received on May 27.

Dear Manolo,

I just spoke with you, and I couldn't hope for you to comprehend the sadness that I feel, the disappointment. After telling you that it didn't matter, I can't help but cry now that I'm writing to you. It hurts me tremendously that my letters have meant nothing to you, that something that I had repeatedly begged of you, means so little to you, because I know that you are no fool and that you were much too laid-back in dealing with it. Could it be that deep down, from the very beginning, you were hoping that it would turn out this way? You could have told Joaquín that I had resolved the matter for you here and that you weren't going to make me look bad (which doesn't matter), or made some other excuse if you thought it silly to say that you'd do it to please me. But you preferred to please him. That's how it goes. I can't be understanding. I can't be so with Joaquín either. I can't forgive him for discouraging you with subterfuges in the interest of going against you. I don't know how you could have believed... but now I'm contradicting myself; I recall having told you that I didn't think you were so foolish.

I might go home on Saturday. I still haven't made the arrangements. The clock just struck 12. Now I know for sure that I will not be receiving a letter from you. Like on other occasions, you decided not to send it. I have waited until the last minute. Although I told you that nothing would make me change my opinion, we can always hope that things won't turn out for the worst. That is why I didn't study this morning, that is why I didn't sleep last night. I know how much this will hurt me when exams come around, but I have a pressing need to be sincere. I don't want you to think that I'm trying to impose my opinion on you. If you know me even a little, you'll know that I've given up many things because I love you, because I thought that we were going to struggle together, but it is quite a different matter for you to take the side of another knowing that you were causing me considerable grief. But you chose him, surely because it is much easier to make up with me. Just three little words, and I'm good to go, right?

María Teresa just walked in and told me to tell you, "While all the other lawyers are chasing after a notary commission, you spurn it like it's a bad thing." I don't want to say anything more because I know that I'll get all . . . I don't know. Goodbye.

Minerva

Written probably on May 25 or 26.[61]

Dear Manolete,

Now I don't even remember what I was saying to you in my letter yesterday. This one, which was going to come out rather ironic, will perhaps come across as lovey-dovey. That's how I feel. You know, you were right: "with three little words." Well, no, after mailing the letter I regretted it. What's the sense in fighting over something that's irreparable? Besides, I understood your reasoning. I would have done the same thing in that situation. Of course, this doesn't mean that I forgive Díaz Belliard, and you, even less so, since you created this situation, but once you found yourself in the middle of it, you were unable to back down for your own good.

Chiqui, I leave for Salcedo tomorrow. I don't know what time, but I'll let you know. Hopefully you can go. I want so badly to be with you, after thinking that you must have been worried. I want to make up with you, cheer you up, make you happy if I can. I'm sending you the book *The Method*.

---

61 Papi had this among the letters from August, but it is clearly a follow-up to the previous letter. Moreover, it refers to a Mother's Day gift for Mamá Fefita, and Mother's Day fell on Sunday, May 29, that year.

How amusing and embarrassing that your mother has received the gift so far in advance. I thought it would take two days to get there and that once they received the notice, they would pick it up the next day, that is, tomorrow. I didn't hear anything that you said to me on the phone. Tell me: Haven't you written it to me? I hope to see you tomorrow or receive a letter before leaving. I'm sending this with Hortensia. She is leaving.

Sending my affection, *vida,* goodbye.

Mine

June 1955

The thief will emerge from his tower one day.
And the invader will be expelled.
All the fruits of life
will grow in my hands
accustomed once to powder.
And I shall know how to caress the new flowers
because you taught me tenderness.[62]

In June Mami begins to refer to "our office" when mentioning Papi's preparations to establish himself in Montecristi. It becomes evident that they had already privately agreed to marry, but I imagine that for political reasons, they did not go so far as to lay out the details of those plans.

The observation of Minerva (and by extension of Aunt Teté) had not diminished; on the contrary. As we will see later on, she remained under extremely close surveillance. I imagine that Mami's constant throat ailments and the fact that María Teresa failed topography class had something to do with their living each day under siege, which they nonetheless overcame trying to live like any other student.

In a letter postmarked June 23 at four o'clock p.m., Mami tells Papi that she is going "to buy the 4th-year books, but for now I only found Criminology. I finally sent them all to be bound." A mere three days later, a note dated June 25 appeared in the "Public Forum," the famous column published by the regime in the newspaper *El Caribe* (*The Caribbean*) to attack and defame enemies and the disaffected. It said the following: "It would be good

---

[62] Neruda, "Letter on the Road," p. 145, with modifications to Devenish Walsh's translation in the first and sixth verses. (t.n.)

for someone to seize the greasy palm of Mr. Horacio Geraldino, who is the book binder at the university and who [. . .] utilizes the material belonging to that house of learning to fill orders for the Law student Minerva Mirabal, for whom he bound almost 20 books [. . .]." Reading between the lines of the letters written shortly thereafter, one can detect veiled references to these kinds of problems that Minerva faced. Nothing she did escaped the perverse scrutiny of the regime and its minions.

Mami and Aunt Teté continued living with Hortensia, and in June they joined the Marcial Silva family in their preparations for the ordination ceremony of their son Rafael. He would be known for his role as a chaplain in the armed forces in those days, and later for his opposition to the provisions for secular education in the 1963 Constitution, and for his role in the coup d'état against Juan Bosch.

In spite of feeling more secure living with this family, the threats did not cease. Luly Caraballo tells me that, one day, while she was studying for final exams at Hortensia's house, Aunt Teté left momentarily to do something, and the phone rang. Mami lifted the receiver, and Luly saw her face turn angry and pale as she responded, "Yes," and "Ah-ha." Luly insisted on knowing who was calling and about what. Mami replied (only after making her swear that she wouldn't tell Aunt Teté, who had an exam the following day), "a calié [. . .] He told me he's going to kill me tomorrow." What most surprised Luly was that, after telling her that, my mother sat down in a rocking chair and resumed studying, out loud like she tended to do. The tension in the air is also evident in the way Papi and my grandmother worried about them, a worry that was not due to the state of their health nor to their studies.

Things at home were not going well either, since almost the entire month, Uncle Jaimito was laid up with a bleeding ulcer at the clinic in San Francisco de Macorís, where his uncle, Dr. José Amado (Cheché) Camilo, practiced. Additionally, Nina Patria had surgery at the beginning of the month. All that, together with exam week and Papi's being far away, added to the weight of the sword that was constantly dangling over Mami's head.

There is an annotation in which Mami sadly refers to the death of Dr. Óscar Lara Rojas from Moca, their friend since before they met. Óscar died in an accident on the highway to San Juan de la Maguana, apparently in unclear circumstances, to which Mami refers in another letter at a later date. The news appeared in *El Caribe* on June 10, and on the subsequent page, there was a photo of Óscar's girlfriend playing the piano. Those days were so ill-fated for liberty and for life that anything published in those newspapers could lead to disgrace or awaken justified doubts.

As for me, it amuses me to realize that my mother was a jealous woman, and I would have loved to read Papi's responses calming down a girlfriend who scolded him even in her dreams.

I also cannot stop thinking about how much my daughter Camila resembles her grandmother and about how much Mami would have enjoyed guiding her and spoiling her. Just as Mami demanded a lot of herself when it came to her studies, so does her granddaughter: "Sweetheart, the exams brought me no satisfaction whatsoever. Actually, I felt way too unsure, and I didn't like the scores nor the material. I would not have given me those grades, but you know that some people think that just because I say it, it's right. But that is not the case." I feel as if I am listening to Camila Minerva.

Undated. Postmarked June 3 in Trujillo City. Received on June 4.

Dear Manolete,

A quick note to tell you that this morning I received a telegram telling me that they had operated on Patria, and it went well. Write to her, my love.

I'm too sad to write a longer letter. Tomorrow will be a very heartrending day, and right now I'm busy sending more flowers with Chiche for Papá's grave. So, forgive me for not writing more.

Sending all my love,
Minerva

Undated. Postmarked June 4 in Trujillo City. Received on June 6.

Dear Manolo,

Milagros did not come today because I'm hoarse again. I was fine for two days, thrilled to be able to study again, and I was thinking of moving up my exam, but, imagine that, it seems that will not be in my best interest. You tell me to study by myself, and I really am getting used to that, but it's just that when it comes to studying, any little thing like what I have is a calamity. Anyway, they have scheduled the first exams for June 21 and the last ones for July 18. How slow this whole process seems! I sincerely would have preferred a week in-between since that way I would have no choice but to just make do and study.

You can't imagine how depressed I've felt since you left. Perhaps it's due to my having become fully aware that I haven't attained the level of education necessary to control my instincts, my nerves, that whole chaos of perverse feelings that we carry around in the back of our subconscious. I really feel quite ashamed in front of you. Maybe that's why I had a terrible dream about you, that you wouldn't listen to me, that you treated me "horribly." That's why you'll notice that I haven't dared tell you in this letter that I have felt lonely without you, very insecure.

I'm going to wait a bit to see if I receive a letter from you. I'm doubting even that. When it's 12:00, I'll continue writing.

Chiqui: I just received your letter, I couldn't possibly explain what I feel: joy, sorrow, almost desperation. How dare you say that I didn't tell you to stay? Don't you remember that I told you to come study with me that day? What's more (affirmative), you knew that I was dying for you to stay. Besides, it hurt me so much that you didn't turn your head when you drove away. I called out to you, and you said bye right away, so I thought it was inopportune, that you were in a hurry to leave. In addition to the million things that have depressed me these past few days, your departure has left me feeling so empty, so sad, but I can't talk about this anymore.

My love, I'm glad that you are studying more. I'm sorry that you will be tired when you arrive, but I thank you from the bottom of my heart for writing to me. I received it on time, thank God, since if I hadn't, I would have felt so dejected. Can you imagine your girl feeling dejected? Well, you wouldn't want to see her like that. Your letter gave me a boost.

Besides, I really like how you explain Law. Always tell me everything that you're studying.

Amore, don't forget my fern roots. Remember that there are several plants and that you should take care of this yourself given that one day, if you'd like, they will adorn your home. To be ready by then, the cuttings should start taking root since they take a while. The stems too.

I was going to write a few lines to "Mamá Fefita," but I don't even have an "Esterbrook."[63]

Love, I would like to bring you the solace you ask of me. I would like

---

63 A brand of fountain pen.

to send in this letter all the comfort I cannot give you personally, but I too am very sad because I love you with all my soul, and you are not here.

Your Mine

Postmarked June 6 in Trujillo City. Received on June 7.

My dear, beloved Manolo,

I was left waiting for a letter from you. I needed it. Love, you cannot imagine how mortified I feel for not having sent your father a telegram. Please give him my apologies. Do you know what it's like to feel distressed? Yesterday was a horrible day: worry, sadness, malaise because my throat was at its worst, and I had such a fever that I didn't get up today, and all my bones ache. But as you can see, I'm still writing to you. This is my third letter, even though you have only written one to me. The same thing always happens; you forget about me quite easily once you arrive in Monte Cristy. What is it that distracts you so much over there?

Oh, Chiqui, I'm not going to take care of myself at all, I'm tired. And I have no energy to study either. I know, I'm going to smoke a pack, and this afternoon I'll go to the university to see Clarita's exams, and if I get wet, all the better.

Manolo, they're calling me to eat. I'm off. The girls send their regards.

You are loved by a girl who feels very down, glum and lonely without you.

Minerva

Undated, postmarked June 10 in Trujillo City. Received on June 11.

Dear Manolete,

Yesterday I received a letter from you. I didn't write to you because I didn't think there was any mail, that is, that they weren't going to pick up letters. I received some very distressing news from home. Jaimito is doing very poorly. They haven't been able to get him up and moving. He has an ulcer, and it hemorrhaged so much that he didn't have a drop of blood left.

Yesterday after receiving the letter, I spoke on the phone with Dedé. Imagine how sad the poor thing is. Love, *mi vida,* know that I don't stop thinking about you even for a moment. If I don't write, it's due to some circumstance. For now, maybe I'll write to you tomorrow, or maybe I won't. It depends on whether I decide to go home, that is, whatever I decide I'll let you know, but sometimes if I'm undecided about something, I wait until I make a decision to write to you. My health has improved quite a bit. How little one knows her own organism sometimes. What I had was a bad case of the flu. I realized that yesterday, after having gone so far as to think that I was developing tuberculosis.

As for my studies, they're going so-so. I'm still alone since my throat hasn't recovered yet.

Amore, I'm sorry that you're down. Share your troubles with me. However, *mi vida,* I don't want you to become discouraged with your work. Keep in mind that this too makes me sad. Go see Danilo, and tell me about it. I hope that everyone at your house is doing well. Give them my affection.

Hortensia is asking me to tell you, well . . . she's telling me to leave space for her so she can write you a few lines. This weekend she's too busy, and it seems that she won't have time, so I'm going to close the letter since I want it to go out in tonight's mail. Forgive me this very choppy letter, but I'm writing it in a huge hurry. Mary sends you warm regards. I don't know what else I needed to tell you and that I have forgotten.

With affection from yours always,
Mine

---

*Postmarked June 10, the same day as the previous letter.
Received on June 11.*

Dear Manolete,

Mi cielo, don't be annoyed that I'm writing to you on this little piece of paper. It is the same one on which your letter came. I'm at Carmen's, and I don't have any other paper on hand.

I've been here since last night. Hortensia and I came to study, and since Carmen is alone, I stayed. They send me my food and everything so that I don't talk with anyone, to see if I improve. I went to see Clarita's exams (by the way, she got 3 outstanding grades) and came back with a fever and nothing has helped me, not gargling or anything. Victoria gave me streptomycin, and this morning I changed my clothes to go to the doctor, but then I decided not to go because I'm tired of so much medicine.

Chiqui, I'm going to send this letter without an envelope so that Hortensia can mail it for me and so that it goes out today. Don't worry about my concerns. I wasn't referring to anything in particular but rather everything in general, to how lousy I was with you, with the girls, etc., in short, with everything. I'm a bad person, but I'm not going to describe the feelings that are bubbling up inside me after having received your very loving and much-desired letter, for fear that the little miss who is going to deliver this decides to take a peek. I still don't have any more news about Patria.

With affection from your
Mine

Undated. Postmarked June 10 in Trujillo City. Received on June 11.

My beloved Fiancé,

I've been savoring your letter since yesterday, as I study Roman Law. How loving it is, and how happy I feel having it with me. I didn't say anything to you in my letter yesterday because I wrote it in a rush. But how delighted I was to receive it! Even your handwriting looked more beautiful on that rustic paper, which in my view it isn't; there was something surprisingly beautiful about it. Oh, my love, you deserve that night out, but don't drink too much because later you can smell it on your breath, and above all, don't forget about me. Give Danilo my best. Mary also sends him her regards.

Well, I'll share with you that I'm feeling better today. I was still at Carmen's, and Victoria called to let me know that your letter had arrived. I bolted out of there like María Moñitos[64] with my hair in two buns that they'd made me. I wanted to get here in a flash to read your letter and to write to you since I didn't have any paper there. I'll go back after eating. Besides, that way Victoria didn't have to go over there to give me the injection. That is what has helped me get better. She herself gave me some of the ones they give out as samples. Maybe one day I'll be healthy. For one thing, my voice has cleared up since I've gone several days without talking. All I have now is a little irritation. Thank you, my love, for being so concerned about me. I think you'll have to use drastic measures. I'm

---

64 A well-known personality for children, whose hair was tied up in little buns with small bows (*moñitos*). (t.n.)

taking good care of myself to please you. The day that I wrote you (Saturday), when they were telephoning Calamidad,[65] a driver answered and gave me the news about Óscar Lara's death. I knew it was going to affect you, but I was so saddened and didn't have the courage to talk with you about any of that.

Patria had surgery in Salcedo, and yesterday they informed us that she is doing better, but there is an awful lot of work to be done at home. Dedé is in Macorís with Jaimito, who took a turn for the worse and had to be brought to the clinic where his uncle, Dr. Camilo, works. All of this has me so worried. You know what that's like, Manolo! I could have taken my first exams by now, since I started to study in half the time (now I realize), but that's like the saying, "the *sancocho*[66] is never without a hair." (Be careful with the one that Danilo prepares for you.) María Teresa has her exams on Friday of next week.

Don Isidro sends you his best. He says that he didn't realize that he wasn't going to see you before he left and that he's very sad that you left so soon.

You haven't told me anything about what you're doing. Why?

Tell me, Chiqui, did you say anything to your father? I so regret not having sent him so much as a card or a telegram. But what are we going to do for him?

Mi vida, I love you more each day. You are the best thing in the world, the most understanding. That's how you've won my trust and my love. It's the only way, the sure and straight path. I adore your generosity, and you.

Mine

This letter appears to have been written on June 11 in Trujillo City. Sent on June 13 and received on June 14.

Manolete, *mi vida,*

Today, Saturday, at 6 p.m. Victoria came to bring me your letter, as Hortensia and I are still here studying. Victoria's husband (I don't know if I

---

65 Reference to a gasoline station on March 30 Street that served as a meeting point for drivers traveling into the country's interior. People would telephone in to ask them to pick up passengers or packages. They also rented vehicles with drivers.

66 A typical Dominican stew made of various meats, vegetables, and tubers. (t.n.)

told you that he came to spend a week with her) got a good laugh because as he shook my hand, I didn't know how nor where it was coming from, and used the other hand to grab your letter, which Victoria was passing me. My love, you don't know how much I miss you. They played the *picot*[67] and that record: "I've Never Told You..."[68] It was as if you were with me, so deep inside my heart. I came for dinner and couldn't hold back my tears. Carmen told me that I was like Lolita,[69] who laughed and cried at the same time. I don't know how you can say that you haven't received a letter from me. Thursday was the only day when I didn't write. Maybe they've gotten lost, or perhaps the mail is delayed again, since this letter from you didn't reach me like before.

I'm finally feeling better, thank God. Now I just have bruises all over my arms from all the injections, but I think that today's will be the last.

Mi vida, I'm quite saddened by the situation with Jaimito, above all because I haven't been able to go home, and because you seem forlorn to me. I wish I could cuddle and caress you. I'd like to be able to tell you that we'll be spending 2 days at home after my first exams, but since you're telling me that you haven't worked, and I know that you need a lot of things, I suppose it won't be possible. It will have to be when I finish, much later, for sure. Oh, my love, if these tears were scented, how fragrant my face would be!

My darling, write to Jaimito or Dedé right away. They are at Dr. Camilo's clinic in San Francisco. I was thinking about surprising you if possible, but I'll tell you now: it's likely that I'll take my exam on Tuesday in place of Leda. If that is the case, I'll send you a telegram, and I'll go to Macorís on Wednesday at 6 a.m. Understand that this is likely but not certain. I'll continue on home, where Patria is (I seem to recall having told you).

Goodbye, my beloved. With this letter, I'm sending my heart, which has been yours for quite some time.

Much love,
Minerva

---

67 A book published in the 1950s containing the lyrics of popular Mexican songs, entertainers' biographies, and advertisements (t.n.)
68 *Nunca te lo he dicho,* written by Ramón A. (Papa) Molina and performed by Lope Balaguer.
69 The song "Lolita the Blackberry" ("Lolita la Zarzamora") was made popular by Amalia Rodríguez and Lola Flores: "What's wrong with the Blackberry / who is always crying / who cries in the corners / the one who was always laughing / and boasting of breaking hearts?"

Note from Hortensia:

Manolo,

You are always so understanding and kind that I can't help but cry when I think of the great friend that I have. When I need to find courage, believe me, I think of you.

Mine and I are studying a lot. I'm dying for her to finish this up and rest. Regards to everyone, from someone who holds them dear.

Postmarked June 17 in Trujillo City. Received on June 18.

Mi muchachito,

I just got back from Salcedo. I was anxious to arrive so I could write to you. I found your letter when I arrived. I didn't write to you as promised because I simply wasn't able to, my love; it was impossible. That afternoon when I spoke with you, I went to see Dr. De la Cruz. I thought I was dying, but apparently it was all in my head, because I'm still alive and kicking. They did a fluovoscopy,[70] but my lungs are all right. It's just my larynx that's affected, that blessed larynx that makes me feel pain from the tip of my big toe to the southernmost tip of my hair. Anyway, I got an injection and left without feeling any improvement. I wanted to stay until Monday but thought that I'd miss you too much, so I came back.

I've been thinking about you the entire way, *mi vida*. I was longing to rest my head upon your shoulder. I was trying to remember the dream that I had about you last night. Later it turned out that in the dream, you "had been unfaithful" to me, and I ended up shouting "I dare you!" Chiqui, the only thing that brings me comfort is that you don't even drink or go out. I don't know what state I'd be in if you did. Look at Jaimito and where it's gotten him. Look at your friend Óscar. What a terrible shame for his girlfriend to find out what he was up to when he was killed. I'm not sure if you noticed in the paper that his death was announced on one page, and she appears playing the piano on the other page.

Sweetheart, the exams brought me no satisfaction whatsoever.

---

70 The original text is unclear, but Minerva could be referring to a "fluoroscopy," a kind of diagnostic imaging that was common at the time.

Actually, I felt way too unsure, and I didn't like my grades nor the material. I wouldn't have given me those grades, but you know that some people think that just because I say it, it's right. But that's not the case. All that matters is that you are happy. Please tell me once and for all what it was about that last paragraph pleased you. Tell me, my love: when did you find out that I was going to take my exams? And all the etc. that you know I want to know.

There is something that makes me both happy and sad: that I'm not going to see you in the next few days. You can't imagine how much it pains me, but I'm happy about the reason. I'm happy that you are taking care of our office. You know that.

Today I receive the first in a series of vaccinations that the Dr. has prescribed me. He told me that they cause fever, which is why I hadn't started them, but hopefully this will make me better. I want to have faith since I need to get better in order to study this material: Civil Law, my precious love.

Tell all your family that I say hello. Thank them for their warm regards. Mary has an exam in a few hours, I'll write to you tomorrow with the results.

Be sure to write me. The doctor (I myself) told me not to fret, and I will if you don't write.

Yours,
Minerva

Postmarked June 20. Received June 21. The envelope includes another letter dated June 20.

My Beloved,

Tonight, while Hortensia is reading for her exam tomorrow, I'm writing to you. I didn't do it yesterday because I had left my paper at Carmen's. But I've thought of you the entire time; that is, in the midst of studying I take a few critical moments to think about *mi muchachito,* who even during exam week objects to my "*non adimpleti contractus*,"[71] and if I don't

---

71 *Exceptio non adimpleti contractus*: Exception for breach of contract, applicable in the case of a bilateral contract when one of the parties fails to comply with their part or does not agree to comply simultaneously. Based on this *exceptio,* the other party can refrain from complying with their part.

write to him, he doesn't write to me. I didn't receive a letter yesterday. How I needed one!

Amore, don't worry about my throat ailment. It will all go away once I'm at home. Besides, since I really enjoy the subjects that I'm studying, when I don't feel like studying one, I study another (that's what I think). And it's all the same to me if I study alone or with someone, so I'll only study with Hortensia since I can't just abandon her. Besides, she reads, and I make excellent progress in the morning just by accompanying her. I'm studying right now, or rather, listening to her study American,[72] I didn't think I'd ever learn it, but I've just realized that I know it forward and backward. Anyway, she is very nervous, but pretty well-prepared after the past year. You can't reproach me for bragging when I say that I made her study. *Mi vida,* I have some painful news to tell you: Mary failed Topography. She knew it. Three topics that she knew came up, and ... I don't know ... you know her: she let herself get carried away with everything they had told her about the exams. She almost thought she was supposed to get nervous, and she didn't put up a fight. She let herself get burned. It was as if she had created her own psychosis. But go figure; she's not very down about it. It hurts me more, especially knowing how she studied. In the two other subjects, the exams went well, thanks to the fact that before leaving, I told her not to worry if she got burned in one subject. That gave her courage, and she took the other exams. What do you think? I didn't even tell her what you told me in your letter. I didn't want to cause her more sadness.

I told Patria that you had written to her. Did you tell me that, or did I imagine it? She's still in bed, but at this point she's being a bit of a baby about it. I wish you could have heard her stories about the day of the operation. And they complain about me! The apple doesn't fall far from the tree.

Everyone here is busy preparing for Rafael's ordination.[73] I imagine they'll send you an invitation. Send him a telegram. You know what, *mi vida?* I agree that you shouldn't come until I finish. That way I'll be *freeeee,* and we'll play all the games from when I was little. And I'll be very happy with all the progress on our office, which will surpass all of my ex-

---

72 American International Law.
73 Reference to Rafael Marcial Silva's ordination into the priesthood. He was Hortensia's brother.

pectations. You should go home so you don't spend more money coming here. Hortensia and I have talked a lot about Monte Cristy. We really want to go there during vacation.

She says she really wishes you were here tomorrow for her exam. Love, I forgot to tell you that some days, I wake up and my throat is better, and some days it's worse. I hope that it improves with the new treatment. All my desires boil down to finishing so that I can be with you.

I love you,
Mine

I'll leave this letter open until tomorrow to see if one of your beloved letters arrives for me.

This letter follows as a continuation.

June 20

Manolete, Sweetheart,

I just received your letter. As you can see, I'm writing to you on the envelope. I was waiting for it to arrive before sealing my letter so that I could include a few more lines. I'm glad that you are triumphing in "your debates." I hope it continues that way through the end. Didn't I tell you about Jaime? How crazy, I thought I'd told you already: a stomach ulcer and as a result, a month of bedrest, a milk-only diet, and the follow-up treatment.

I'm still studying with Hortensia, who studies for a few hours if she's focused. You know, I'm a glutton for punishment. I'm jealous. I love you so much. Don't you stop writing to me either, my love. Whenever I don't write, it's because I've had my share of problems these days. This afternoon I'll go to the University with Hortensia. I have no choice but to go, even though my throat hurts a little. I'm thinking about buying two 4th-year books that I still need. Oh, Love, I feel so whiny, and I'm missing you so much that it's killing me.

Yours,
Mine

Postmarked June 23 in Trujillo City.[74]

Dear Manolete,

I've been waiting the whole morning for this moment, when I would receive word from you. Thank God I've received your two letters, *mi vida*. I wanted them so badly! What can I say? I didn't feel like studying today. I tried to sleep a bit so that I wouldn't feel tired this afternoon, but Morpheus[75] treated me badly and refused to surrender me. I thought a lot about you.

I'm glad that you've won the case. Keep it up, my love. Triumph is a great incentive, but I don't think that you need it as such. I've had the immense satisfaction of witnessing your tenacity.

Stop telling your family that we're going. Don't you see that these are just plans? In the event that we do go, it would be when Hortensia has vacation. By the way, Hortensia earned three "Very Good" grades. Her exams went well, which made all of us happy. She was very nervous.

I don't know if I told you that I was going to buy the 4th-year books, but for now the only one I found was *Criminology*. I finally sent all of them to be bound. *Procedure* is the only one that I left for later because I needed it, but I'll do it later. This makes me feel much better.

I'm sad, Love, because you say nothing about when we will see one another again. What's more, for the past few days, I've felt an unjustifiable jealousy, and time passes so slowly.

Your Mine

Postmarked June 23 but dated June 22.

June 22

By beloved Fiancé,

I wrote to Mamá today, explaining what happened with María Teresa's course. Then I replied to a letter from Danilo. I hate to think that I'll miss mail pickup without sending you a few lines. I've gone two days without

---

74 This letter and the next one were postmarked 4:00 p.m. that same day.
75 Ancient Greek god associated with sleep and dreams. (t.n.)

a letter from you, my love. Why haven't you written to me? I've missed them so very much.

You know what? My throat hasn't hurt for three days, I believe I'm going to heal.

Chiqui, I long so, so very much to see you, to talk with you, even to write to you, but it's a 1/4 to 3 o'clock. This is going to be left behind if I don't hurry up and give you a hug and a very, very loving goodbye. Until tomorrow, my love.

Your
Mine

Postmarked June 27 in Trujillo City. Received on June 28.
It includes a note from Hortensia.

My Beloved,

You say that I write you very little. I don't recall having done so, but if you say so, it must be true. I've been very busy. Alba, Hortensia's sister, arrives from New York today, Sunday, at 9:00 a.m. She's coming for Rafael's ordination. In preparation, I tried to help her fix up the house, paint the furniture, etc., and that is why I've been so busy. That is why I didn't write to you yesterday. Besides, *mi vida,* I have a lot to study because various circumstances have made me fall behind with reviewing, and I need to study. My exam is on the 11th. How happy I'll be to see you again! You know, your letter from yesterday filled me with happiness. It contained a vague hint of tenderness. By the way, my love, I don't know in which book I've put it, and I've grown tired of looking for it to reread it. You can't imagine how harebrained your fiancée is.

Do you know the reason why I write shorter letters to you? It's because I want to save everything for when I see you. But you can't complain. I have replied to each one of your letters, and I have written you several extras. But this is not a dispute, Manolete; it is simply an explanation. I dream about you every night (except for a few).

Mamá called me just now because she was worried.[76] Everyone there is doing well. I too am doing so-so.

Manolete, I'd love to write you more and more, but I still have to get

---

76 She was mentioned in the "Public Forum" the day before.

ready to go to the airport with the girls, and they're waiting for me. Say hello to your family, I too love them very much. You know that.

Sending all my love,
Mine

Below is Hortensia's note:

Manolete: I want to write to you, but it's impossible. I am very busy right now. Imagine: exam, ordination, and on top of it all, my sister's coming from New York. I'm happy about your victories but saddened to know that you aren't coming.

Regards to everyone, to don Manuel and your little brother. Tell them I haven't forgotten them.

As always, your little sister.

JULY 1955

> But nor can I
> forget my people.
> I am going to fight in each street,
> behind each stone.[77]

In July the correspondence starts being correspondence. Three of my father's letters, which I managed to recover, enrich our understanding of this epistolary relationship.

Mami's texts are short and hurried at the beginning of the month, due to exams and the end of the academic year. Her letters became considerably longer once she returned to Ojo de Agua, leaving behind María Teresa and Hortensia.

Two important things draw our attention this month: the familiarity with which the couple treat their respective families and the escalation of the threats against Papi due to his romantic involvement with Minerva Mirabal.

When Hortensia's brother is ordained a priest, Mami meets Eduardo, Papi's brother, who was a seminarian. Their letters reveal my father's affection

---

77 Neruda, "Letter on the Road," p. 147, with modification to Devenish Walsh's translation in the first verse. (t.n.)

for Mary (Aunt Teté). By now, the Mirabal Reyes family considered Manolo part of the family, to the point that my grandmother defended him to his jealous girlfriend. In one of the funniest anecdotes in the correspondence, Mami tells Mamá Chea that she had dreamed about an act of infidelity and that she saw herself ending the relationship. Mamá Chea listened, and to bring her back down to Earth said, "Remember that it's a dream." Dedé, Jaimito, Patria, María Teresa, Margot, Tonó . . . everyone by this time was doting on my father. As for Mami, the letters also reveal her deep closeness with Papi's family. (There are jokes that suggest that my paternal grandmother would tell my mother everything that my father was doing in Montecristi.)

It is precisely in July when Manolo makes plans to bring his family to Ojo de Agua the following month so that everyone can meet and to celebrate the "first" anniversary of their courtship. My aunts Edda and Emma, the twins whom my parents often mention in their letters, spent that summer vacation at Mami's house. This is lovingly documented in an article that Aunt Emma published in the December 9, 1974, issue of the magazine *¡Ahora!* (*Now!*).

But a shadow threatened the lovers' plans, not only for that summer, but for the rest of their lives. Trujillo's talons extended their reach to the farthest limits of the half island and beyond. At the end of his July 27 letter, almost in passing, Papi mentions the news that he is still receiving "the warnings." This has to do with the arrival of anonymous letters meant to notify the family that Manolo was romantically involved with "a red communist." Around that time, a friend of the family went to visit my grandfather, Papá Manuel, bringing the message that "his son should end that relationship because it is dangerous." My Aunt Ángela told me that she has never forgotten the calm with which my grandfather stood up and responded to the emissary as he accompanied her to the door: "I thank you for your suggestion, but I do not know what your intentions are. I will also thank you to never return to this house with such messages."

Papi signed all of the postscripts in his letters with a "V." According to my Aunt Ángela, that was the initial of the pseudonym under which my father wrote poetry and a novel about native peoples, a few chapters of which he asked her to read. She was unable to preserve any of those texts once the dictator's thugs dismantled my parents' house and life in 1960.

Postmarked July 1 in Trujillo City. Received on July 2.

My beloved Fiancé,

While everyone is at the "office," I am writing to you and thinking of you. *Mi vida,* forgive me for not having written in these past few days. There has been so much to do around here, and I can't stay out of things, although I wish I could. It's not in my character. I have to get involved in everything. Even just now I was at the Casa España[78] helping them prepare the tables. But when the commotion inevitably began, all my phobia of meetings washed over me like a tidal wave. Regardless, I know that I'll go toward the end because I want to see Eduardo if he is, in fact, coming, as Rafael told me. It is the only thing that can drag me there. My love, forgive me, too, for not being able to offer you the joy of an upcoming exam. I've lost too much time and don't feel well-prepared. My exam will be on the 11th, just like Leda's. The second round begins on Monday. I haven't forgotten you, Manolete, but you have. Or is it that you're tired of that litany that I never tire of hearing?

Kisses,
Mine

Postmarked July 5 in Trujillo City. Received on July 6. The envelope contains three brief notes that were apparently written on the same day.

My beloved Fiancé,

I just spoke with you on the telephone. It had been so long since I felt such happiness. I'm lonesome and sad without you, without your letters. I'm also nervous and swamped with exams. I'm sending the letter I had already written you. You never did tell me what you were doing yesterday. I called you three times. It's just as well. You saved me the quarters for the operator. (They didn't charge me for the calls.) As you can see, I'm in a joking mood. I'm happy. I've heard your voice. What a beautiful, sweet feeling. Even though I told you that I was only going to write once, hopefully I'll have time to buy paper and write to you a few more times. Although you may doubt it since I don't write, I think about you all the

---

[78] A social and cultural center for Spaniards living in the Dominican Republic. (t.n.)

time. You fill my thoughts so completely that I have to make an effort to concentrate on my beloved "Civil." You see!? Now because of you, I haven't been able to cover certain material: "The Transfer of Credits." Read it, maybe it will be on my exams.

You haven't told me what day you want me to go to Salcedo. Hopefully it's soon since that means that we'll see each other soon. In any event, this "credit," without "right of refusal" is yours. Do you agree to that?

I love you so much,
Mine

On another small piece of paper, inside the same envelope:

My dear, beloved Manolo,

I am writing to you at naptime since it saddens me deeply to think of the days that go by without you receiving a letter from me, thinking of you so much. But that's life. There is so much work to do these days. I thought I'd be prepared, but to date I haven't prepared even half of the material in each subject. But don't worry, I just ask that you not pay me any mind this week if you don't receive my letters as often as I would like.

I received your letter yesterday. It's the only thing that lifts my spirits. Now I'm studying with Clarita in the mornings, afternoons and evenings. Don Pachi is coming to pick her up at ten. I haven't seen hide nor hair of Hortensia, since, as you can imagine, she is always with her sister, and I can't be wasting time.

If you could only imagine how much I long to be with you. The day I finish my exams and we can see one another will be glorious!

I was left waiting for Eduardo yesterday. Why did he not come to the parade? Or did he come and I did not see him? How is your family? Give them my warmest regards. And to you I send all my life, all my love.

Mine

Although the following is dated July 6, it was in the same envelope as the previous two.

July 6, 1955

Dear Chiqui,

I received your letter this afternoon. It's a shame that they arrive in the afternoon, after they've already picked up today's outgoing mail. Otherwise, you could receive this tomorrow.

Oh, Love, how sweet your letter is. I must be crazy to not take my exams tomorrow and dart off to Ojo de Agua, to wait for you to arrive, *mi muchachito,* to lean against your shoulder and put to rest this one month and nine-day marathon of loneliness-induced exhaustion (breathe). But my nerves won't allow me. I have a feeling that the material I've neglected will appear on the exam, and I haven't dared run the risk.

Chiqui, I have to go settle my situation regarding Philosophy. Guerrero told me to complete the seminar right away, that he was going to lend me the books. If you're not going on Tuesday, I'll stay and do that. So just let me know, because if you do go on Tuesday, I'll leave in a hurry. Eduardo was here just now. I set this aside because some visitors arrived. I can't tell you what a positive impression Eduardo has made on me. Everyone here sends you their regards. Dedé and Jaimito are coming tomorrow. As inspired as I was writing this, and then they came, interrupting me. What a shame.

Don't forget your
Mine

Postmarked July 9 in Montecristi. It bears no stamp of receipt.

Monte Cristy

7/9/55

Miss
Minerva Mirabal
Trujillo City

My beloved, cherished Fiancée,

Do you know what it's like to feel blissfully happy? That's how your *muchachito* feels. The cause? The most wonderful thing in my life: you, my most beloved!

You are the best, the most understanding. I appreciate all your efforts. You understood how much I needed your letters and, in spite of all the storms and work that surround you, you wrote to me as always. And this time your letters were enchantingly simple, full of tenderness and affection. How could I *not* adore you?

Yesterday, as much as I desperately wanted to write to you, I wasn't able. I was in court all day. Naturally, I ate at home and rested, but it is such an inadequate time for writing, and when I got back, it was too late to send mail.

Eduardo is here. If he struck you as nice, the impression he has of you is even greater than you can imagine. I so enjoyed hearing him describe his impression of you. He congratulated me for being with you, and he wishes us tons of happiness. "Under the grace of God,"[79] of course!

Everyone here says hello back to you. Mamá is very content and as always is "keeping an eye on me for you." I don't do half what she writes in her letters.

My love, I'm thinking of going on Friday the 15th. I have a trial on Tuesday. I'll wait until you defend your Philosophy seminar, as long as you're all ready by Friday. I don't think my impatience will endure any longer. Regards to everyone at home. Give Mery all my affection.

I adore you.
Yours,
Manolo

P.S. Excuse me for not writing you a longer letter, but today I went with my old man to the fields—it had been about 15 days since I'd last gone—and we got back just a bit ago. I still haven't bathed, but I didn't want tomorrow to come and go without you receiving word from me and all, all my affection.

My love, try to soothe your nerves, and believe first and foremost that as always, you will triumph on your exams. You deserve it. I already have a candle lit for you. Go get 'em, *bien mío!*

V.

---

79 Eduardo was in the seminary, studying to be a priest.

Postmarked July 20 in Villa Tenares. Received on July 21.

July 18, '55

My Beloved,

See? This is a page out of the notebook in which I'm trying to do my Sociology assignment, but if you keep disrupting my thoughts like this, I'll never finish. It feels like you're still here and . . . I have here a paradox! (In one way or another I had to use this term that I saw in Durkheim's book.[80]) It seems like a century has passed since you left. I reach out my hand to touch you, and it tightens in a fist against my chest. I hear your voice and feel deep within me the tenderness with which you called me "beautiful" yesterday. Nothing I say can convey to you how I've spent the morning without you and at the same time *with* you.

Chiqui, it's nighttime already. I was writing during the day, and the tip of my pencil wore down, but I want to finish this no matter what so that I can mail it early tomorrow. It turns out that my work wasn't so difficult. I'm pretty far along, and if I weren't so indecisive, and if I thought about you less, and I weren't busying myself with pruning the bushes, and taking care of my feet, thinking about you, etc., etc., I'd have finished this blessed Sociology assignment by now, and tomorrow I'd be able to work on another one. But who knows how long . . .

Chiqui, don't say anything about us going to your house. If the twins come, we'll go pick them up, but I forgot to tell you that we were planning on returning the same day. We'll drive from here with Patria, either with Pedrito or with another driver. But we have to come back. I still don't know if I'll go to the capital on Friday or on Monday. It depends on my literary activity in the next few days.

Tell me, *mi vida,* do you think you'll have any problem finding the fern roots for me? If so, don't worry, I'll swap them for *higüero*[81] trunks. It's all the same.

You know what, Chiqui? I'm very sleepy. I'll write to you again tomorrow. *You,* write to *me* and console me for this terrible void that your

---

80 Apparent reference to *The Rules of Sociological Method* (*Les Règles de la Méthode Sociologique*) by the French politician, economist, sociologist, and anthropologist Émile Durkheim (1858–1917).

81 The Dominican *higüero* is a medium-sized tree that bears a large fruit whose outer casing has traditionally been used to make bowls, jars, and handicrafts. (t.n.)

absence has left in me, and give me a little assurance that you're happy with me, that you love me as I am, and as deeply as I love you.

Yours,
Mine

Postmarked July 21 in Salcedo. Received on July 22.

July 20, '55

My beloved Fiancé,

I was thinking that I would be able to send this to you in time for it to go out with today's mail, but that will not be possible. Don't forget that your girlfriend lives in the farthest corner of the world.

I have been here at Patria's since last night. I came with Peter.[82] I was thinking about leaving early, but I've been reading, and it's already nine in the morning. I finished the Sociology assignment yesterday, and it is so delicious to be able to read a few magazine articles. It seems that my neurasthenia[83] is subsiding. This morning I was thinking that you've had to put up with me and my nerves, even now that my exams are over, which has been no fun at all. To tell the truth, I was in a really bad state. Don't go worrying about me, *mi vida,* thinking that I'm suffering. I'm sorry for your sake, of course, but since I'm feeling back to normal, I'm feeling calm about it.

When I get home, I'll type up my assignment and work on the other seminar. I'll most definitely take it to the capital on Monday, and I'll be there until Wednesday. If in fact you come the following Saturday (or on Friday, perhaps) I'll be led to think that life is beautiful. I would like to be able to hand in my four seminars so that I don't have to think about my studies at all until next October. In the meantime, I'll think about the lovely things that I can make and embroider for our home. You know that this makes me immensely happy! Manolete, sometimes I have to laugh at all the people who come up to me and say that they are going with me to Monte Cristi. Everyone is making plans, so prepare to house and feed an army. There are about four girls, various cooks, and some servants. We'll have to bring over Buckingham Palace, at the very least.

---

82   Affectionate nickname for Pedro, Patria's husband. (t.n.)
83   Nervous exhaustion. (t.n.)

Today I'm thinking of checking at the post office to see if your first letter has arrived, at the very least.

Ugh! How annoying! I've been talking to you in my mind all day, thinking all day about the things that I was going to tell you when I wrote to you, but when the time comes to write, I don't know if it's because they're waiting for me, or what, but my mind goes blank. Is it all right with you if I just tell you that I adore you more and more each day?

Yours,
Mine

Typewritten and unsigned. Postmarked July 21 in Salcedo. Received on July 22.

July 21

Mister
Dr. Manolo Tavárez
Monte Cristy

Dear Manolete,

As of now, as I am writing to you, I still have not received a letter from you. I hope to receive one today. If not, I'll despair.

I continue to work on the seminars, but I'm happy because I have a bit of time each day to read and "evidently" my pessimism and bad mood have improved. By the way, *mi vida,* tell me if you have this book of mine: one that's all bound, called *The Renaissance,* by Walter Pater,[84] if you do, please mail it to me as soon as possible, as I'm thinking about using it as a guide for one of my assignments.

There occur to me a thousand things to tell you, but I'm having a hard time with this monologue. So write to me. If I receive a letter today, I'll write to you again.

---

84 Walter Pater (1839–1898), English essayist, literary critic, and art historian who was very influential in his generation precisely for this book that Minerva mentions, *The Renaissance: Studies in Art and Poetry.*

Postmarked July 22 in Salcedo. Received July 25.
There is a fingerprint on the letter, apparently hers.

My beloved *Muchachito*,

Yesterday afternoon I went to Salcedo. I waited for the mail to arrive, and your letter came after all. You want me to write every day. You complain if my letters are brief, but be fair. I never leave any letter of yours unanswered, but if I don't write to you, you don't write to me either. I have to tell you that according to my count, we're now at 4-to-1, as always. But when I point this out, you dispute it. I don't know if it's for fun or because you need glasses. Besides that, you find a thousand things wrong with my letters, which recently, I know, are far from perfect.

But enough with complaints and quarrels. I "have the pleasure" of telling you how delighted I am that the twins are coming. I hope they come soon. Hortensia wrote to me yesterday and told me that they haven't yet assigned a date for Mery's exam but that it will be sometime next week. So, we eagerly await them here. Hortensia sends you warm regards. She says she's had a very sore throat and that Carolina was there studying with her.

Chiqui, I can't correct myself and stitch together a neat, coherent letter if my thinking is so unraveled. How am I supposed to write you a proper, methodical, and systematic letter? Such a letter might come from one of your other lady friends, but not from Minerva. The night before last, I dreamed that you had fallen in love with I-don't-know-whom and that we had broken up, and I was headed for I-don't-know-where. I was telling Mamá about it yesterday, and I was so convinced that she had to remind me that it was only a dream. I think it all came up because Margarita is thinking about all that stuff and everyone here (Antonia) asks, "What does Manolo say about this?" Well, I don't know what Manolo says; he hasn't said anything to me. But, do you see? I don't know where I was going. What I was going to tell you is that yesterday I forgot to sign a note that I typed you. If you want, I can send the signature along with this letter, but I don't think that's necessary, my love; certainly, you've recognized and identified it.

Mi vida, I'm sorry you've been ill. Poor thing! I thought you had already recovered. I hope that you have by now and that you take good care of yourself.

The thousand things that I wanted to tell you are about something that happened. You almost ended up working in the court here. A man came to talk with Mamá, asking her to recommend an attorney. For several reasons, she didn't dare notify you. You can laugh; it was nonsense, having to do with complicity in that felony that we've discussed so much. The guy was released. They gave $60.00 to the lawyer, who didn't have to do anything since the district attorney dropped the charges, and there was no evidence. And Uncle José was telling me that after all that, he made so many asinine comments that some people wanted to knock him down a few pegs. You would have done a better job. The question arose because they drew connections between Mundo's death and the brother's revenge, and since there were so many parties with opposing interests, there weren't enough lawyers in Salcedo. And that's without taking into account that one of them was being represented by Sánchez Morcelo. You can't imagine how much it pains me that Mamá didn't tell you. But Uncle José told me that he was going to keep an eye out to secure anything he could for you here. Let me know if you'd like that.

Ah! I almost forgot. I think I told you that the case is being appealed. I want us to go, so prepare yourself. I'd like for us to go together. I have never been to a trial, and besides, we can hear the famous "Morcelo Sánchez."

Chiqui, Chachita is going to Haiti. I think you know that. She told me that if I needed anything, to just let her know. I might ask her to buy Garraud's *D'instruccione Criminale*.[85] Anything from France is cheap there. A thousand congratulations on your wins. That makes me so happy!

                              I love you and think of you often,

                                           Mine

Postmarked July 25 in Salcedo. Received on July 27. The envelope was typewritten, apparently by Dedé.

My beloved Manolete,

Your harebrained fiancée has lost her paper, pen, and good sense. Dedé is getting her packages and boys ready to leave, and I don't want to miss the chance to send this. I didn't write to you yesterday because I went to

---

85 René Garraud (1849–1930), *Traité théorique et pratique d'instruction criminelle et de procédure pénale*.

the post office, and they told me that there was no letter. I slept over at Patria's, and this morning when I got back, I had the unparalleled delight of a letter from you. Dedé won't let me write, asking me how to spell your name and your town's name so she can prepare the envelope. I don't know how I'm even managing this. Tomorrow I'm leaving with Chiche at 5 a.m. I'll write to you from the capital. Write to me there, and tell me which day you all are coming. It's impossible to write more. Jaimito is revving up the engine.

Sending all my affection,
Minerva

Postmarked July 28 in Montecristi. Received on July 30 in Salcedo.

Monte Cristy

7/27/55

Miss
Minerva Mirabal
Trujillo City.

My beloved *Muchachita*,

Since Monday I haven't received any more of your cherished updates, your letters. I don't understand why our correspondence to Salcedo takes so long now. In your last letter, postmarked the 22nd, you told me that you had only received one letter of mine, when by that time I had already written you four. This latest one of yours took almost five days to reach me. I'm sending this one to Trujillo C. with the idea that you must be there by now. Tell me whether or not you've handed in the work for the seminars and how Mery and Hortensia's exams turned out.

Tell Mery that I'm eager to see her, that I always think of her with all my affection. Hopefully this last course went well for her!

About my trip there with the twins: it can't be this week. Some difficulties have come up, one of which is pressing. It's an issue related to my Mandatory Military Service. Yesterday they called me from the fort. I don't know who started the rumor that I was intending not to march. I enlisted and ended up required to go on Sundays. The march will last two hours every Sunday (except for leave).

I'm thinking of going with the twins the first week in August, on Saturday or Sunday. However, my love, I was thinking that on August

15, when we celebrate the "first" anniversary of our relationship, I could bring Mamá, Ángela and Jaime, and the twins. What do you think? For me it would be an enormous joy. So, tell me if I should postpone the trip for that day instead.

Last night I left court at ten (10) at night. The deliberations went on forever. It was a child abduction case. The plaintiff was represented by a lawyer from Santiago. Antonio Grullón and I worked on the defense. The judge reserved the verdict for the next hearing. There was a huge audience; they were even standing on the benches and in the street. This has me feeling a bit "emboldened." A number of colleagues have congratulated me. Blow away the "puff" of smoke with which I'm telling you this! I'll write to you again tomorrow, my guardian angel.

I'm kissing you passionately.
Yours,
Manolo

P.S. Regards to everyone there. Don't forget to go to the University to pick up my ring and diploma. I've started receiving the warnings again.

V.

Telegram from Hortensia to Manolo, sent from the capital on July 28, 1955.

Minerva left today. Hugs.

Telegram from Minerva to Manolo, sent from Salcedo on July 28, 1955.

Without letter from you. Don't know when they'll come. Let me know.

Postmarked July 28 in Montecristi. Received on July 30 in Salcedo.

Monte Cristy

7/28/55

Miss
Minerva Mirabal
Trujillo City.

My beloved and cherished Fiancée,

Today I received your latest letter from Salcedo. (I presume that by now you must be in the capital.) Yesterday I wrote to you in the capital thinking that you would still be there. I remembered that you had told me that your trip would be on Monday or Wednesday of this week.

I have faith and immense hope that Mery and Hortensia have taken their exams by now and that they have done really well. Each time I think about them still studying, my soul aches, especially for Mery, who has been studying so diligently for such a long time.

In my letter from yesterday I told you about some of the obstacles that have made my trip to Salcedo this weekend impossible. I also asked you about the possibility of bringing almost my entire family on August 15. It depends on our patience, and on what is possible on my end, because if I bring the twins this week, I don't think I'll be able cover the expenses of returning so soon and "with so many people."

I assure you that for me, going such a long time without seeing you means making a sacrifice that is almost greater than all my strength, but my desire to introduce you to my whole family is also immense. You have known this for a while, my love, and you also know why I hadn't done it sooner.

I just now received a telegram from Hortensia, notifying me about your return to Salcedo. "Miraculously," this letter doesn't share the same fate as yesterday's, given that I sent it to the capital by "intuition."

Surely Hortensia will send it to you as soon as it arrives. Oh, darling, my heart falls when I think about us going a few more days without seeing one another!

As always, I am studying and reading a little. I have worked quite a bit these days. I have a trial tomorrow. It's an assault and battery case. Antonio and I are representing the defense again. This afternoon I am planning on reviewing everything regarding Provocation (legal justification) and intoxication, as the specific mitigating circumstance.

Regards to everyone there. To Mery, who surely went with you, I send an effusive and affectionate hug and hope that all went well for her.

Sending all of my adoration.
Yours,
Manolo

Postmarked July 30 in San Francisco de Macorís. Received on August 1.

My Beloved,

I received your telegram just a little while ago. What a shame you can't come this week! What is it that's come up? I assume that you'll tell me in the letter that I hope to receive from you today. You haven't written to me in 6 days. When I got back, I found two from last week (thank goodness), which brought me immense excitement and happiness. They brought back the beauty of those last days that we spent together.

But in spite of... (Great. They've interrupted me and I don't know what I was going to say.)

Manolete, what a huge shame that you won't be here to see some roses that I know you'd really enjoy. There was something that I deliberately placed so that it would be the first thing you saw.

I'm at Dedé's. We are going to Santiago this afternoon. Jaimito says for you to see if it's true that bran is less expensive there, and that you let me know. Dedé says for you to give us the answer when you come "so you don't go and write."

You tell me that "tomorrow I'm going to make reference to your letters," and you don't say anything about the many things that I mentioned. That thing about the orchids: don't think it was for no good reason that I told you, so that you wouldn't worry; it was because they gave me another idea, and I was thinking of perhaps following through with it. But I'll be delighted if you bring me the roots.

I did not hand in any other assignment because I didn't have time, but I will try to do it now. I was going to send you the copy of the Sociology assignment, but quite frankly it's not worth it. I really like that you have a bit of an ego to compensate for the huge one that I have.

Write me a lot. I don't want to feel like this, so lonely and far away.

Chiqui, we'll be delighted to bring the twins; we're delighted that they are coming. However, because of the logistics of the trip, and because Mamá won't allow us to go alone, we have to return the same day. Oh, Love, why haven't you come? I miss you so immensely.

I have so much to tell you, but I've lost track of our conversation, and all I want is to see you. How thrilled I am that you will finally be setting up your office! It's a good thing you put up with me expressing my opinion and sticking my nose into everything, and you even welcome it.

Everyone here sends their regards. Jaimito arrived with the car and, as I said, we are going to Santiago to run an errand for Mamá.

I send you a kiss, with my hopes that you are completely well.

Your fiancée,
Mine

August 1955

Love, I am waiting for you.
Farewell, love, I am waiting for you.
Love, love, I am waiting for you.[86]

At the height of August, my mother regarded that year as the worst of her life. Of course, she was referring to the constant moving, the lack of security, the harassment, the surveillance, the tension, the "Public Forum," and all the circumstances that kept Dominican men and women from breathing freely, and her more than anyone. As far as her engagement was concerned, it is evident that their marriage plans were taking shape in concrete ways.

Mami had learned to live with the stigma of being a dissident of the regime, an enemy of "the Chief." She tried not to outwardly project the vertigo that undoubtedly kept her in a state of constant anxiety. However, these letters show indisputably that on the inside, she was waging a heart-wrenching struggle for the normalcy she so deeply desired.

In the process of publishing this correspondence, I read the newspapers from those years, spoke with almost all of the remaining individuals mentioned in the letters, and listened to countless anecdotes from those days. These have helped me to better understand Mami's character, her courage, and above all, to confirm the paranoia that the dictator's intelligence service tried to stir up in her and in her family.

But in August, the month of vacations, in the maternal and fraternal refuge of home, Mami recovered a healthy complexion and gained weight. The infirmities disappeared as if by magic. She rested, resumed her love of literature, lost herself in books that had nothing to do with law, and recited poetry while standing in the garden, just like Mamá Dedé remembers her today. She wrote letters insisting that Papi come to visit her, and she made plans.

---

86 Neruda, "Letter on the Road," trans. Donald Devenish Walsh, p. 151. (t.n.)

The August 16 holiday was the first time that Minerva, Patria, and María Teresa visited Montecristi. When they returned, they brought with them my aunts Edda and Emma, Papi's younger sisters, to spend their vacation. The twins' stay in Ojo de Agua distracted and involved the entire family. Mami embroidered the towels that would adorn their kitchen in Montecristi, and the Tavárez Justo and Mirabal Reyes families further tightened the ties of affection in a bustle of activity that involved two cities, parents, brothers and sisters, friends, and a growing intimacy.

Fortunately, I also have some of Papi's letters from August. In them we see that both lovers were anxious to lessen the distance, that they both kept a close count of the letters they sent and that "were due," that by then their conversations were like essential nourishment, and that one longed as intensely as the other to express their affection physically: resting her head on Papi's shoulder, the sofa where they would talk and kiss, gazing at the stars, listening to a romantic song, a kiss . . .

On August 20th, the entire Tavárez Justo family, with the exception of my Uncle Eduardo, traveled to Ojo de Agua to meet the Mirabal Reyes family. Mami, absentminded or distracted, tells Papi that she hadn't recognized Reynaldo (Papy) Bisonó when she ran into him at El Gallo, a store in Santiago. This friend of my father's had close familial and commercial ties with Papá Manuel. Papy—whose father don Arturo Bisonó owned a rice mill that financed harvests for my father and grandfather—made it a custom to have lunch with my father every Thursday in Montecristi.

It seems appropriate to share a story that I heard directly from him. On one of those Thursdays, Papy Bisonó was with my father and Claudio Luna Morales at a bar when a marine patrol arrived. My father said out loud, "Trujillo's thugs have arrived." His companions were shocked but calmed down because the look on the marines' faces suggested that they hadn't understood a word. Nonetheless, they left to inform the commander on duty, Lieutenant Neftalí Cabrera, an acquaintance of my father's. He appeared at the bar immediately and asked them to leave so as to avoid problems. The marines realized that "whatever Manolo had said about 'the Chief,' it wasn't anything good." In his meeting with me, Papy concluded, "Manolo wasn't like us. We all supported Trujillo, until he came along with that movement."

My father had to postpone almost all of his visits to see his fiancée because he was supposed to participate each Sunday in August in the obligatory marches (to which "my truck and I have been cordially invited") to pay homage to Trujillo.

As if that weren't enough, on the 26th he informed Mami that he would have to be in the capital with his professional association to attend a national ceremony at the Trujillo-Hull Monument, known today as the *Obelisco Hembra* (Female Obelisk). The ceremony was in "reparation" to the dictator, and in repudiation of Drs. Eduardo Sánchez Cabral and Federico C. Álvarez, who on the 6th of that month, at a private event in the Matum Hotel in Santiago celebrating the former's 40 years of practicing law, "in a reprehensible collusion of silence, failed to mention and exalt in their speeches the magnificent work initiated by the illustrious ruler." That is how the newspaper *El Caribe* describes it on August 28th, in a summary of the bazillionth "activity of reparation and repudiation" that had taken place throughout almost the entire month of August, including in the farthest corner of the nation's territory.

As for Mami, life at her home during those days was marked by sadness due to the rapid decline in the health of Martina de la Cruz, Nina Patria's mother-in-law, who finally died on August 18th.

Postmarked August 2 in Salcedo. Received on August 3.

August 1, 1955

My beloved Manolete,

I just received two of your letters: one that Hortensia sent me from the capital, and the one that you mentioned in the telegram. (My God, from the 28th!) In addition, there was one from your dear mother and one from Hortensia. What an abundance of letters!

Even so, they have left me in low spirits. I don't know if it's because the time between now and the 15th seems like an eternity or because the youngest of your letters has "little wrinkles," it's so old. It feels like I am isolated and alone. If it's possible, I'll have to get used to your letters taking so long, but I feel like I'm sinking into an abyss of loneliness without recent news from you. It's horrible, my love. Do you know what I mean?

I am infinitely delighted that your entire family is coming here. I love them deeply and am eager to meet them. But does that mean that I won't see you before then, even for a bit? The choice is a terrible one. My selfishness surrenders between a thousand inevitable sighs and an insufferable malaise. (I'm in love.) Mamá and everyone here are delighted that you all are coming, and, for now, Mamá only knows part of it. I assume that you and the twins will stay over, right?

I have here your snazzy new ring, your diploma as befitting such an honorable attorney, as well as the ties. It might seem as if I were collecting them, but actually, I hadn't given them to you because I kept forgetting to bring them and because Mary didn't like them. (All of these are resigned to waiting.)

I am reading *Headless Angel,* extremely interesting (by Vicki Baum),[87] and I have three unfinished seminars that I have yet to touch. Hortensia wrote to me, as I mentioned, and I am planning on responding to her this afternoon. I will bring them to the post office myself. This includes the letter for doña Fefita. I would like for Hortensia to come spend a few days here, as she has become quite thin.

Do you recall our last quarrel, *mi cielo?* And after that, you don't want me to object, yet you know how difficult it is to be here all day in this restlessness, yearning and loving. I think about that bit about "if you put off coming for more than fifteen days," and . . . Anyway, you should not have gotten angry about this feeling being stronger than I am. You reason through all my theories about living in tranquility, as if you didn't know that I adore this feeling that you inspire in me, which makes me suffer and feel human. You speak to me of "sacrifice" as if it were a foreign concept to me, but you are just a grumpy old man who likes to torment me.

I'm embroidering some dish towels to dry the dishes (if they ever manage to become soiled with some kind of food) and so many jokes come to mind, about our food, our stomachs, etc. But I'm not going to tell them so that you don't go and laugh thinking that I'm dreaming, "though it may be true." The thing is that the embroidery shows a very industrious little gal (unlike the one you will have), doing each of the chores corresponding with certain days of the week: "Wash on Monday," "Iron on Tuesday," "Sew on Wednesday," "Market on Thursday," "Clean on Friday," "Bake on Saturday" and "Church on Sunday." (Eduardo would like this last one.) Anyway, Noris is here and is helping me. It's really simple.

But surely you think that I'm being selfless writing at length and twice a day (at least today). Well, that's not the case, Mister, think again. Like any intelligent person (without vanity) realize that reciprocity is called for, and that you, Sir, are obligated to give me details about everything going on in your life, and to write to me at length, at great length, and

---

87 Vicki Baum (1888–1960), a very prolific Austrian writer who was popular at the time. Several of her novels were adapted to film.

respond to all the little things that I've told you in previous letters and that you have let pass. If not, you shall come to the "wake" of a young woman who died of overwhelming nostalgia, and then write the plot for the film, *One Can Also Die from Absence*. But don't be grief-stricken now. Remember that when all was said and done, I never told you that I went to El Gallo and became quite jealous, so you've saved yourself from something. You, Sir, are undoubtedly a very lucky young man; you always end up with the best. For now, could it be that the best is that sweet, tender kiss that yearns for correspondence, for reciprocity? Did you receive it, my love?

Your Mine

Undated. Postmarked August 2 in Salcedo. Received on August 3.

My cherished Love,

I still haven't received the letter that you were talking about in the telegram. I did receive one on Friday, which was the only one from last week, but it was written on Monday, which is to say that it took 5 days to get here. (I almost said fifty, but it seemed longer than that.) Oh, *mi vida,* I knew that going so long without seeing you would be even more insufferable during vacation. What a Sunday it was yesterday! I didn't think of anything but you, and it pained me to see our sofa, our rocker, and how I longed to rest my midday drowsiness upon your shoulder! Uncle Fello and Aunt Lilia were here and asked about you a lot, telling me to be sure to bring you by. They spent a few days, and yesterday Uncle Mon and his wife came to congratulate me, supposedly on my exams.

Do you know who Benjamín is? He is Milita's husband. He is going to do me the favor of taking this to the post office. He's "saddling up" his horse as a signal for me to get a move on, so I won't be able to write as much as I'd hoped. But he'll surely bring me your letter, and this afternoon I'll write to respond and to satiate my hunger to talk with you.

Mary says to tell the twins to bring their bathing suits so that we can go to Jarabacoa on Sunday. We're crazy excited awaiting their arrival. I'll do my best to write to Mamá Fefita, but it's still not easy for me, I never received the letter that you told me about. Regards to your family.

Yours,
Minerva

Postmarked August 5 in Salcedo. Received on August 6.

My beloved Manolo,

I was planning on writing to you earlier so that this letter would go out in the mail today, August 3, but some visitors came, and it was impossible for me to do so. The boy went to Salcedo, and if there is a letter from you, he'll bring it to me, so this will do double duty, covering today's material and the response to your letter, if I have the pleasure of receiving it. Yesterday I brought one to the post office. I was going to Santiago with Mamá to run an errand. We passed through La Jagua to La Vega and from there took the Puñal Highway and returned by way of Moca, quite a tour.

We saw Sánchez Morcelo's house, and I thought of you. You know which one it is, right? It's just as you enter Jarabacoa. A beautiful country house, made of wood, with its pool and everything. I know you would have really liked it. Upon my return, I found the letter you sent in response to the one that I had written from the capital. I felt terribly anguished when I saw the empty envelope. I thought that it was very brief, but it's that the paper was thin. In any event, it seemed brief to me because now that you're not coming, I need to hear a lot from you, that you fuss over me. I need you to show me that you miss me and love me too. Yesterday I was jealous. I was trying to ask myself if I would be flattered to know that some old admirer was still in love with me, but I couldn't reach any conclusions because none of them interest me. All this to try and understand what it must be like for you to know that some girl is thinking of you. But it was her fault that I thought about all this since there's no other reason for her to behave like that. The thing is that I'm like a guy when it comes to these things, and the worst part is that I can't help it.

I saw Papy Bisonó in El Gallo. As always happens with me, he had to identify himself as "Manolo's friend." He asked me if we were still doing all right, and he told me that don Manuel had been to his house and "had spoken a lot about me."

My, my . . . why hadn't you told me that your farm had been turned into a landing strip? You've all become quite popular. (Every day I thought of it and forgot to ask you.)

You don't tell me much of anything, and I want to know all your thoughts and what you do from the time you get up until the time you lie down.

My love, I set this letter aside, and in that time, Pedro arrived from the post office and told me that it was closed when he got there. What a shame! Chiqui, there is a beautiful moon right now, but it's pale and sad because you're not here, and I miss you. It was a year ago yesterday that I sent you a telegram letting you know that I had postponed that trip. Remember? Aunt Fefa died a year ago today. I've been quite sad thinking about her. She loved me so much.

You know something? The fact that you've thought to celebrate the first anniversary of our relationship by coming with your family has moved me deeply. It reveals a sensibility on your part that makes me love you even more, if that is possible. I adore you.

Mine

Kept with another letter in an envelope postmarked August 24 in Montecristi, though it does not contain a letter from that date.

Monte Cristy

8/8/55

Miss
Minerva Mirabal
Salcedo.

My Everything,

Yesterday I was telling you that today I would write to you again, and indeed here I am again with all the immensity of my love and this immense, magnificent need that I have for you. I'm writing to you in a rush, *bien mío,* because the mail is going out, and I want to be sure to tell you a few things that make me very happy, blissfully happy.

Yesterday I went to the Farmers' Bank, and with Papá's consent and using part of the livestock as collateral, I am going to take out the money that I told you about to start the project, the dairy business about which I've talked with you so much. I'll get around $900.00. I'm very happy. You more than anyone know how closely tied to our plans this little endeavor is ... lovely, cherished because of the end that inspires it ... Oh, darling, I can't live without you! I'm burning with the need to have you by my side. All my struggles and my efforts are directed toward realizing my greatest, only, incomparable ideal: that of creating our love nest.

I just arrived back from the office. I was with a client until now. That's why I'm not writing more. I want to catch the mail so that tomorrow you can share in the joy with which I'm writing you this letter. Mamá, in her manner of speaking, which by now you know well, sends you all her affection and hopes that soon you come to your home. She says, "if she doesn't write to me tomorrow, the young lady is a tad bit awful."

My regards to everyone there, most especially to Mamá Chea and to my dear girls. I adore you with all my soul.

Your Manolo

P.S. Excuse the envelope, my beloved. I didn't have any other on hand.

Yours,
V.

Postmarked August 11 in Salcedo. Received on August 12.

August 10

My beloved Manolete,

I haven't written to you since you left. Today is Wednesday. However, I haven't forgotten you even for a moment. I was reading just now and got up feeling impatient, thinking: How can I possibly go on reading this boring book and not write to my love as soon as possible? The pen that I'm using to write to you is yours. I found it among my things. It seems that Mary borrowed it from you and forgot to return it. Have you missed it? Today I went to Salcedo to bring Dedé, who brought us the car, and I didn't find your letter, which I was eagerly awaiting.

How did everything go with the march?[88] It worries me. If you had not been able to come with your family this weekend, it would have hurt me so much! Three nights—all three—I have dreamed about you. Once I dreamed that I was visiting at your house and you almost, almost, ignored me. You were out and about with Acosta, and later it turned out to be with some girl. It must be that my subconscious is worried. I don't want you to feel lonely either, *Amore*. Before, you were excited about

---

88 The obligatory march in honor of the dictator. He mentions his summons in a previous letter.

your studies, and I assume that you still are. I understand that you need a distraction, and I want you to have some fun, but the things I don't know or with which I am unfamiliar make me uneasy or make me suffer. I was under the illusion that if I wrote to you every day, you'd feel less lonesome, but now I realize that this is not enough. I have to be more open. Maybe when I go there it will be easier for me to get used to thinking about things differently.

I was reading *The Ways of Love,* a true lecture on tolerance and love for others, but the truth is that I find it difficult to read books that give advice. What really did inspire me was Aeschylus's *Prometheus,* a marvelous work from antiquity that raises for the first time the question of justice. Right now, I'm reading *The Great Mouthpiece.*[89] It's rather tiresome since it's full of unnecessary information. I'm planning to finish it tonight even if that means skipping half of it.

Chiqui, I don't know how I've even managed to write you this letter: there is a lady here who talks more than a parrot. Prepare yourself, because she's eager to have a chat with you. The other day, the first thing I found was the box of your ties. How it pained me! Chiqui, when are you going to give me the little picture that I've asked of you? I really need it, but you don't think of me.

Come soon. I'm sending my love. Forgive all my resentment.

Your Mine

This letter bears no postmark. It seems to have been delivered by hand.

August 13

My Beloved,

Today is Saturday. I have all afternoon to write to you, which is barely enough time since I did so only once this week, and I would like to reestablish that closeness that we sometimes have when it seems that we can't live without writing to one another, without sharing our thoughts with one another. You have asked me if this is a contract, and you stop just short of congratulating me for how well I comply with what is tacitly stipulated. Isn't that why I fittingly oppose the "*Non adimpleti contractus*" exception typical of synallagmatic[90] contracts? Well, no, my love, I didn't

---

89 *The Great Mouthpiece* by Gene Fowler (1890–1960), American journalist and author.
90 Bilateral. (t.n.)

write to you the first few days because a doubt was casting its shadow over my soul, and I always find it difficult to write in that state of mind. Then, until yesterday (Friday), I hadn't received a letter from you, and I thought that you would be coming tomorrow and, in any case, I would talk with you on the telephone, but before that, I needed a note explaining this silence of yours. I recalled that you had told me to write to you at least three times, which was a tacit promise that you would do the same. I was so worried thinking that maybe there was something wrong, because of the march, or for some other reason. But, *mi vida,* if you know me so well, how do you not know that the temperature of my letters fluctuates according to yours, and that without even thinking about such a "contract," my behavior in this sense—except for when my anxiety gets the best of me or I feel like being generous—can't be anything more than a reflection, an impulse, a reaction, given my temperament? Before, you would at least send me a telegram, and now you let me wait impatiently for five days without word from you. Oh, *vida,* forgive this super-intolerant, ultra-sensitive and extremely rash fiancée of yours. These defects, and she, have belonged to you for some time, and you can censure and criticize them as you please.

With this in mind, I've thought and meditated quite a bit, *mi cielo,* on the fact that you—perhaps rightfully so—consider me rather intolerant. In spite of everything, *mi muchachito,* I don't want you to lose your faith in and affection toward people *ad referendum.* I'd rather that you be convinced of my intolerance. I've spent some time contemplating my behavior. Haven't I done the same thing for which I reproached them? If I remember correctly, I told you about my feeling disgruntled when I was coming back from some trip, of it being the same old story, about the gossip my girlfriends were telling me and my later conviction about who had started the rumor. Am I not doing the same thing right now? I know from experience that you dislike it when you observe these defects in my behavior. Maybe you noticed them before, but with affection, or perhaps you were unaware. Even though I don't have the same intentions, nothing justifies this. You, I, everyone is spiritually better off thinking well of humanity.

And in regard to my studies, don't worry, Chiqui, hopefully there's nothing worse than what I've experienced this year . . . and I've already come through it.

Last night, accepting an invitation from the Governor, I went to Salcedo to the inauguration of the "Salcedo Athenaeum." I slept over at Dedé's, and this morning I ran into Chelito. She said hello and treated me the same as always. We had a nice time visiting, and I'm so glad that we did.

Mamá wants me to tell you that she's so sorry that the trip didn't materialize. We hope that it can very soon. If I could, I would go pick up the twins so that you all could come later to get them, but it can't be, because Dedé is going to Sosúa with Jaimito, and Patria doesn't leave town due to doña Martina's worsening condition. They have invited me to go to Sosúa, and María Teresa is going, but I have no interest in going out without you ... Chiqui, you tell me that nothing gets past me. However, something is getting past me. Have you told me the true reason why you've postponed your visit? Or is it that you are hiding something else? Why have your letters been so non-explicit? (Forgive the scribbles, my desk is made of air.)

I'm glad that you have been driving the tractor (almost) and that you've gone to the fields with your dad. This has made me very happy.

I set this letter aside because (finally!) the architect has come. I'm so thrilled, and I hope to transmit to you my delight regarding the whole house situation. As usual, I have gotten my way, and everything is going to be according to my taste, or almost everything, because we still don't have the estimate ... and it's possible that it won't be according to my taste.[91] Speaking of taste, I'll share with you that, although it may not make you feel as smug as it makes me feel, he found my taste to be very refined, intelligent, practical and a few other things. He even asked me about my fiancé, because he would find it difficult to deny me anything given how "convincing" he found me to be. (How do you spell "perceive," as in "observe"?)

Anyway, don't worry; it seems that it is *I* who doesn't know how to deny *you* anything. You see me with this head full of curls, right? Me, who is always sporting the latest, loveliest hairstyle, etc., etc. But no, I had them looking very lovely today because even though I had a sense that you would not be coming tomorrow, I gave myself a home permanent, and the curls turned out nicely. But sadly, your telegram, and then your letter, confirmed that I wouldn't be able to show them off to you.

---

91 Mami designed and participated in the building process of Mamá Chea's new house, which today houses the House Museum.

I've read quite a bit and embroidered even more. The towels are coming along nicely. When you come, I hope to show them to you finished, cleaned and starched.

Tomorrow I am going to Salcedo for a wreath-laying ceremony. If it's possible to reach you by phone, we'll talk. Among the things that I've heard today, one is particularly interesting: that advancing in the legal profession is very easy, that all one needs is honesty and good faith, because with so many lawyers being scoundrels, people these days are looking for no more than that. I liked that a lot, *amore*. I don't want you to collapse from exhaustion. Lie down upon this chest to rest for a moment, and hear this tender heart that beats for you.

Yours,
Mine.

Postmarked August 9 in Salcedo. Received on August 20.

August 18, '55

Here I am, delighted with my dear little girls, who are very well-behaved. They are quite content and are going to stay . . . well, Edda says not, that they won't stay more than two months. Emma is now quite plump. They've only been here for two days, and they've already been rejuvenated by the fresh Ojo de Agua air, or at least I hope so.

You know, Chiqui, yesterday the girls were telling me that you were going to come, and it surprised me that for the first time, I knew nothing about your plans. Did you tell them that you were coming? That's what they understood. *Amore,* doña Martina, Pedrito's mother, is still doing quite poorly. She's not in agony, but I doubt that she will last more than a few days. We are all very saddened by this.

Yesterday I received your letter from the 13th. I thought there were two of them. In any event, it made me so happy. In it you talk about "your distractions," and I am so grateful for all that you say! You tell me about your dreams, etc. I had one to share with you too. It seems that we still had a lot to talk about. On the way back, it was as if I were satiated by your presence and at the same time (What a paradox!) thirsty for you. It seems like it's been a century since I last saw you. I interrogate the twins all day long about what you do, what you eat, when you sleep, how you are when returning home after being here, in short, all those details that point to an acute case of Manoloitis.

Manolete, your family, your house, everything pertaining to you . . . I liked them all so very much, and I feel like they are a little bit mine as well. True, my love?

On the way back, I was thinking about finishing a painting for you to hang in your office, or in the little reception area. I also really liked your friends. I regret not having chatted more with them.

The tender and loving presence of your arm lingers on my back. How happy I felt with you that day. When are you coming, *mi vida*?

I was going to write to doña Fefita to thank her, don Manuel, Ángela, in all, everyone for being so loving toward me. But I'm writing this in a hurry since I'm going to bring Mamá to spend the day at Patria's. The girls are going with me, but we'll come right back. We'll stop by the post office to bring this for you. Be sure to pass along the message. Emma is writing to them too.

If you all come this weekend, send me a telegram, and don't do like I do. But then again, I'm useless. I have to finish. Mamá is waiting for me. The girls have made too good of an impression on everyone. Everyone here thinks they're precious. It's just that they're a bit more grown up than we had anticipated.

Jaimito is doing better. He didn't suffer any setbacks, thank God.

Sending all my love. Write to me soon and at length, just like you like.

Kisses from
Mine

Postmarked August 24 in Montecristi. Received in Salcedo on August 26.

Monte Cristy

8/24/55

Miss
Minerva Mirabal
Salcedo.

My beloved Chiqui,

These past few days, I've been in better spirits. As always, you miraculously rejuvenate my spirit! The moments we spent together were so beautiful!

Mamá has come back charmed by the treatment she received from everyone there. She found Mamá Chea to be especially delightful. It's beyond me how they managed to talk so much in such a short period of time. Now that we're back, she's been talking about you all nonstop. She is—we are—very excited about your upcoming visit. I forgot to tell Mamá Chea that Dedé can come too, as a chaperone. I hope that she can and that everyone wants to come.

The trip back was very quick and without any problems. We were home by a quarter to nine. I attended the event promptly and covered my turn. Afterward, the association went "in mass" from here to the Ramfis, where there was a toast. I went home as soon as it was over. I wasn't in the mood for a party.

All of the shrubs made it here all right; they barely showed signs of motion sickness. Mamá planted them almost right away, and she is delighted because it seems that they will take root. She was fascinated by your garden. She tells me that when you're here, I'll barely have time to talk with you.

Darling, I won't be able to go this weekend. I have to be in attendance with the association in Trujillo C. on Saturday the 27th. I will use the day to take care of some professional errands. Just as I told you in that letter, my love, I'll go from Thursday to Friday to pick you all up. Oh, what a joy, *bien mío,* to have you all with us again! Everyone here is delighted and is talking about everything that needs to be done for when you come.

Excuse my handwriting, but I'm writing to you with an eighty-year-old fountain pen, and my fingers are covered in blue ink.

Tomorrow I'll write to you at length. You'll see that I've written this letter in a rush. Last night I dreamed of you, that you had shaved your head, Mery too. What's that all about?

Regards to everyone there.

Yours,
Manolo

P.S. Say hello to the twins and tell them to behave themselves and to be helpful to Mamá Chea. Give them a kiss for me.

Yours,
V.

Postmarked August 26 in Salcedo. Received on August 27.

My beloved Torment:

Don't laugh, don't quarrel with me if you haven't received letters; quarrel with the twins, who have taken up all my time. I do have just two minutes to write this to you since Benjamín, the father of your future pupil, Milita's husband, is going to Salcedo, and I'm taking advantage to send this to the post office. How was your return home? I was worried because I didn't give you all so much as a glass of milk when you left. Moreover, everyone here has given me a complex saying that apparently, I didn't tend to doña Fefita because I was being "lovey-dovey" with you.

I spoke with Hortensia on the telephone and she told me that she was coming to the Mass for doña Martina, (it's on Monday) and she'll stay over and surely go with us to Monte Cristy, but don't say anything at your house yet because it's not for certain. You know that she has a lot on her plate, but since this is what she told me, I'm telling you.

Let me know if you are coming this week or if you are going to wait until we go to bring the girls. But they're not leaving just yet. Understood? They are behaving very well, and there is no reason for them to leave so soon.

I still haven't received a letter from you. I hope for one today. Is it that you, too, have me on a diet? I saw your name in the newspaper, and Joaquín's. I see that you arrived on time. Do you find this letter insipid? No? Well, my soul is yearning for you and I adore you as always.
Your Mine.

Postmarked August 29 in Montecristi. Received on August 31 in Salcedo.

Monte Cristy

8/29/55

Miss
Minerva Mirabal
Salcedo.

My dear Chiqui:

Hey, what's going on? Don't you understand what it means for me to go eight days with only one little letter from you? I can assure you that had

I known that the twins were going to be the indirect cause of so much worry and anxiety, I wouldn't have left them for so long. Perhaps it's too selfish or, I don't know what, but the fact is that I'm not satisfied with your writing me so little (that you forget about me) because of them, or because of anyone.

Is this the real reason for your silence? "The fact" is that going so many days without word from you has made me a little sad and at times all too worried . . .

As I was telling you in my previous letters, I did, in fact, go to the capital. I attended the function and fulfilled all my duties satisfactorily. On Saturday afternoon I went to Hortensia's and didn't find her there. I saw her the next day about to get into the car to go to your place. I asked her to tell you hello for me and to express my regret for not being able to go. Besides my immense desire to be with you, I would have liked to have gone to the Mass for doña Martina. But at the time, I still hadn't finished my obligations and, what's more, I had a case pending for today. (Civil court; a divorce case.) Fortunately, Thursday is just around the corner. We'll get into "a big dispute" over all that you've made me suffer . . . and my parents and another darling little boy will have the pleasure of having you with them.

Regards to everyone there, most especially to Mamá Chea, Mery, and the twins. Since we're on a diet (though yours is broader and less strict) I can't write any more, in spite of how deeply I adore you, *pelúa*.

Yours

SEPTEMBER 1955

I have not left you when I go away[92]

Now that I have my parents' letters, they bring me back to the places where the fond memories of my existence have unfolded. They make me long for the sultry noontime air, the cool of evening, and rainy nights under the zinc roofs of the houses where I grew up, even though they do not mention these things. When Mami speaks of summer Sundays in Ojo de Agua, I can smell and hear the familiar sounds of home, the hustle and bustle in the kitchen or

---

92 Neruda, "Letter on the Road," trans. Donald Devenish Walsh, p. 145. (t.n.)

in the patio; the slow, steady strides of Mamá Chea; Javier Solís playing on the old radio in the living room; the early morning crow of the roosters or the trill of the little birds in the garden. I imagine that today's readers might also feel a certain melancholy for the almost forgotten vernacular landscapes, as well as anguish over that murderous era, destroyed in part by its many unforgivable and unacceptable deaths. As for me, they allow me to feed my memory by seeing my parents there, in those places where I was never able to observe them before. I see my mother from behind, wrapped up in her love-struck daydreams, and my father arriving to visit, with a huge smile.

So distinct in style: Papi, very comfortable writing those detailed, somewhat formal and romantic letters. Mami with whatever she happened to have on hand: memory, pencil, pen, stationery or notebook paper, getting right to the point and almost always forgetting about the date and sometimes spelling.

In the early days of September, Minerva and her sisters, this time including Dedé, made another trip to Montecristi. By now both fiancés were loved in the homes of their in-laws, and the depth of this affection breathes throughout their correspondence. At least for the time being, the danger didn't seem to contend with the love that was in the air.

They saw one another frequently and conversed often. Mami memorized Papi's childhood shenanigans, which she heard from his lips and from those of his family, and upon returning home, she told them to Mamá Chea. It was from those same lips that I would later hear those stories from Papi's childhood. They remained etched in my memory only to reemerge through these letters.

During his adolescence, Manolo belonged to a kind of fraternity formed by Domingo A. Peña Castillo, "La Cuca," who organized cultural and athletic activities. Part of the group's activities consisted of cultivating bravery, loyalty, and other values through exercises like crossing the municipal cemetery at midnight, barefoot and alone. On one occasion, someone reported them, and that night the police waited for them at the exit. Although Papi managed to escape, they went to arrest him at dawn. Neither the police with the shoes that he'd left behind in the cemetery as irrefutable evidence, nor the thorns that were stuck in his feet, nor Papá Manuel's threats were enough to make him confess to his participation nor give away the names of the other members of the fraternity. As a consequence, my grandfather grounded him for an entire month and later decided to send him to study in the capital in order to get him out of Montecristi. Papi was thirteen or fourteen years old, and in his memoirs, "La Cuca," one of the first members of the 14 of June Movement to be imprisoned, points to this episode to illustrate the courage and valor that Manolo demonstrated in the face of the horrendous torture in the prison called La 40.

On September 13, Mami tenderly recalls a conversation with Papi, and she imagines him taking his nap, lying on the "dear bed" in which he had come into the world and in which he still slept. Papi was born in the home of his grandmother Mercedes Ramos, which via the rear patio was connected to my grandparents' house by means of a little old wooden door that was always open. This house where Manolo was born was inherited by the Petit Tavárez family: Eugenio Petit, Uncle "Eño," and Aunt Delia Tavárez Ramos.

She also speaks to Papi of the "loneliness" of the couch where they used to talk and cuddle, and where she probably learned to kiss, considering that my dad was her first and only boyfriend.

The letters speak of plans for the home they would establish, and the happiness is so evident that it's palpable. Mami, in an untimely prophetic way, writes, "Oh, Love, I'm so afraid that what we have will end. I don't know why, but I have something like a premonition; it's as if there were a question mark in the future . . ." She was far from knowing that those omens of absence and loneliness would mark their few years together. Or maybe she wasn't far at all, but rather too close. My mother was like that.

With her heart full of somber premonitions, Mami didn't resign herself to the coming storms, but rather she flowed along with life in Ojo de Agua, enjoying the harmony of daily life there. Sometimes Mamá Dedé slept over in the country with her sisters, and they all stayed up late talking. They were planning a trip to Higüey, across the country's eastern region, to fulfill a promise that my grandfather had made before he died, and they made trips to the capital to run errands for Aunt Teté or my mom at the university or to go shopping. As it says in a certain poem, everything was moving along, approaching its clearest definition.

Postmarked September 8 in Salcedo. Received on September 9.

September 7

My beloved Manolete:

I was planning on writing to you when I got up today, but this morning I couldn't shake the sleepiness, and it seems that you're not going to receive this as soon as I'd wished. How was your trip back, my love? I hope that tomorrow I receive your letter with details about the trip. I miss everyone so much. I'd like to write to everyone today, but I don't know how I'm going to arrange that, and moreover, Mamá is asking me to write her some business letters.

My dear *muchachito,* you are so present within me that everything I say or do, it seems like you are hearing or seeing it. It is as if I were conversing with you at all times, and every now and then I have to call myself to order: "But Minerva, are you going crazy? Don't you see that Manolo is in Monte Cristy?" But I believe that we are united and together, wherever. I'm sending you this little poem by Manuel Magallanes Moure:[93]

> Do you remember? A beautiful summer morning.
> The solitary shore. The flight of large, heavy wings.
> Sun and wind. Florid the blue sea. Do you remember?
> My hand was gently squeezing your hand.
>
> Later on, together, our slow gazes
> rested upon the shadow of a ship that appeared
> over the tired brim of the blue distance,
> silhouetting in the sky its unfurled sails.
>
> Now I close my eyes, reality fades away,
> and the vision of that radiant morning long ago
> is reflected in the dark lens of my soul.
>
> I see the shore, the sea, the far-off sailboat,
> and the prodigious illusion is so vivid, so vivid,
> that feeling my way like a blind man, I search again for your hand.
> The end.

It's beautiful, isn't it, *mi vida? Amore,* I wasn't able to finish this letter, I'm taking advantage of an opportunity to send it to you. I'll continue writing to you with all my soul.

I adore you,
Your Mine

---

93 Author's note: Manuel Magallanes Moure (1878–1924), Chilean romantic poet. Translator's note: the translation is mine.

Postmarked September 11 in Salcedo. Received on September 12.

My Beloved,

This afternoon, Saturday, I received your letter. Each one of your phrases, Love, moved me deeply. It was like the most marvelous music I've ever heard. I don't know, Manolo, I felt so insignificant! You are so good, so good to me, and your love is the most beautiful thing that life could have given me. I want nothing more than to preserve it and to make you happy, to live for you. Do you remember, *mi vida,* all my anxiety about traveling, etc.? Well, nothing seems to matter to me anymore. I only want to be by your side; it is the only thing that matters to me. Now my dreams are woven solely around you and your happiness, which is mine. But, *mi vida,* I don't think it's necessary to tell you this; you have guessed it, right?

You can't imagine the things that I've wanted to tell you these days. The other day I cut short the letter that I had barely started; I sent you only a fraction of everything I wanted and planned to tell you. I remember that when I had to stop writing, I was thinking of describing for you the emotions that stirred in me when I mended that shirt of Papá's that you wore. Do you remember that it had a small tear? Well, I went to sew it in order to preserve it since it's a reminder of my dear father. That's when I noticed the scent of the powder that I had put on you. But it was your scent, and I was dying of nostalgia.

You tell me that you'll write, letting me know about plans, errands you have pending, etc. I'll be so delighted to read and listen to everything you tell me. I've made many plans too. The only thing that discourages me is how inconvenient it is to get the mail. Even writing to you is difficult because I don't know their schedule. Chiqui, I'm feeling very sentimental. All my memories move me. Each action you take delights me. Even the fact that you painted your house is something that brings joy to my soul, and the fact that you helped your mother when we went there, are gestures of yours that fill me with pride and joy. But you must be getting a big head with so much praise, my precious *muchachito,* and for the time being, as one announcer says, I'm going to let you have that pleasure. I think it's well deserved because you are my L. I'm overcome by such tenderness when I remember your childhood shenanigans. I've even told Mamá about the fraternity. I adore everything about you. I remember the dark highway when we were coming back from Manzanillo, and I'd like to be underneath the wing.

Your letter brought back all those delightful, very beautiful memories. Oh, Love, what good does it do me to yearn? I need to see you . . . I promised to help you, that is, to not insist that you come, to write to you often so that you would feel at peace. But, *mi vida,* I don't feel I have the courage to fulfill my promise. How could I be far from my beloved for long? I feel too weak to the bone.

It delights me to know that everyone there is growing to love me. But you're such an optimist! Who has led you to believe that not everyone here adores you? And I'm jealous of it all.

This afternoon I went to Salcedo to call you on the telephone, but then I decided not to or to leave it for later . . .

. . . Manolo, I had set this letter aside and I am continuing it today, Sunday morning. I'm going to send it to the post office right now and see if there is one of yours there. Yesterday I brought the ones for Mamá Fefita and Ángela since I had them ready. Tell the dear twins that I will write to them today but that it probably won't go out with this one because I don't have time. Tomorrow, Monday, I have to go to T.C.[94] with Mary to enroll. We'll see if she can since enrollment for final exams closed on the 10th, that is, yesterday. I'll write explaining all this to you or I'll call you from T.C.

Regards to everyone. I adore you always,
Your Mine

Postmarked September 11 in Salcedo. Received on September 12.

My beloved Manolete:

Yesterday I had to go to the capital with María Teresa because they notified her that registration for final exams closed on the 10th, and it's now the 12th. Can you believe it? But thank goodness everything turned out ok, and she was able to resolve the matter. I think I told you about this in my previous letter.

So, anyway, we went with Chiche and returned with him around 8 p.m. and slept at Dedé's. I've gotten up early to write to you so I can mail this before going out to the country.

---

94 Trujillo City, the capital. (t.n.)

My love, there are so many things I want to tell you. I won't write down all that I desire, all that I think, because it would seem like a very dramatic letter.

I have the vague and uncertain hope that you will come this weekend. If so, and if you want us to go meet you in Santiago (whatever you want), let me know in advance. We'll take the opportunity to run an errand. Anyway, let me know when you come so I can wait for you in Salcedo.

The case that we're going to hear on appeal is on the 6th of next month, although that is not definite. Since that is so far off, I hate to think that you won't be coming until then. This poor little heart wouldn't be able to take it. Oh Chiqui, I'm feeling very blue, and I have so many things to talk about with you.

I still haven't written to the twins. Give them my regards, and tell them that I'll do it later. Rita did not bring the letter for doña Fefita to the post office for me, which is why it took such a long time to arrive.

How are you, my love? It seems like it's been a century since I last saw you. Tell me, *cielo,* did you take care of the paperwork for the notary commission? [95] Don't you want to please me? Is it bad, my love, that I'm asking you to come? I'll make up for it when I'm in the capital! I'm unbearable. But I love you a lot.

Yours,
Mine

Postmarked September 14 in Salcedo. Received on September 15.

Darling "Manuel,"

About 4 hours ago I mailed you a short letter written in a hurry at Dedé's. When I went to mail it, they gave me your two letters and one from Emma. Oh, *mi vida,* my one love, what joy! I knew you had written to me. That's why I didn't say anything in my letter. But I was eager to hear from you, for you to reach out to me with your loving hand, the hands that I adore, through this distance that separates us. Manolo, how bittersweet it is to dream of you, of your generous love, so full of

---

95   The responsibilities of a *notario* in the Dominican Republic are greater than those of a notary in the United States. The former requires extensive legal training. A *notario* is responsible for drafting legal documents and advising clients. (t.n.)

understanding, and to feel you so far away. I need you too. When will I be able to lay my head upon your shoulder once again and rest from all these mundane concerns that besiege us? You see? Right now, Mamá is calling me to eat. Won't they let me write to you in peace? There are so many things that I want to write to you but don't know how; they get all jumbled up and render my thoughts incoherent. That leif-motiv (in "What is art?" you will find the correct spelling) anyway, that "lei motiv" as I was saying, is like the pulsations in my brain when I write to you. If the brain has pulsations (like those radio stations that don't tune in well and are interrupted by a chirp) you won't be able to tune in to my thoughts, because a chirp, which I'll say is the radio station of my feelings, is constantly sounding: "I miss you—come—I miss you—come—I adore you—come." "Ad nauseam!"

It's true, right? One has to grow accustomed to things little by little, and I cannot get used to being without you so abruptly.

What you've told me about your plans to obtain "our daily bread" and how that plan is taking shape, moves me and makes me immensely happy. Don't say that I'm rambling. You know that it's because I adore you, and I laugh about our affairs and make comments to you about "providing," etc. because laughter and happiness are sisters. And, notice, Manolo, I have stopped writing for a moment without realizing it in order to think, and the conclusion is that you can rest assured: that's your Minerva for you, the one who pokes fun of sentimental things, perhaps to hide her own sentimentality. When I'm not like that it's because things are going poorly. But I don't know if that was what I was going to tell you. Mamá has interrupted me, and I've forgotten.

You know something, Love? I brought you something from the capital. I hope you like it. I was going through the album to send it to you, but what if you come? I have to add some photos that are lying around. Why don't you bring the ones that you have, and we will include them so that you have them all together? I'm going to buy the photo corners in Santiago, if you come and I go to pick you up. Just thinking about it makes me hum.

On our way back we stopped in Bonao to buy something, and in the café, they played the record that reminds me so much of you " . . . And yet you remain united with my existence . . ." Oh, Chiqui, I adore you! Aren't you tired of hearing the chirp? Sorry, I can't tune in to any other station, and you'll have to hear it or turn off the radio. That would be best.

Doña Marina died, Margot's[96] Marina. Tell Emma. Tell her that I'm not writing to her right this moment because I am going to the funeral. I'll take it as an opportunity to think about you. (More chirping at the funeral.)

Sending all my love.
Your Mine

Postmarked September 14 in Salcedo. Received on September 15.

September 13

Chiqui,

I'm writing to you again in case I can't do it tomorrow. Tomorrow is the Mass for Papá, and I have to inspect the car and after that the time flies by without me knowing how. I started reading Emma's letter so I could answer her, and I couldn't resist the urge to read over and over again the letters I received from you today. I realized that in mine I never mentioned to you the tenderness that fills me when you tell me about your arrival in that dear bed where you now take naps, my precious *muchachito*. Now, in that bed, you are newly born for me.

Love, I've pretty much decided to go to the capital in January. If by chance I go now, it will be for a week, to see what the situation is with my attendance etc. But, as you know, no one studies at the first of the year. Anyway, I'm planning to read Josserand now. I'll start tonight, God willing. I'll also spend time with Mamá and help her with matters related to her house. Most importantly, I feel close to you, and I'm taking care of things for us, which as you know fills me with happiness. It's the only way to make the time pass more quickly, so I'll study the other six months and will be in 5th year.

And now, to say goodbye I'm going to send you this little moment: we are on the sofa. (By the way, the sofa is jealous because it's thinking that apparently, they prefer another and that they've abandoned it. It's been so very long since they spent as much time with it as it wants; for months now it hasn't seen more than the occasional, brief rush, and it doesn't like that.) So then, we're on the sofa, but I'm not trying to push you off of it. I prefer that you draw me in as if you needed me closer, and essentially, you "pull" me in and with all the happiness in the world, I give you (too bad

---

96 Apparent reference to the mother of Margot Mora, the cook in Mamá Chea's house.

we only have mail) the sweetest and most tender kiss you've ever shown your *pelúa,*

Mine

Postmarked September 23 in Salcedo. Received on September 25.

My dear Manolete,

You can't imagine how I've spent the past 26 hours since we parted. I have been sad, so sad. I've felt depressed, empty, alone, uninterested in reading, studying, doing anything. I haven't stopped thanking you from the bottom of my heart, or with all my soul, that you stayed with us for a few days. If you hadn't, I don't know what would have come of me. But do I have to tell you yet again that you are too good to me? Love, there is only one thing that I don't want you to do in order to please me. As you can imagine, that has to do with the notary commission. I mean to say that before, I was asking you to do it to make me happy, but I no longer want you to do it for that reason. If your only interest in it is my interest, or you are only interested in it because of me, don't do it, my love. I swear I will come to understand or I will try to. I don't know if I have expressed myself clearly. What I mean to say is that if you don't think it worthwhile, if you think it is more beneficial for you to invest your money in something else, although my opinion weigh in the balance, with all my heart, I am asking you to not do it. Maybe this is because I realize how much I have insisted and have really nagged you about it "without reason," and I am convinced that two people who love one another are better off when each one maintains a certain amount of independence. My love, forgive me for my rather forceful way of expressing this the other day when we were in the car on the way to Santiago. It was difficult for me to approach that subject when I still wasn't in enough control of my emotions to speak calmly, and please forgive me, my love, for having been so unpleasant and nitpicky these past few days.

Today while looking for some old papers, I found the photo that I am sending you so that you can enjoy a moment of distraction during these three short weeks, ok? I also found all my letters to Mamá and Papá from when Mary couldn't take the exams due to her age, in short, everything we talked about previously. How I thought of you!

Last night I dreamed of you, my love. There was a number 25 in the dream, but I don't recall in which part. The thing is that you were a close friend, like a brother, and I was engaged to someone who did not appear in the dream. But you were calling to me and sitting me on your lap, which made me very happy, but it mortified me as well because of what people would say or, just the same, because of what Pedrito, who was witnessing the scene, would think of me and my infidelities.

Oh, Love, I'm so afraid that what we have will end. I don't know why, but I have something like a premonition; it's as if there were a question mark in the future, and you are not always at the end, like you were before, with the certainty of before. All of this makes me very fearful, fearful that you won't always be sincere, but please, my love, don't go fretting about everything I'm saying to you in this letter. It's that, as I was telling you, I still haven't managed to keep my state of mind in check. Maybe we can go to Santiago on Tuesday to see you. Hopefully it works out. Be sure to let me know if you're coming.

Give everyone at home my regards; tell Mamá Fefita that I'll write to her later. My warm regards to don Manuel, Ángela, Emma, Edda, Jaime, and don't forget to pass along a kiss to La Curra and to her little sister. Say hi to Lala, Eugenia, Gerardo and everyone else for me. Write to me soon, *mi vida.* When you come, I think we'll go to Jarabacoa or perhaps to the capital to bring Mary to school. Bamby says that you should love her a lot because she is the one who is whitening me (she's putting glycerine with lemon on me for my sunburns) and Raúl says that love is colorblind and points to Felipa, whom Macario[97] loves in spite of her not being pretty. What do you think about that?

I love you very, very much,

Your Mine

Postmarked September 23 in Montecristi. Received on September 25 in Salcedo.

Monte Cristy

Sept. 23, 1955

Miss
Minerva Mirabal
Salcedo.

---

97 A reference to the popular comedic series of Macario and Felipa, which was transmitted by Dominican Radio and Television.

My beloved, cherished Fiancée,

You know that old song, "With You at a Distance?" Well, my love, I've been singing it since we parted. How well it says what I want to tell you! "Not for a moment can I distance you from me, it all seems like a lie, because you're not here with me!"

Oh my sweet baby, how I thirst for you! ... I've become once again that sad and withdrawn guy that almost nobody knows ... You are my source of inspiration and life! Love me always, my friend and companion! Thank you, *bien de mi alma,* for having given me with your love all the deep and human meaning of this word! I adore you and cannot live without you. This situation cannot go on much longer ...

Yesterday I wrote to Isabelita and recommended that she let me know right away. Among other things, I told her that if she wants to talk about this with me personally, I would go as soon as they let me know. Hopefully we can resolve all of the apparent difficulties, and you girls can go there. You can't imagine how it saddens me to think that people in school might feel like they did before.

As soon as she replies, I'll let you know at once. Hopefully I'll have her letter in hand before Mary has to go to the capital. If it is possible for you two to move there, we'll have time to take care of all this well before her exam date.

How did it go having the veil made? I didn't think you'd have time. What time did you arrive? I was here around 2:30 p.m. Aunt Tulia sends her most sincere thanks. She had searched for the shrubs all around here. They (the shrubs) arrived in good condition; they seemed barely unaffected by the trip. Mamá sends you countless "things," lots of love. She received the "wax plant."[98] The twins, Papá, and everyone here send their warmest regards. Give my warmest regards to Mamá Chea, Mery and the girls. Since arriving I've found some things to do. At the end of the month I will send you some twigs for our nest. Oh darling, how I loved that bed and that lovely furniture! I'm anxious to pick them up! I want to start buying some things that we are going to need. We'll talk about this tomorrow. The mail is going out.

I adore you. Forever yours,
Manolo

---

98 Common name of the *Hoya carnosa* plant, enjoyed for its small, fragrant, white flowers. (t.n.)

Written September 24, postmarked the 25th and received on September 26.

My beloved Fiancé:

I was planning on getting up really early to write you, but last night I had a terrible time sleeping, and it was almost morning when I was finally able to fall asleep, so I'm afraid it's already a little too late and that the post office is closed. Today is a holiday. Anyway, I'm hopeful that you will receive this on Monday, and at the same time I will receive one of yours. Today is Mamá's name day (Our Lady of Mercedes Day), so we are waiting for the girls to arrive. It is also Patria and Noris's name day. We always used to spend it together while Papá was alive, and I wanted to tell you to come, but I knew it was impossible since you'll be there until Wednesday. I dream about you every night, my love. I'm longing to see you again! If I can, I'll go to Santiago on Tuesday. We'll talk. It looks like we will be going to Higüey next Saturday. It is the trip I have told you about. There is a seat in the car for you. Will you be able to come? Last night as I lay awake, I recalled over and over again the last night we spent together. Remember? You told me how difficult it would be to part. Oh, Love! It's agony not receiving even a few lines from you. Didn't I tell you that you owed me three letters from the last time? Write me, my love, if you miss me as much as I miss you. Remember that a woman has her high tides and low tides, and this is my low tide. How can I avoid this wave of pessimism that washes over me?

    You always understand me. You always know how to say just the right thing to me. You are there when I need you most. That is my hope.

Kisses from your
Minerva

P.S. Chiqui, if we go to Santiago, remember about the Dr.'s visits.

Dear Emma:

Just a quick note to say hi and to tell you that Mary asks if you can send her the little figurine. Send it with Manolo on Tuesday because we might go to Santiago. She says that she has to make clothes for college. Forgive her. If not, ask Manolo to send it. How are you two dear *chiquis*? Have you already forgotten Ojo de Agua? All of us here think of you often.

Love to everyone,
Minerva

Postmarked September 25 in Salcedo. Received on September 26.

My beloved Fiancé,

I'm up this morning, Sunday, to see if there is a letter from you at the post office, and I'm taking the opportunity to write you. Yesterday Mamá received the telegram you sent her on everyone's behalf. You can't imagine how thrilled I was when she called for me to come see it. I would have kissed you had you been here! Around here each day that passes is the same, somewhere between missing you immensely and my wave of pessimism, which thank Goodness is finally passing. Last night I thought of saying several sweet things to you in this letter, but today I can't remember them. Dedé slept over last night, and time flew by as we stayed up talking. We went to bed after 12, which means that I've woken up a little sleepy, and on top of that, I had a very unpleasant dream about a snake. When I woke up and told everyone about it, they brought up the widely held superstition that this is a sign of betrayal. But I laughed, remembering that my dream was undoubtedly provoked by the novel *Salambó*[99] that Joaquín (?) lent me and that I read yesterday. The novel describes part of the Punic Wars, full of cruelties and human sacrifices. Salambó, daughter of Hamilcar, is a Carthaginian priestess who keeps a serpent and dances with it in honor of Tanit (the moon). All very unpleasant and depressing. You can imagine that it haunted me even in my dreams.

   I don't know if we'll definitely go to Santiago on Tuesday. Neither Dedé nor Patria knows if they can go, and Mamá might not want "her girls" to go by themselves. Almost every day I go to the farm to plant. Every day I think about you more than I should, and every day I adore you more.

Yours,
Mine

---

[99] Historical novel by Gustave Flaubert, 1862.

Postmarked September 29 in Salcedo. Received on September 30.

My Beloved,

It is impossible to tell you in a quick little note the countless things that fill my soul for you. I also need to respond to your letter and, most importantly, give you an update on the trip: it seems like it will definitely happen. We waited for Hortensia until last night since I didn't dare tell her to cancel the trip, but today I will have a telegram sent to her, along with this letter and another telegram for you. I will tell her to wait for us there. She will come back in Mary's seat. She will request her exam for either Monday or Tuesday, so she'll be finished with that and will come back here until the 17th.

Love, since Mamá and the girls want to buy some things in the capital, I thought it might be easier for you to meet up with us there at some point during the day, and then we will continue on the trip together.

I hate to think that you're not coming. We are going to visit all the towns in the East, God willing, and besides, it was Papá's promise to take the whole family. And you are part of the family! If you end up not going, be sure to let me know, but if there is not enough time for a telegram (two days), telephone asking them to let Dedé know.

I can't begin to tell you how remorseful I felt reading your letter. I have such nerve! I'll never tire of telling you how good you are, and knowing that you are right makes my remorse taste sweeter. And it convinces me! Love, it's getting late, I have to mail this. I didn't write to you yesterday, so you can imagine my uncertainty regarding Hortensia's trip. Thank Goodness she solved that problem by dragging her feet. Don Isidro is already back to work.

Love, I adore you. Goodbye. Do go. You'll find us with Hortensia or shopping along El Conde St., Palo Hincado, Siglo XX or any of those places. Call Hortensia's place, and they will tell you. I will be waiting for you anxiously. We're going in Chiche's "Cadillac." I hope you understand this letter.

Kisses from your
Mine

P.S. Yesterday afternoon was when I received your second letter. Give my regards to everyone.

OCTOBER 1955

> I shall scratch the earth to make you a cave
> and there your Captain
> will wait for you with flowers in bed.
> Think no more, my sweet,
> about the anguish
> that passed between us
> like the strike of a match
> leaving us perhaps with its burn.[100]

The October letters are an invaluable legacy for understanding Manolo and Minerva, as they reveal their intrepidness and the intensity of their reflections and convictions.

It becomes clear that Papi's mind was fixed on one thing: marrying, as if his love were growing impatient with the distance, as if he knew without knowing that time was a fairy tale and was nothing because there wasn't enough of it, nor would there be enough. It's as if for that reason, for precisely that reason, he felt an extraordinary urgency to unite his body and existence with her, with Minerva, the one, the woman he loved. Something tells me that he also felt the urgency to protect Minerva in light of the increasingly intense threats that both were receiving, evidence of the horrendous stalking to which they were subjected.

As for Mami, in love and open to being persuaded, she mounted a brief but staunch and carefully weighed resistance to a rushed wedding. She lucidly confronted her impatient fiancé's intrepid temperament only to be convinced in the end by "three little words" from Papi, by love and by destiny. It's a good thing! If he had not convinced her, perhaps I would not have been born.

Her reaction was to reanalyze the obstacles: economic factors, her studies, the fact that they would not be able to live in their own house, her inability to be a traditional wife, her hang-ups, the possibility of becoming pregnant before finishing her studies, among other things. Overcoming the migraines that he suffered throughout his life, Papi fixed up "the loft" in his parents' house, which would be their first "nest," and he talked of headboards, nightstands, lamps, and other furnishings.

Amid all this discourse, Papi, feeling anxious and accompanied by two friends, drove to Ojo de Agua one night, apparently to calm Minerva down

---

100 Neruda, "Letter on the Road," trans. Donald Devenish Walsh, p. 143. (t.n.)

after she discovered her fiancé's real age while taking care of paperwork for the wedding. He succeeded. All of this happened in a matter of one month. That is the kind of whirlwind in which they lived.

Meanwhile, daily life marched on, and they continued sharing it through their letters. The family made the trip to Higüey in fulfillment of Papá Enrique's promise. I have not been able to confirm whether or not Papi, who by then was part of the family, was indeed with them. Memory is imprecise, and some of those who went say yes, and others no. My brother Jaime Enrique recalls that they stayed at a hotel in the capital whose breakfasts he will never forget, and that they slept there more than one night. Trujillo City was so small back then that Mami writes to Papi, "you'll find us with Hortensia or shopping along El Conde St., Palo Hincado, Siglo XX or any of those places." That's how tiny my parents' world was, making it easy for the forces of evil to reach out their claws until they destroyed everything. Papi and his truck continued being invited to the regime's proselytizing activities. An invitation in the time of Trujillo was an order, and failure to comply could mean paying with one's life. People paid that price all too frequently. In the year 1955, with the preparations for the Fair of Peace and Fraternity of the Free World, the despot's megalomania had degenerated into delirium.[101]

October is also when my mother became involved in the design of Mamá Chea's new house in Conuco, located along the Cibao's main highway, between Tenares and Salcedo. The house later became the Mirabal Sisters House Museum. With Mami about to marry and move to Montecristi, and María Teresa studying in the capital, the most prudent thing for my grandmother to do was to move "out into the open," to a less isolated place, closer to her siblings, Carmela, Toña and Lalía, and to Uncle Tilo, her beloved brother-in-law and close friend.

---

101 The year-long Feria de la Paz y Confraternidad del Mundo Libre was a kind of world's fair held in Santo Domingo (then Ciudad Trujillo) starting December 20, 1955, in celebration of the twenty-fifth anniversary of Trujillo's rise to power. It was a time when criticism of the regime was mounting at home and abroad. The fair, which was accompanied by a book fair and similar events, was a spectacle organized by the regime to showcase the country's agricultural, industrial, and commercial achievements and the cultural "progress" it had achieved under the regime's stewardship. Present-day discussions of the fair frequently note its exorbitant cost at the public's expense and the self-aggrandizing nature of the event. As a case in point, Trujillo's daughter, Angelita, was crowned "Queen" of the fair and wore a gown that cost some $80,000 in present-day standards. The modern structures erected for the fair transformed the area of the capital now known as Centro de los Héroes, in honor of the 10 conspirators who assassinated the dictator in 1931 (a turn of poetic justice). For an in-depth analysis of the fair as spectacle and propaganda, see Derby, pp. 109–111; 122–134. (t.n.)

Mami makes multiple references to her work on the small "farm," a plot of farmland that Mamá Chea placed in her care and that my brother Manolo and I inherited.

My Aunt Teté would return to the University of Santo Domingo alone and would move into the convent where Minerva had previously lived. During one of Hortensia's visits to Ojo de Agua, Mami suggested to her that it had become difficult for them to live together, perhaps due to differences in character or maybe interests. Following that conversation, she shared with Papi her decision to not continue living in the home of the Marcial Silva family. My grandmother never tired of repeating that she felt eternally indebted to this family for having welcomed my mother and aunt, knowing the risks incurred by sheltering known enemies of the regime during that fateful time in our nation's history.

As October draws to a close, so ends the correspondence that I have recovered from the days of my parents' courtship. Manolo triumphs in his efforts to move up the wedding date, and the proposal contained in the verse of the poem "Invitation to Home" that he sends to Mami, by the Argentine poet Baldomero Fernández Moreno, would be consummated in the "loft" at my grandparents' house in Montecristi: "Climb the stairs to my home and stay with me forever!" Mami has given in, and after several conversations she finally writes: "If you still want to marry me, do me the favor of quickly resolving the matter of the bed and whatever else you have to resolve. If so, it will be sooner than you imagine."

It would, indeed, be sooner than Papi imagined. The letter that closes this chapter of their correspondence and of their lives was sent exactly one month prior to the wedding.

Postmarked October 6 in Montecristi. Received in Salcedo on October 8.

Monte Cristy

October 6, 1955

Miss
Minerva Mirabal
Salcedo.

My beloved Fiancée:

The return trip went quickly, even though we were in Mao longer than we had wanted. Upon arriving I developed a headache and upset stomach that kept me in the house, unable to go to the office on Tuesday afternoon and all day yesterday. That is why I didn't write to you yesterday, as I had the burning desire to do. I was more worried than ever about your trip. I was thinking about you driving back alone and about all the problems that could have occurred. In short, I worried for Mamá Chea. I felt very pessimistic, but none of that compares to the immense joy that you brought us. Your attitude about not wanting to part from me was so beautiful; it assured me that you would follow me "until the end of time" if necessary. Tell me, my angel, how did the return trip go? Did Mamá Chea worry? Because surely you arrived late. Tell me if you told her everything. I'm afraid of losing her trust. But fortunately, soon we'll put an end to these constraints and this annoying adolescent arrangement. Darling, how happy I feel! Soon I'll have you with me forever! I'm insanely happy!

"Climb the stairs to my home and stay with me forever!"[102] What beauty and what indescribable emotion I hear in these verses. Since yesterday they seem even more beautiful.

My love, I am determined to set up our little nest. Today I bought wood, and tonight I am going to ask Santiago for everything I need to at least fix it up. I want to paint it too. You can't imagine how excited I am. Today I spoke with the carpenter who fixed my desk. He is willing to make everything for us, including the headboard, in the design of your choice. So, if it's all right with you, you can pick it out and send it to me. This guy does really good work.[103] I'm sure he will do a professional job. Tell me if you want it in mahogany or pine. I think that the latter color is more modern, youthful and attractive. What do you think? If you don't like that idea, my love, we'll make it however you choose and out of whatever you want. I just want you to like them.

I've been thinking about the hearing today in Macorís and if you ended up going. Tell me about it, and if they proceed with the case, tell me all the details. Tell me what you think of S. Morcelo as an attorney, what you thought of his performance, and the main legal points of his

---

102 From the poem "Invitation to Home" ("Invitación al hogar") by Argentine poet Baldomero Fernández Moreno, 1886–1950.

103 His name was Ricardo Vargas. Papi gave him the nickname "Malmente" ("Badly") because he said this word often. He worked with them on the loft and on the house to which they later moved.

defense strategy. I know the case, more or less. I really regretted not being able to stay.

Just as I had predicted, they did not end up releasing on Saturday that client that I told you about, in spite of the fact that everything was ready for his release on bond. They could not give the release order that day because the district attorney was not present. He was here this afternoon. In the next few days, I'm going to look for the cow that I told you about in order to sell it. I took advantage of an opportunity that is undoubtedly magnificent.

You can't imagine, *bien mío,* how heart-warming it was for me to flip through your album. It's as if I too had lived those undeniably happy days of your life with you. I see in each photo your cheerfulness, your carefree spirit, that smile that makes you so innocent, so enchantingly happy and ... so beautiful. I'm certain, my love, that from the first moment—from the first moment and from that time forward—I would have fallen crazy in love. I firmly believe, my beloved, that we were born for one another, and it escapes me why we didn't come together sooner. Now I sadly realize, *bien mío,* all the time that I missed out on living. I'd have loved you yesterday, today and always! Oh! How happy your love makes me!

Everyone here says an affectionate hello, and they hope you'll come soon, very soon. My warm regards for Mamá Chea, Mery and Hortensia. To Patria. For you, my angel, all my soul.

Yours,
Manolo

Postmarked October 10 in Salcedo; Received on October 11.

My dear Love,

I received your letter tonight; so beautiful, so sweet that it filled my soul with tenderness! This morning I got up early to write to you, but Mamá had me answer a letter for her, and I missed "the mail," the opportunity, and then I had to go to Patria's. I slept the afternoon away. (Your pen is what's making these smudges. It seems to have brought a little hair from the capital.)

Oh, Love, I can't begin to tell you how worried, taken aback, I am by what you have said to me. Chiqui, you know how much I want to be with you. Each breath I take, each beat of my heart is for you; I breathe because of you. But, *vida,* they're telling me here that they don't think I can marry you and go to the capital in a month. Think, Love, how difficult that will be for me. And, *vida,* I was hoping we would fix up our little home modestly. I've always told you that I don't want luxury, but it's so delightful to dream about a little love nest for us, and if you spend money setting this up, realize that it will be unspeakable for us to even think about setting up a house. You know that I adore your family and that it will be nice living with them, but don't you think it would be easier for us to wait 9 months, of which time we'd have to be separated more than half? Now, my *muchachito,* all I want is to make you happy, but think about all this, Love: look into the future and ask yourself if it won't be more complicated this way than if we were to continue being "adolescents" for nine more months. Do you think I will have the strength to leave my beloved husband so soon? I don't know. Besides, you know all that I have to do this year given that I've lost so much time already.

I have good news to share with you: Mary spoke with Isabelita and told her that you didn't think it a good idea that we go to her cousin's, but she didn't have to explain it to her; she understood. So, then she told her how she regretted that we weren't going, etc., etc., and she told her that she was thinking of fixing up the garage and even installing a bathroom to see if César wanted to go. And when Mary told her that she was going to school and that I was staying until January, she was delighted because that way "there was time to resolve things." In other words, she didn't make any assurances, but she showed interest, and maybe it will be possible for us to go there.

Tonight I'll look for the bed design. I'll be sure to send it tomorrow, I'm not sure if it will be made of pine or mahogany since Mamá gave us the mahogany armoire, but that doesn't matter if you prefer pine because later we could put it in another room, if it's only temporary. But tonight I will look for the design.

They rescheduled the hearing for November 16. They have scheduled three days to wrap it up since a key witness failed to appear. We were there for two days and thoroughly enjoyed it. How I missed you, and how I would have loved to share all the proceedings with you, but I have to be patient to tell you the details. I'll write again tomorrow. As I said, I'll send you the design for the bed, if I find it. This week I'll go to Santiago. Let me know if there are no alternatives for buying the things I need. Oh,

Chiqui, don't scare me! After all, I was saying that a month prior, I would have nothing left to do. The return trip went really well. Of course, I told Mamá, and she said nothing.

With all my soul, a kiss from your
Mine

Postmarked October 10; Received on October 11.[104]

My beloved Fiancé,

Last night I barely slept. I lay awake thinking of you, my love. And just as I said, I've gotten up early to write you. Do you want me to tell you in detail about the trial? It was very lively and interesting, especially the first day. But it's better that I tell you about it in person. The most interesting figure, the one I like most, is the presiding judge. I knew him from before, but I really like how he handles things. Of course, I haven't had much opportunity to observe him, but I can't say that I'm surprised given what people have told me about him. Moreover, I'm demanding, and I find that he gives of himself what one would expect, what one believes she would do in a similar case (the listener). In other words, one accepts as quite natural that which is fine and criticizes or loses patience with attorneys who aren't to our liking. But of course, this is nothing out of the ordinary. What is surprising is "the miracle," and that still hasn't happened. What an opinionated fiancée you have!

I will tell you about one incident. On the first day the judge called S.M.'s attention, beseeching him to not prolong the trial by elaborating on each question with considerations that pertained to the defense strictly speaking, that if he did, the two days allotted for the trial would be insufficient. The judge is a very polite, educated and impartial person, logically. Sánchez M. carried on unintimidated and ignored him, which the judge seemingly did not take into account. And so, the attorneys carried on indulging themselves. The next day there was a crucial discussion, but when Amaro elaborated, Dr. Toca gave the same warning as the judge, along with his usual moderation, albeit ironically. He said that he was glad that the defense was keeping in mind what they'd been warned about the day before, when it fell on deaf ears. However, he decided to

---

104 The letter includes magazine clippings with written commentaries, showing the bedroom sets and other furniture that she would like.

give each attorney the opportunity to elaborate all they wanted and to make all the observations they deemed pertinent to each question. Dr. Toca "defended" himself saying that the comments they had made were crucial but that Amaro had elaborated and had "stung" him, which was why he was making that observation. The judge responded, "Today, yes, but yesterday?" So then S.M. stood there very pompously, like someone who was above all this and said: "I have several observations regarding these statements, but considering that there was an opportunity to state them during the defense, and not wanting to prolong the trial (looking down his nose at those who do) I will refrain."

I'll tell you in person the bit about "Varita," "Negrito López," and Zacarías,[105] the most peculiar of the witnesses that testified.

Love, I am sending you those bed designs. If you think you can make it the same color as your desk, pick the one you like. And I want to tell you, Love, that you have to help me (too much). When I am with you, I am not strong, and I cannot think about anything else. I don't want to contradict you; your desires are my desires, which is also the case when you are not with me, but my sense of practicality sometimes disquiets me, and you have to help me. Think about it, Chiqui, I won't be able to study if I get married, or, supposing I can, this year will pass, but I have two left, and if during all that time there's a baby, I'll have to take care of it, and then I won't finish, and one thing that I want is to share in your work, qualified to help you. And you know, *mi vida*, I wouldn't want to put off having children. I imagine that nature would seek revenge against me when I wanted them. I'm superstitious. But there's more, and how it pains me to disagree with you! But if you want, *mi vida*, you can fix up the loft in your house, buy the bedroom furniture, and when I come in July, I promise that I will take my exams first thing, and we will get married immediately after, without any ceremony. You will have paid off the furniture and will have your diploma and notary commission, and I'll bring my desk to the office, and we will continue living at your house until I graduate. Or, if you prefer, Chiqui, I'll attend university now for one month, I'll take care of my attendance for this semester, and I'll attend the next one, and when I come during Holy Week, "I will stay with you forever." That way I will only have to go back to take my exams. But if you wait until July, we will keep seeing one another as often as before. I will

---

105 It was not possible to identify the trial in question.

go with Mamá one day and as many times as we are able to get together. I will do whatever possible. You'll go in January, for example, and we'll spend a week going to the fair, and at Christmas, I'll go and you'll come, and we'll be together a lot.

Mi vida, if you want, come next weekend and we'll go to Jarabacoa. Then the next time, I'll go with Patria and Pedrito to spend a day there, and we won't go a long time without seeing one another. Then you'll come for the trial, and we'll go those three days, and we'll have such a great time. I know because of how much I enjoyed myself this time. What will it be like with you?

Well, my love, I'll end here. Until tomorrow. Write to me soon. I'm sorry that you're suffering from that headache. Mamá didn't see anything wrong with my going there to take you; she said that she'd let me return, if that's why you want to move up the wedding. Manolo, I want to be with you more than anything, but I know that you want me to finish my studies. Don't you think it's worth making the sacrifice for a few more days? You'll see how they fly by and, besides, I've decided that it will be at your house. That way it's not so much on you to come here.

I adore you,
Mine

Postmarked October 17 in Salcedo. Received on October 18.

My Beloved,

I've had all night to savor your precious letter, and I still have goosebumps as I write my reply. Even the telegram has given me goosebumps. I love that you ask me to come, but unfortunately, I haven't been able to go, as I desperately want to. But yesterday one of Jaime's sisters got married, and Dedé, with her usual carelessness and with all she had to do, forgot to send it. It ended up back in my hands too late. It was pouring rain, and I couldn't get in touch with Patria, but I don't think there was any chance she could have sent it. Remember how my eye was red? Well, I didn't take good care of it, overheating and bent over planting at the farm. It got really bad. I even had to lie down. It wasn't until yesterday that it started feeling better. Imagine, it is still a little closed and watery. Poor little eye! And you don't write to me! After I sent you those two letters, I waited Monday, Tuesday, until Thursday, and since you said to me in that letter that maybe you would come this weekend, I didn't write to you at that point since there wasn't time. I received the latest letter yesterday (Saturday). You'll say that we are 3 for 3, but I always write you first, and the anxiety of awaiting your letters is what keeps me from having time to respond to you, for one reason or another, as you say. Uncle Mundo is here and sends his best regards and asks that you tell the twins to come soon, that he'll find some spirited steeds for them.

Hortensia is still here. She is leaving tomorrow. Just imagine, with my eye the way it is, I haven't been able to go out, which makes me feel bad because I would have liked to be more attentive to her. I can't resist sharing a little story with you. You know how Mary is, she was telling me, "Mine, she's going to lynch us. You know what that means?" So, apparently Hortensia has everything, everyone is her friend (her mother's) and her relatives are illustrious. She has seen everything and knows better than anyone. She has read everything. And here comes Mary with a photo of the Santiago Monument and she says to her, "Look!" And she replies, "Oh, yes! I've been there. I've climbed up to the top." Mary says, "And did you see how lovely the city of Santiago looks through the eyes of the Angel of Peace?" She says, "Oh, yes! Marvelous! Just imagine!" Mary died laughing and replied, "Liar! You can't look through the eyes of the Angel of Peace." Manolo, I couldn't contain my laughter, I'm still laughing, but she said that she had replied without thinking, and she tried to control the damage the best she could.

I'm so glad that you liked the photo of the bedroom set that I sent you, and it makes me sing with joy (if I knew how)[106] that you are arranging to have it made. I would like you to purchase the bed frame that costs about $70 because that way, all we'll need is the mattress, which you can leave until the last minute. In the meantime, you could go ahead and have the dresser made, if you want. After that, I want you to purchase the small dining room set, but don't put more than one thing on credit at a time, so that you can pay it off in less time. My love, I have good news: last Sunday I won $150 on number 1214, which was something like fourth prize. I had dreamed of Papá again. Remember? And I got half a ticket. I was thrilled. I took a bit of the cash and saved the rest to see what we're going to do. That was one reason why I was going to write to you every day and—you

---

106 The family always teased her about singing out of tune.

see?—today I was going to forget to tell you. If the ticket vendor hadn't come, I'd have forgotten.

Another thing that I wanted to mention is the most up-to-date and complete work that Sánchez Morcelo uses, like *Criminology, Penal Law,* etc. I'm not sure of the title, but it is by Pierre Lusac[107] (I think that's how it's spelled). In Moca there's a bookstore that orders it. It's in France, in a bookstore whose name I don't recall. We will find out the day of the trial. It contains the pre-delinquent and post-delinquent states and the differences between "evidence and presumptions." As you can imagine, Sánchez Morcelo felt very full of himself when Dr. Toca called him "Pierre Lusarito" in front of us. He was the one who recommended the work to us. We'll go to Moca to order it if necessary, right?

Let me know if you're coming next weekend. We have a lot to discuss, and if I go there, we won't be able to talk at all, because it will be a very short visit. Besides, I'll go there in the interim so that you can come for the trial. I almost forgot to tell you that I told Hortensia that I wouldn't return. She was mortified. I told her that if I go for a few days to take care of my attendance, I'll go to her house because I still don't know where else I would go. But she told me absolutely not, that it was my house, and that if we made an effort, we could get along, that her dad was giving her an earful: "Now they'll think that I've done something to you." But I explained that it was impossible. "Imagine, after all the time that we've been friends, each day I have to tiptoe around you more and more because I know you better. Before, my interactions with you were natural and relaxed because I didn't know you, but that has faded away the better I've gotten to know you. I know that I share much of the blame, that I'm not very tolerant, but I'm convinced that I'm no good at diplomacy. I wasn't made for delicacies, superficiality, and formalities." She began to cry and told me that those were "hang-ups" that one develops and asked me to excuse her, that everything that happened at the end of the semester was the result of nervous tension. I told her that I hadn't factored that into my decision and pointed out that I had tried in vain to revive the camaraderie. So, in order to save our friendship, it was best to spend the year apart. You can imagine the rest.

---

107 Pierre Bouzat. The book is *Traité Théorique et Pratique de Droit Pénal* (Paris: Librairie Dalloz, 1951).

Hortensia has just arrived. These are her exact words: "That we've missed you a lot, that it's a shame that you haven't come, and that I'm sure that he (how smug!) is going to come when I leave."

Mary leaves tomorrow. She sends warm regards and asks if you gave the dear twins the medal. I've talked so much! However, the only thing on my mind is the memory of your love.

I adore you.
Minerva

Postmarked October 19 in Salcedo; Received on October 20.

My beloved Fiancé,

You see? I can't find a way to begin this letter, *mi vida*. How inadequate words are, and how poorly I would express myself with them! There are no words to express all the turmoil in my soul, which is filled with you. Last night I made the trip with you. Oh, my love! Forgive me. I am paying for how I made you suffer. I was still awake when the car came to pick up the girls. Now I understand how Mamá worries when we travel. I was even afraid that your windshield wipers wouldn't work well. What nasty weather! Thinking about what your trip means fills me with remorse and tenderness. Oh, Chiqui, I was careless, but ... I don't know ... one can sometimes lack common sense. Looking back on my state of mind this time yesterday as I wrote to you, I just remember feeling so certain that you knew that I wasn't going, that I didn't even mention it in my letter. And I berate myself repeatedly for not having realized that you were awaiting a reply, and waiting is painful. And you say that I don't feel the same way you do! When do I ever not want to be by your side? What I wouldn't have done to make the trip had I received the telegram in time!

My love, there is something else that I want to discuss with you, but please don't respond with that look of disappointment that you had on your face last night when we talked about this. You know that my life is yours; it is yours to do with as you please, but I have to reason with you about certain things because it is my duty for your sake and for mine. Hasn't sincerity been the cornerstone of our love? I don't think about my reactions when I'm speaking with you. I could care less about giving up certain things. I think about the two of us, about the normal reactions of any human being softened by affection. Two months ago, you said to me, "I'm not getting married until I'm fine in regard to . . ." I don't know, those were more or less your words, and I felt hurt (so much so that I reminded you from time to time). I seem to recall telling you that I didn't need to be very well-off, and then you said to me, "It's not for me, but for you. I have always told you that I'll marry you one way or another." *Vida,* I don't remember the exact conversation, but I'm asking you today: Do you love me more than you did back then, when you said those words, which I interpreted as a lack of interest? Or have your thoughts changed? Listen carefully, my one and only love: if you ask me to marry you tomorrow, I won't be able to tell you no, because I adore you, because my desire to be by your side is so deep that it hurts being the one to place an obstacle in our way. I only want to reach a mutual agreement. That is why I want to reason with you, not because I am any less idealistic than you, but rather because they made me manage a household and business for years (that is why I'm terrified of debt), and that is why when I'm with you I think only about that beautiful moment and the infinite Heaven of our love. But when I'm alone, I think about the broom, the ironing board, the basket of dirty laundry, and all those mundane things that one must keep in mind at a wedding. (Laugh, my love.)

Another thing: everyone here tells me that I couldn't live with anyone, and you should know their opinion of me. They say that I am too fussy to live in a house that is not my own, that I would be miserable. My love, you know how much it hurts me to be practical, how it saddens me to say these things to you, to bring you down to Earth. But you told me last night, "Even if I wanted to, I wouldn't be able to get a decent house in Monte Cristy right now," and I responded: but the thing is, if we marry now, it is impossible for us to even think about setting up a house. We'd be crazy. That is why I wanted to wait until July. But I want us to be together as much as you do. My dear *muchachito,* I beg you to oblige me. As much as I love your family, I ask that we set up our house before I finish my studies. Otherwise, I might feel inhibited. It doesn't matter if it's not the yellow house across from the courthouse. So what if it's a modest little house? I'll make it beautiful for you with my own two hands. It will be our home, and together we will watch the gardenias and jasmine grow, the ones that I have planted to adorn it, and I will place their flowers on your desk every day. My love, you'll see that we won't need riches to make us happy. I prefer spiritual tranquility and love a thousand times over. Mamá and Papá were happier when they were poor and struggling than once he had achieved all the economic comfort he could have desired. I don't believe in Acosta's theories, and it scares me a little when you say that you are very ambitious. Of course, I want to travel. I would like for us to travel before setting up the house that you want, if possible. Now while we are still young and full of energy, it would be ideal for us to build a house at the price you want for when we have our children and are longing to rest, once we've seen the world a bit. But another thing, Love, if we have a child, I won't continue my studies; there isn't anything nor anyone who could make me abandon him. If this doesn't matter to you, then *in that case,* I could care less about abandoning them (my studies). I swear! But I don't want to impose my ideas upon you. Now I'm just rambling. I can't express my thoughts clearly today, as I've said.

Love, write me a long letter, and soon. Tell me that you're coming. Don't forget that I'm sad about having worried you and that I think about you every minute of the day.

Yours,
Mine

Postmarked October 18 in Montecristi. Received in Salcedo on October 20.[108]

Monte Cristi

October 18, 1955

Miss
Minerva Mirabal
Salcedo

Bien mío,

I was waiting for your letter to arrive before writing you, and I'm thinking about how nice it would be if all of them were as long, even though everything you wrote to me we had already discussed during my spontaneous nighttime trip. We arrived back all right and in time to sleep a few hours. As you can imagine, the return trip ended up being a little less lively than the trip there; at that hour, my dear friends were beat. Acosta slept on the trip as if he were in his own bed, but as for me, none of this affected my

---

[108] On the envelope from his father's stationery, Manolo altered his father's middle initial "F" to make it look like an "A."

mood. I had a lot to think about, about us, about what we discussed . . . Anyhow, I wasn't as tired as one would expect for a trip at that hour, from here, under those circumstances. I needed to go, to see you, and I don't regret it. I feel calm and content. That's how anxious I was, how worried.

I have never been able to keep away from my deep desires, no matter the risk!

There is something in your letter that lifted my spirits; it has made me die laughing. Tell Mery that I said congratulations. I had no idea she was such a pill. That bit about the monument would make anyone laugh.

It's too bad what happened with Hortensia. I have always told you as much, but I admire your frankness when faced with an irreparable situation. Hopefully she's able to understand everything you said to her. It would certainly be in her best interest to follow your advice. She's a good person, and hopefully we'll always have her affection. I sincerely regret not having been able to spend more time with her, there at your house. I am saddened to think that these most recent moments might be the last. All goodbyes are sad, most especially when it comes to cherished friends, and I, just like you, cherish her greatly, even with her flaws. Some, most of them, haven't surprised me; I recognized them some time ago, but as the saying goes, "A friend is someone who knows all about you and still loves you."

I am extremely excited about the book you've told me about. Maybe it's the one that I'm looking for. I desperately need it. I'll buy it as soon as I can. I'm sure that the bookstore in Moca will order it. It's the one owned by a gentleman, an attorney by the name of Antonio Rosario, if I remember correctly. If I go this weekend, we'll go see if he has it, to buy it. Hopefully the price isn't too unreasonable.

I had two trials today, and luckily all went well, or more precisely, it went well for the client. One was regarding a "robbery" and the other "domestic violence and abuse." All cases are interesting, even the very simple ones. A novice like myself always learns something new, naturally.

I can't promise that I will come on Saturday because they are holding a political rally in the town of "La Gorra," in Libertador Province,[109] and our truck—which is in my name—and I are "invited." In any case, I'll let you know. On Thursday the 27th I have a trial in Santiago, at the court-

---

109 After the tyrant's execution, the province reclaimed its original name: Dajabón.

house. That day, as soon as I leave the courthouse I'll go to your place to spend a few days with you, until Monday. I want so much to have a long talk; we have so much to talk about.

About the headboard, if we're definitely going to need it for November, they won't have time to make it here. They have a lot of work. If I can get a hold of the tube or something like it, I'm thinking about having two really pretty little night lamps made for me. The guy who makes them is the son of the owner of that workshop that I've mentioned to you. I'm referring to Maney, the same one who used to go by Chico. They're amazing, but I have to get a hold of the tube or something similar to what the old carbine lamps used to have.

Tell Mery when you write to her that Acosta was really impressed. He thinks she is intelligent and cultured. I have thought a lot about what you told me about her, in spite of having barely heard you. We'll talk about all this, but to me there doesn't seem to be anything at the moment. In the past, a friend I know well, who is a close friend of his, brought up that topic based on something he had insinuated. I think I mentioned something to you about this. I've thought a lot about Mamá Chea and what this means for her, and I can't stop thinking about us, our wedding, etc., etc.

Everyone here says hello and are left feeling disappointed because I mistakenly announced your visit.

My warmest regards to everyone at your place. Ask Mamá Chea to excuse me for the poor timing of my visit. But she too was once like us; she experienced all this and will be able to understand us. Besides, and I mean this seriously, I feel we have that trust.

I'll see you soon, my sweet, beloved torment. I adore you.

Yours,
Manolo

Postmarked October 20 in Salcedo. Received on October 22. This is the last of the letters exchanged during their courtship.

My Beloved,

If only I were with you, if only you could read my thoughts! I live only for you and because of you. I have gone two days without writing to you, and yet I have been doing it the entire time. My heart hasn't stopped telling you a million things. I miss you so deeply that I'm only going to write you a brief note because I have to see you, not write to you. I wish you were here this weekend. I'm planning on going to the capital on Tuesday. If you still want to get married, do me the favor of quickly resolving the matter of the bed and whatever else you have to resolve, for then it will be sooner than you imagine. I still haven't received a letter from you. I would like to be able to talk with you on the phone, but I don't know if that will be possible. I will attend classes next week and will buy my dress in the capital and whatever else I need. Mamá says that if we are getting married, the sooner the better. We have to talk, I cannot go without seeing you.

I adore you and send many, many kisses.
Your Mine

Today I went to Uncle José's and told him that you wanted to get married, and he told me that it was the best thing I could do. So then Mela told me that for her it was a struggle to make the decision and say yes, that I not do the same thing. But I think that I already have.

Oh love, don't go another day without writing to me. Do come!

Telegram from Minerva to Manolo. Salcedo October 22, 1955.

Impossible to go. I hope you come next week.

NOVEMBER 1955

> Now I am going to tell you:
> my land will be yours,
> I am going to conquer it
> not only to give it to you,
> but for everyone,
> for all my people.[110]

There were no letters in November. Life happened so quickly that it impeded any chance of sitting down to write them. Wedding preparations filled each day of the second to the last month of 1955.

My mother went to the capital to attend a week of classes at the university

---

110 Neruda, "Letter on the Road," p. 145, with modification to Devenish Walsh's translation in the fourth verse. (t.n.)

and to prepare for an itinerant life between Montecristi, Trujillo City, and Salcedo. She would return there repeatedly for the rest of her life.

She purchased her bridal gown in Casa Virginia, between obligations at the university. Her classmate, Yolanda Vallejo Pradel, recalls that she accompanied her to purchase part of her trousseau and that Mami, who was still in mourning for Papá Enrique, purchased colored undergarments to lift her spirits. Doña Yolanda writes:

> I didn't go to the wedding because I would have had to travel to Salcedo. I think Hortensia went. We organized a bachelorette party in a restaurant called Mario, which at that time was right in front of Independence Park. I don't remember what we ate and drank. We had little money, which we collected from a select group of her classmates. I remember fondly that once we were already at the restaurant, Minerva wanted to go get her sister María Teresa, and I too wanted to go get my sister Mirtha. We both left and returned with our sisters.

During those days in the capital, and with the intention of inviting them to the wedding, Mami visited her friend Emma Rodríguez and her husband, the poet Rubens Suro, who tried to convince her to send Trujillo a telegram announcing her marriage. I spent many summers with them and their daughters during my childhood and adolescence. I remember that he used to tell me that Mami didn't want to do it, so he helped her write it, but he wasn't sure whether or not she had actually sent it. I found the draft of that telegram, written on the inside of an envelope, and I transcribe it here. As I stated, I don't know for certain whether or not it was sent nor if it arrived at its destination:

> This telegram is to notify Your Excellency of our upcoming marriage, which will be celebrated on the 20th of this month. We also want to take this opportunity to bring to your eminent knowledge that the home that we will establish in Monte Cristy under the protection of your glorious era of peace and progress is one more house that Your Excellency _____ly[111] has at your service. Respectfully. . . .

On November 18, two days prior to the wedding, the press published the zillionth report on the dictator's visit to the United States during that time. One can infer from the reports that the trip was for health reasons, but it was disguised as a trip to see the Menorah Medical Center in Kansas, reception

---

[111] The underscore indicates where the original handwriting was illegible. (t.n.)

included. Even the photo captions emphasize that "in spite of freezing temperatures, Trujillo has walked habitually through the streets of the city." In Ojo de Agua it was raining torrentially two days later, on the morning of Sunday, November 20, when my parents celebrated their marriage surrounded exclusively by close friends and family. In the only surviving photograph of the wedding, Mami's face is a poem of happiness, while Papi gazes at her with a dreamy look.

Those who attended the religious ceremony in Saint John the Evangelist Church in Salcedo and the luncheon in Ojo de Agua remember that moment as very intimate and simple. Tonó, who as usual was there working and organizing everything like a busy bee, remembers that they left around three o'clock in the afternoon and that their car broke down about two kilometers away, in Villa Báez, in front of her father's house. They had to wait a long time for a mechanic before continuing on their way to the Montaña Hotel in Jarabacoa, and after that, to the Princesa Hotel in Constanza, where they had planned to spend their honeymoon. I can imagine how disgruntled my father must have been after those final days of longing, feeling eager and desperate to hold my mother in his arms.

The despot returned from abroad that same afternoon. The news filled the newspapers on November 21. I like to think that on that Monday, the newlyweds, precisely for being just that, had neither the time nor the interest to look through the newspapers.

December 1955

Beloved, I am going off to my battles.[112]

Naturally, there are no letters from this month either. Papi and Mami were in their honeymoon phase, and everything they had to write to one another they did so with a look, with their hands, with their voices, and with silence, together in the loft that Papi had set up for them. A lovely photograph was taken at the foot of the staircase leading up to their first home. They appear seated, very much in love, with Mami clearly expecting. It is one of my favorite photographs of them, and a large reproduction hangs in the entrance to my office at Congress. From there they give me strength to fight the battles that in their memory I continue to wage through democracy and thought,

---

112 Neruda, "Letter on the Road," p. 142, modified from Devenish Walsh's translation. (t.n.)

with a spirit of resistance, and by virtue of hope in a Dominican Republic that is better off than the one they passed on to me.

That "loft" did not have a private bathroom, which meant that they had to cross the balcony to use the one in the main house, an uncomfortable situation for both of them, but especially for Mami, given her pregnancy. After that, they moved to a house very close to my grandparents, a little house in which my mother could finally fulfill her promise: "I'll make it beautiful for you with my own two hands."

The next letters in the collection, which open the second part of this book, are almost entirely from Manolo to Minerva. They begin well into the year 1956, following my birth. Evidently, my mother became pregnant with me as soon as they married, because I was born nine months and eleven days after the wedding.

On December 5, the newspaper *El Caribe* published an article with poems by and information about Minou Drouet, a child prodigy whose poems sparked great controversy in the literary world of the time, specifically with regard to the authenticity of her work. In a way, this preceded the editorial "Boom" that extended beyond the borders of France and involved numerous writers. *El Caribe* echoed the controversy and even dedicated one of its daily caricatures to the child poet. Doing the math, I could have been conceived that same day, and Mami, with astounding intuition could have decided on my name when she read the publication, which she carefully clipped and saved. Yolanda Vallejo remembers that when they returned to the university in January, Mami—instead of saying that she was pregnant—told her that she was "expecting Minou."

December 20 saw the official opening of the Fair of Peace and Fraternity of the Free World, which concluded on February 27 of the following year.

As planned, at the beginning of the month, Mami went back to Trujillo City for another week in order to satisfy the attendance requirements at the university. The three semesters that she had remaining would be stretched out over nearly two years of extraordinary effort and hard work to obtain the degree about which she had dreamed and to practice law alongside Papi. But the tyrant's forces of infamy and harm were weaving other plans.

II
Marriage
1956–1958

Figure 2.1. Manolo and Minerva's wedding on November 20, 1955. Courtesy of the Fundación Hermanas Mirabal.

Figure 2.2. Manolo, Minerva, María Teresa, Leandro, and Patria in Montecristi. Courtesy of the Fundación Hermanas Mirabal.

Figure 2.3. Manolo and Minerva, pregnant with Minou, on the staircase leading up to the loft at the Tavárez family home in Montecristi, 1956. This was Minerva and Manolo's first home as a married couple. Courtesy of the Fundación Hermanas Mirabal.

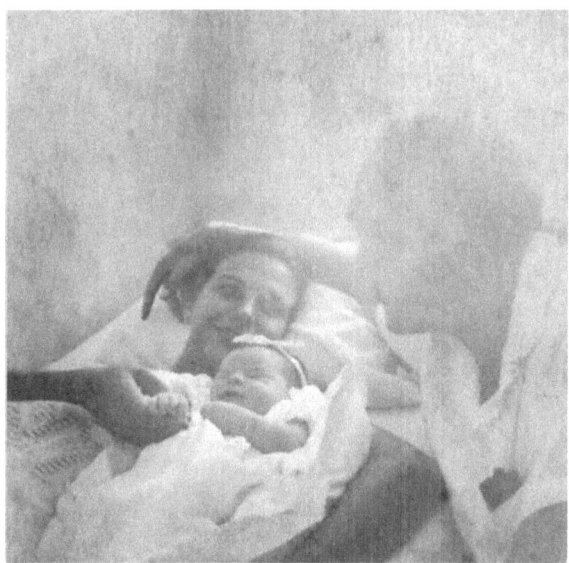

Figure 2.4. Minerva and Manolo with newborn Minou at the clinic of Dr. Fucho Alba in San Francisco de Macorís on September 1, 1956. Courtesy of the Fundación Hermanas Mirabal.

Figure 2.5. Manolo with Minou on her first birthday. Courtesy of the Fundación Hermanas Mirabal.

Figure 2.6. Minerva with Manolo on the day she graduated with her law degree on October 28, 1957. Courtesy of the Fundación Hermanas Mirabal.

THE YEAR 1956

> From our love lives will be born.
> In our love they will drink water.
> Perhaps a day will come
> when a man
> and a woman, like us,
> will touch this love and it will still have the strength
> to burn the hands that touch it.[1]

The only letter from 1956 in my possession is especially significant to me because in it, Papi tells Mami how their marriage and my birth have enriched his life. While the passing years tinge in sepia the memory of his figure and of his voice, this letter is a testament to the eternal nature of his unending tenderness. It lifts the veil on that first year of marriage.

I was born on August 31 in the clinic of Dr. Fucho Alba in San Francisco de Macorís, in the same clinic where my brother Manolo and my sibling-cousins Jacqueline and Raúl were born. This means that when my father wrote to her (on November 25!) I was just under three months old, and they had just celebrated their first wedding anniversary.

Beginning in early January 1956 and until she finished her turbulent studies in October 1957, Mami stayed in the capital at the home of Aunt Isabelita Tavárez, widow of Enrique Lithgow, Papi's cousin. She allowed her to stay in the garage that had been converted into an apartment for her nephew César Lithgow. My mother lived there while attending the university in the capital, with me in utero and later with me as an infant. Some of her friends have told me that she used to bring me to class and that they themselves would help her, holding me and giving me milk during the lectures. Papi, concerned about Mami's health, recommended that she visit her gynecologist, Dr. Asela Morel. A few years later, possibly won over by Minerva's passionate resistance, Asela joined the 14 of June Movement and, together with Mami, was one of the seven women detained in the dictator's torture center, La 40, in 1960.

For professional and economic reasons, they were planning to move to the capital definitively within the year. Their plans would never come to fruition, as time and political events were rapidly accelerating. In fact, the only residence that my parents would share in the capital was prison.

---

[1] Neruda, "Letter on the Road," trans. Donald Devenish Walsh, p. 149. (t.n.)

Papi continued working in Montecristi, both at his legal practice and at agricultural enterprises. During that year (1956), in addition to cultivating rice, he, Uncle Jaime, and Papá Manuel invested in a crop of onions and poured all their savings into it. Aunt Ángela told me that it was a successful harvest but that when they went to sell the crop, the government had already imported large quantities of onions, which financially ruined not only them, but also the majority of Dominican producers.

During that year, my mother wrote several letters to her family in Salcedo. In them she describes her daily life, Papi's struggles with agricultural production, their difficulty making a profit, and her exhaustion from having to constantly move from one place to another, first pregnant, and later with me in her backpack. She traveled back and forth between the capital and her homes (Salcedo never ceased to be home for her), and navigating that hustle and bustle, she finished up the fourth year of her studies. Thanks to a comment that Aunt Teté sent to Uncle Leandro, we also know that Papi sometimes visited her in the capital: on February 29, she and Mami had lunch with him at a restaurant and later went to the Fair of Peace and Fraternity of the Free World, which had officially ended two days prior.

Around the same time, Mami wrote to Mamá Dedé, describing her visit to the fair. Like any young homemaker, she was interested in certain household items and urged her sister to acquire them. Around the middle of March, Aunt Teté wrote to Mamá Chea: "Minerva left today to spend a week in Monte Cristi. I lent her almost all the money I had left, so send my monthly remittance soon..."

This year also saw the completion of Mamá Chea's new house in Conuco, and Mami went to help with the move. After a few months, Mamá Dedé and Uncle Jaimito began residing in the family home in Ojo de Agua, where Dedé still lives.[2]

The new house was of a modern architectural design, in which my mother was integrally involved. It would be the last place that she and my aunts Patria and María Teresa would call home, as they lived there while their husbands were in prison. Mami carefully supervised the construction not only of the house, but also of the garden. She herself placed the slabs for the walkway leading to the main entrance of the house, whose door my grandmother

---

[2] She lived there until her death on February 1, 2014, after this book was originally published. (t.n.)

closed forever when they murdered my mother and aunts. "Until they return," was her response to our questions as curious girls and boys.

Both houses, without distinction, would be my home and that of my siblings. My most cherished memories of childhood and adolescence took place in those two houses: one in which the sisters were born, and the other from which they parted and only returned to occupy the graves that, with their monument, are now part of that lovely garden that my mother so carefully tended. Today this garden forms part of the Mirabal Sisters House Museum. With the gravesite and the garden that surrounds it, the museum was officially declared an Extension of the National Pantheon in November 2000, forty years after the murder. It is currently the most frequently visited site of the National Pantheon in the Dominican Republic.

Pregnant with me, and soon after giving birth, while studying, recently wed, and always busy, Mami's correspondence with her family describes ordinary, day-to-day things, the things that filled her busy life. I love the respectful and affectionate tone that my mother uses with her family. Each time she addresses Mamá Chea, she does so with carefully chosen language, with a scrupulous tone of affection. While not part of my parents' intimate correspondence, these letters provide invaluable insights into the spaces and circumstances in which everything was taking place.

My parents were happy in the loft in Montecristi, a fact that I do not doubt in the least. Mami got along exceptionally well with Papá Manuel, her mother-in-law, and her brother- and sisters-in-law, and she very quickly became an integral part of her new family. Nor is there any doubt that my parents' conversations in that loft often centered around the latest in national politics and that they remained in close contact with their friends and companions opposed to the dictatorship. Aunt Emma used to tell me that when the two of them would start talking about political preparations, my mother would say to her, "You know that what we are talking about is dangerous. You had best go downstairs to your house." But since Aunt Emma refused to pay her any heed, she would compare her to Aunt Teté, who at her age used to follow her around all the time, wanting to participate in adult conversations. By that time, both of them were resolved to join in the resistance that was forming underground to bring an end to the savagery that "*in crescendo*" was suffocating Dominican men and women.

Attached to the letter is the receipt for a bank draft in the amount of $20 from the Reserve Bank, dated November 27, 1956.

Monte Cristy

11/25/56

I received your letter just a moment ago. As always, news from you has filled me with happiness and joy. The heart is insatiable; although we were together until some days ago, everything that you tell me about your life, and about my daughter, seems new and even surprising to me. I don't think there is ever a moment in my life when I do not think about you and my beloved daughter. You two are always with me.

Etched in my memory is the image of our daughter and her tiny little mouth trying out a smile, that smile that you know well "and that makes Papi happy." How I miss you two! It is only thanks to my well-trained patience that I am able to live under these circumstances, without you and without that beloved "doll," who, being so tiny and by simply being the miraculous fruit of our love, has brought me to experience all the dimensions of what it is to be a man. Thanks to the two of you, I am more complete, a slightly better and more just person, more understanding and aware of my destiny.

Until you two came into my life, I was lost, tangled up in my own restlessness. I barely knew who I was, what I truly wanted. I was always a dissatisfied man, lacking any clear, defined, worthwhile purpose in life ...

I continue this letter today, Tuesday. Last night while I was writing to you, a gentleman came to discuss a matter with me. I talked more than a parrot. But it turns out that he will give me some work. This morning I was very busy with hundreds of errands and at the office. I have just now arrived back from the fields, and here I am with you, my love.

Attached I'm sending the check for $20.00. I think it will cover your expenses for the time being. If you need anything, let me know. I hope that the baby is already feeling better. They tell me that all children experience this and that it's caused by the stomach not working properly. As for you, I assume that you are feeling well since you haven't mentioned anything about your health. But, *mi bien,* if you continue to have pain in your bladder or any other ailment, go see the doctor. Don't worry about expenses. Even though our situation in that regard is just now "starting to become clear," it is for events like this that I work.

I am still very excited about the prospect of us going there to live. Naturally that will be within a year, at least. I am preparing for that. Tomorrow I might talk with Mr. Breet[3] about the banana issue. Sully was here for precisely that reason, but I wasn't able to see him. His trip coincided with my stay there. But he told me that he was as excited as ever. In my previous letter I mentioned something to you about a business plan that Papá, Jaime and I are developing through a mutual agreement. If it is successful, we will have more than sufficient financial means, which will allow us to weigh anchor and move to a different environment.

You know very well how sad it will be for me to leave my dear hometown, but I am compelled by serious motives. You know the economic situation around here, the intellectual desertion, and their perspectives. This reality has brought me to the following conclusion: here we would become stagnant in our profession and lead a mediocre life.

We have a lot to talk about. I want to share my ideas with you, hear your opinion, and feel your encouragement.

Regarding the date of your trip, I think I'll run out of patience before then. I had already become accustomed to the idea that it would be Dec. 5. From here we can go to Salcedo for that sad day[4] ... We could bring the baby and spend two or three days, or leave her and return the next day. But in the end, this all depends on the circumstances regarding your studies. Hopefully you can arrange matters like we discussed.

The check is in Eduardo's name because it will be easier for him to cash it since he has more free time than you. Give him my thanks in advance. For Isabelita, Chelina and everyone else there, my warmest regards.

This letter isn't longer because I want it to go out tonight and reach you as soon as possible. Keep writing to me, each letter longer than the last. To my darling daughter, I dedicate my entire life, which has been yours for so long. As soon as they give you the photos, send me some. In the meantime, *bien mío,* I'm sending you all the love that you have inspired in me.

Yours,
Manolo

P.S. Let me know how Uncle Mimo is doing. Ángela might head over

---

3 According to Simón Tomás Fernández, the correct surname is Breck, assistant manager of the Grenada Company in Manzanillo. At that time, Manolo was also positioning himself in such a way that the Grenada Company might contract his legal services.
4 Likely December 14, the third anniversary of Enrique Mirabal's death. (t.n.)

there the day after tomorrow. I believe she is going to stay with my Aunt Isabelita. Keep writing to me. I'll write you again tomorrow.

V.

The Year 1957

> When they tell you: 'That man
> does not love you,' remember
> that my feet are alone in that night, and they seek
> the sweet and tiny feet that I adore.[5]

Not a single letter between my parents in 1957. I call it the time of love and of the sea, in Montecristi. However, family memories, the historical timeline, and letters from my parents to their relatives and friends chronicle an apparently routine year for a young newlywed couple with a very young daughter. I say apparently because in my parents' life, there was no place for that tranquil monotony reserved for those not destined for the turmoil of an extraordinary fate.

We know that the regime never stopped monitoring Minerva closely, never stopped harassing her, and by extension, Manolo either. As an adolescent he had belonged to the Democratic Youth. Even before meeting one another, they shared the same sentiments about freedom. As soon as my father began his relationship with my mother, he was labeled an enemy of the regime, dragging his entire family down with him. Thus, the Tavárez Justo family joined the Mirabal Reyes clan as two families who had "fallen into disgrace," as people would often say.

Until mid-year, Mami kept up with her nomadic life, which she lived between the home she shared with her husband, her mother's home, and her accommodations when studying in the capital. In July of that year, she finally took her final exams and concentrated on writing her thesis: *The Principle of the Non-Retroactivity of Laws and Dominican Jurisprudence*. As a child I would spend vacations with my grandparents in Montecristi. I remember Papá Manuel reminiscing that my mother used to sit and write her thesis underneath the vine arbor that he had built at the base of the balcony. She used to say that in order to concentrate on her work, she needed the opulent natural landscape of the Cibao countryside.

---

5   Neruda, "Letter on the Road," trans. Donald Devenish Walsh, p. 147. (t.n.)

The thesis has a few dedications. The first: "To my beloved husband: Dr. Manuel A. Tavárez Justo, whose kindness and understanding have made it possible for me to complete my studies." The second: "To my beloved daughter Minou. May this thesis provide encouragement for you in the future." The third was a mandatory dedication required for any student to graduate: to the tyrant. She had certainly demonstrated how much she wanted to graduate.

This brilliant work, written with academic rigor, diligence, and courage, still serves as reference for those who study this topic. There are those who think that its content further enraged and provoked the tyrant and his minions, given that the mere selection of this topic was an act of opposition to Trujillo. It was a country in which there was no rule of law, in which there were no laws except for those dictated by "the Chief."

By that time, they had moved into the house where my mother could finally plant the garden that she had dreamed of creating around their nest. My parents lived in that house on Santiago Rodríguez Street in Montecristi, two blocks away from my grandparents, until their imprisonment in 1960.

In addition to her new passion for the sea, Mami found a friend about her age with similar interests: Tamara Díaz, the wife of Carlos García Tavárez, Papi's first cousin. It was with Aunt Tamara that she began learning the arts of sculpting and photography. She had a talent for those arts and immersed herself with the same enthusiasm that she demonstrated in all that she did. What she learned would eventually help her endure the days of her final incarceration. On display in the House Museum are two of the plaster busts that she sculpted in prison: one of my face, which she sculpted from memory, and another of Aunt Sina, her cellmate, who served as her model.

Papi moved his office to the house, and Mami, fulfilling her promise, adorned his desk daily with flowers that she herself had planted. But the forces of infamy and defamation were carefully laying their plans.

After having faced numerous refusals throughout her academic career, Mami suffered one more. She graduated with a law degree on October 24, 1957. My father was her graduation sponsor, and although her grades and thesis warranted her earning highest honors, she was denied them. In 1989 the Autonomous University of Santo Domingo, in an act of reparation and justice, christened the law school auditorium in her name and conferred upon her a new posthumous degree, the one that she had earned: Doctor of Jurisprudence, Summa Cum Laude.

But immediately following graduation, something even worse happened. The despot committed one of his customarily vile acts. After having caused her to lose sleep year after year, making her wonder whether or not she would be allowed to register for classes, he delivered a final blow, assaulting the pride of the woman who had defied and despised him: Minerva would never be allowed to practice law. The denial of her exequatur while my mother was pregnant with my brother Manolo was one of the worst punishments inflicted upon her for being "enemy of the Chief and a red communist." He never allowed her to take her place in the courtroom. He also made sure that she would never have time to.

With thwarted aspirations of forming a law firm with her husband, Mami could only work as his consultant and assistant, which she did, as evidenced by numerous notes in each one's handwriting about various aspects of cases they were preparing, notes that I found among their law books. Among these papers I feel compelled to mention the draft of a notarial act that my mother must have taken great pleasure in writing, as it shows that she finally got my father to become a notary: "I, Dr. Manuel Aurelio Tavárez Justo, Notary of the Municipality of San Fernando de Montecristi [. . .] certify that Mr. Gabriel Socías has appeared before me . . ." The draft suggests that the majority of their clients were limited to extended family, for on the back of the paper, my mother wrote some "Pleadings in the Jaime Ricardo Socías case" for a property violation in which the victim was related to my uncle by marriage. This was jotted down alongside my father's note containing information for a notarial act for a woman by the last name Morel and calculations of the expenses they had incurred for the onion crop.

Mami continued spending the majority of her time caring for me and for herself, since in November or December of '57 she became pregnant with my brother Manolo. In spite of his initial fears, my paternal grandfather described her as "an excellent homemaker."

She also continued reading a great deal and sculpting. She often went to the beach at El Morro on family outings and visited her mother's home in Conuco. In those years, they closely followed both the international political situation and the national situation, which was reaching its boiling point with rampant repression and the tyranny's excessive brutality.

Elsewhere in the region, important liberation campaigns were taking shape, such as the struggle of the Cuban revolutionaries in the Sierra Maestra, the development of which Manolo and Minerva followed closely. Concurrently, the region's dictators were seen in an increasingly negative light and as less useful to their longtime associates. In the eyes of the world, the tyrant's impunity began to crumble definitively due to events that fundamentally impacted his image. These were terrifying events like the kidnapping in the middle of Manhattan and the subsequent murder in Dominican territory of the Basque intellectual and politician Jesús de Galíndez.

It was nearing the hour of the furnaces,[6] and my parents were in the middle of the bonfire.

THE YEAR 1958

> Love, when they tell you
> that I have forgotten you, and even when
> it is I who say it,
> when I say it to you,
> do not believe me,
> who could and how could anyone
> cut you from my heart
> and who would receive
> my blood
> when I went bleeding toward you?[7]

Resonating with the indignation and foreboding storm emerging throughout the nation's territory, Minerva and Manolo's lives were also very intense in 1958. This intensity is seen in their personal relationship as well as the deepening truth and transparency of the commitment they established. The country was submerged in a bloodbath. In order to retain power, the tyrant's repression became increasingly brutal. The lethal delirium with which he ruled during the epilogue of his "Era" was directly proportional to the lucidity and commitment with which my parents dedicated themselves to the struggle to end his regime.

The storm was intensifying in my mother's soul, and my father was forming an awareness of everything that would be paramount and truly fundamental both for his sake and for THEIRS. They were forged in knowledge, in rebellion, in the refusal to submit, and in resistance. The time to act was approaching. It was time to get on with the work of liberation that today is an important part of the history of the Dominican people.

---

6   Phrase from an 1891 letter by Cuban revolutionary, writer, and icon of political resistance, José Martí (1853–1895). Ernesto (Che) Guevara opened his 1967 *Message to the Tricontinental* with the same phrase. (t.n.)

7   Neruda, "Letter on the Road," trans. Donald Devenish Walsh, p. 147. (t.n.)

Perhaps it is best to describe what was happening during that time before diving into an interpretation of the only two letters from 1958 that I have been able to recover: one letter from Papi and two poems that my mother copied down and sent as a reply.

On February 14, Aunt Teté and Uncle Leandro were married in a civil ceremony with the intention of going abroad to study. They were denied permission to leave the country with an irrefutable argument: María Teresa belonged to a family of "hostile enemies of the Chief." They had an intimate religious ceremony in May and established residence in Santiago, where my uncle was working as an engineer. Mamá Chea was left practically alone with her loyal employees, although they were truly family to her and to us. Concerned about the effect that not having her four daughters at home was having on Mamá Chea's spirit, and suffering complications toward the end of her pregnancy with Manolito, Mami traveled to Salcedo more frequently, where she received care. During her first years as a student, she had written to Mamá Dedé that when she was ill, she wanted and needed to be at home with her mother. These frequent absences, as we will see, would have a negative impact on her marriage.

The deceivingly pleasant calm that characterized Minerva Mirabal's life at her home in Montecristi, with me as a small child and Papi always nearby, would be shaken in April with a malevolent reminder that she was still being incessantly pursued by her eternal tormentor's relentless obsession.

The venomous "Public Forum" was once again merciless with Mami's reputation, and this time with Papi's too. On April 6, 1958 it published a note signed by one Gumersindo Almonte titled "He Lives with a Red." Along with other fallacies, it accused Papi of cohabitating with a communist. I can only imagine what this libel must have meant for Mami, who was so proper, so dignified and as honest as ever. My father responded in writing. As a result, and as was customary, the paper subsequently published a "Note of Clarification," this time drawing even more attention. The note by Luis E. Suero, Attorney General of the Republic, was titled "They Are Legally Married," which is the conclusion he reached after a "full and thorough investigation." The note also informed the public of my existence.

My brother Manolo (Manuel Enrique Tavárez Mirabal) was born on August 14 at the same clinic in San Francisco de Macorís where I had been born. The delivery was not in the least bit like the previous one. Mami suffered serious health complications as a result, and she had to spend time in the capital to be treated by her gynecologist, Dr. Asela Morel. She was forced to leave Manolito in the care of Nina Patria and Mamá Chea.

The only stain that exists in my parents' relationship came about during her absence. In her memoirs titled *Alive in Their Garden,* Mamá Dedé calls it Manolo's "indiscretion," while Mami, naturally, would consider it an act of betrayal that was very difficult for her to overcome, given her characteristic transparency and staunch loyalty.

In Montecristi without Mami and laboring away at his legal practice as well as his crops, in which he was deeply involved, Papi found time for a romantic entanglement with a young woman who worked at the court. For my father, the insignificance of this person in his life was always clear, but for Mami this was quite serious. She found out through the evil tongues of anonymous third parties (probably the same ones who hid behind names like Gumersindo Almonte). Going so far as to risk her own life, given her precarious health, she darted off to Montecristi, gathered her things, and showed up in Conuco, prepared to leave Papi. My father was petrified, cut off the fling right away, and did not give up until he won back the love of his life, his other half, his best friend, his confidant, his partner. But approaching her was not easy given my mother's proverbial stubbornness.

Mamá Dedé recalls how she shared her own personal experience with Mami once my mother stopped ranting, raving and crying, jeopardizing her health with all the emotional stress. She advised Mami to think it over very carefully, that this experience—common among women at the time—was no reason to get divorced, not even close. We can only guess what was going on in Papi's mind during that time. I can imagine that for a man as courageous as Manolo, the risk of losing Mami had to have been one of the few moments in his life when he was truly afraid. If his "indiscretion" was considered typical in those days, the confrontation it provoked with Minerva must have made very clear to him that neither he nor she was a typical person.

No one knows, nor will they ever know, what was said between the two of them. What we do know is that some time into this separation, while my two mothers—Minerva and Mamá Dedé—were seated in the rocking chairs on the porch of the house in Conuco, Papi pulled up in his car. Mami sprung to her feet, and they got into an intense argument. From a distance, her sister watched her argue, gesticulating. Over time, Dedé's recollection of this episode in my parents' lives would become legendary in our family: "Minerva adored Manolo, and for him, there was never any doubt about what was truly important. With three little words he convinced her, and they made up." When Mami reentered the house, a little calmer and more or less reconciled with Papi, she fixed her large dark eyes on her sister and with her index finger made a gesture that meant, "Don't you dare say a word."

It took time, however, for things to run their course. This is evident in the two poems that Mami copied down and sent to Papi and in his letter to her while she was receiving medical treatment in the capital. He updated her on Manolito, who was still under two months old, and he explained that he had slept in Conuco with me. "As always we woke up wet," he wrote. Papi's letter can be interpreted in many ways. It has the cautious tone of one who knows that their stability is still in the phase of "we'll see," and it reveals the exhaustion and loneliness brought on by this episode.

As for Mami, the two poems that she sent to Papi were more than telling. The first is by the Colombian poet Miguel Ángel Osorio, better known by his pseudonym Porfirio Barba Jacob. It is prefaced by a quote from Montaigne: "Man is a vain, fickle, and wavering thing," and is missing a stanza, which she omitted on purpose, as she herself indicates. It is the following:

> And there are days when we're so wanton, so wanton
> That women offer us their flesh in vain:
> After girdling a waist and caressing a breast,
> The roundness of a fruit makes us tremble again.[8]

The second poem is one of the "ghazals" from *Diván,* the collection of poetry by Persian poet Shams al-Din Muhammad, better known as Hafiz. The book was a gift to her from Pericles Franco in the late '40s. The poems are written on a sheet of notebook paper, which Mami pointedly sent in an envelope intended for a sympathy card. In the same envelope, I also found Papi's letter. I'm not sure why (as they were written much later), but they were in the same small box in which Papi had meticulously organized and preserved all the letters, telegrams, receipts and little pieces of paper from when they were dating. I wonder how often and in what different circumstances my father reread these letters.

As if out of the blue, I just now realize that I have never referred to my mother's extraordinary beauty nor to my father's good looks. But in that situation, I imagine them with furrowed brows, wading through the floodwaters that in the end would be "drizzling rain" compared to what fate had in store

---

8   Barba Jacob, Porfirio. "Song of the Profound Life." Translation by Nicolás Suescún. (t.n.)

for them. This was perhaps the only shadow cast upon the harmony, the immense love, and the solidarity that existed between my parents. The future was fast approaching, and they would face it united, as the ONE that they always were.

This letter seems to have been hand-delivered. It had been placed in the same envelope as the subsequent note and the two poems that Mami sent.

Monte Cristy

10/3/58

Dear Minerva,

Yesterday I received your letter, and today Eduardo brought another one. They have brought me peace and tranquility. They have allowed me to taste a bit of happiness. My desire to have you here at home soon has me feeling feverish. This loneliness is so immense! Send me a telegram letting me know when you leave so that I can go meet you in Dajabón.

The day before yesterday I was running errands in Santiago, and I went to Salcedo. I was at Patria's and doña Chea's, where I slept. Our dear children are doing very well. Manolito is so beautiful and much more alert. By now he clearly looks like an almost two-month old; he laughed a lot with me. I brought him a box of milk, which he needed. In regard to eating, he will be like Minou, fortunately. I took her to Patria's, and we slept together: As always, we woke up wet. It pained me deeply to leave her, especially after having told her that I would bring her with me, but doña Chea wanted her to remain until you came, and I did not want to contradict her. However, the child longs to return to her own home. As soon as this absence crosses her mind, her longing becomes an obsession. She speaks of nothing else, and she latches onto anyone or anything that could bring her home. This girl senses and understands too much.

When you return home, we will discuss the article on sexology that you sent me. It is really very interesting. It has broadened my horizons regarding all of this.

Carlos and Tamara are here already. Their arrival has made my loneliness more pronounced. They invited me out for drinks last night, but when I got home, they had either gone to bed already or they had gone out. I went to the fields and later had dinner at home.

As you know, Ángela has already delivered her daughter. She is very big and beautiful. In spite of having had a Cesarean, she is doing very well, and the baby as well. Jaime must be very happy.

I'm writing you from the Magistrates' Court. I'm still here. I have such a huge headache that I see fireflies. We left some hearings very late, and you know that always kills me.

I'm afraid you won't receive this letter because you are already on your way. I'm waiting for you with open arms,

Yours,
Manolo

From Minerva to Manolo, undated, in an envelope meant for condolences.

"Song of the Profound Life"[9]

1) There are days when we're so variable, so variable
As the light blade of grass to the wind and chance.
Maybe glory smile to under other skies heavens,
For life is clear, billowy and open like the ocean.

2) And there are days when we're so fertile, so fertile,
Like the fields in April, trembling with passion:
Under the generous influence of spiritual rains
The soul sending out bowers of illusion.

3) And there are days when we're so sordid, so sordid,
Like the obscure entrails of obscure flint:
Night surprises us with its profuse lamps,
Measuring out Good and Evil with sparkling coins.

4) Missing[10]

5) And there are days when we're so placid, so placid . . .
—Childhood at sunset! Sapphire lagoons!—
that a verse, a trill, a hill, a passing bird,
and even one's own sorrows make us smile.

---

9   Miguel Ángel Osorio (Porfirio Barba Jacob), "Canción de la vida profunda." Translation by Nicolás Suescún. (t.n.)

10 The stanza that Minerva identified as fifth is actually the third in the original poem, and the omitted stanza is not the fourth, but rather the fifth. I have modified Suescún's translation to reflect Minerva's rendering. (t.n.)

And there are days when we're so gloomy, so gloomy,
Like in a gloomy night the crying of a pine grove.
The soul moans then with the pain of the world,
Perchance not even God himself can give us solace.

But there is also, oh Earth, a day ... a day ... a day
When we weigh anchor never to return ...
A day when ineluctable winds blow by,
A day when no one can retain us any longer!

End

Manolo,

I seem to recall telling you about Hafiz. I'm going to copy this little poem for you so that you can see what lovely language this oriental poet uses.

"The Captive Heart"

> It seems that my life is reaching its end, but my desire is unfulfilled. My fortune still lives in my dreams. My hours pass, void of thought, and the wounds that you gave me do not heal into scars.
>
> My heart must have remained captive in your black curls, undoubtedly content in those perfumed webs, because I know nothing more of it. Being faithful means surrendering the entire heart. Leave—Oh Hafiz!—if you are unable to break free from her.
>
> From *Las gacelas de Hafiz*, p. 43.[11]

---

11 My translation of Minerva's transcription (t.n.)

Figure 3.1. Founding members of the 14 of June Movement. Manolo, Minerva, and Leandro appear as the first three individuals in the first row. Two of the seven women imprisoned at the time, Dr. Asela Morel and the engineer, Tomasina (Sina) Cabral, appear in positions two and three in the second row. These images were created and used by Trujillo's secret police, the Servicio de Inteligencia Militar. The source of this reproduction is Pérez, Milvio. 1J4. *Del sacrificio (1959) a la inmolación (1963)*, published by the Dirección General de Aduanas of the Dominican Republic.

III

Letters in Prison

1959–1960

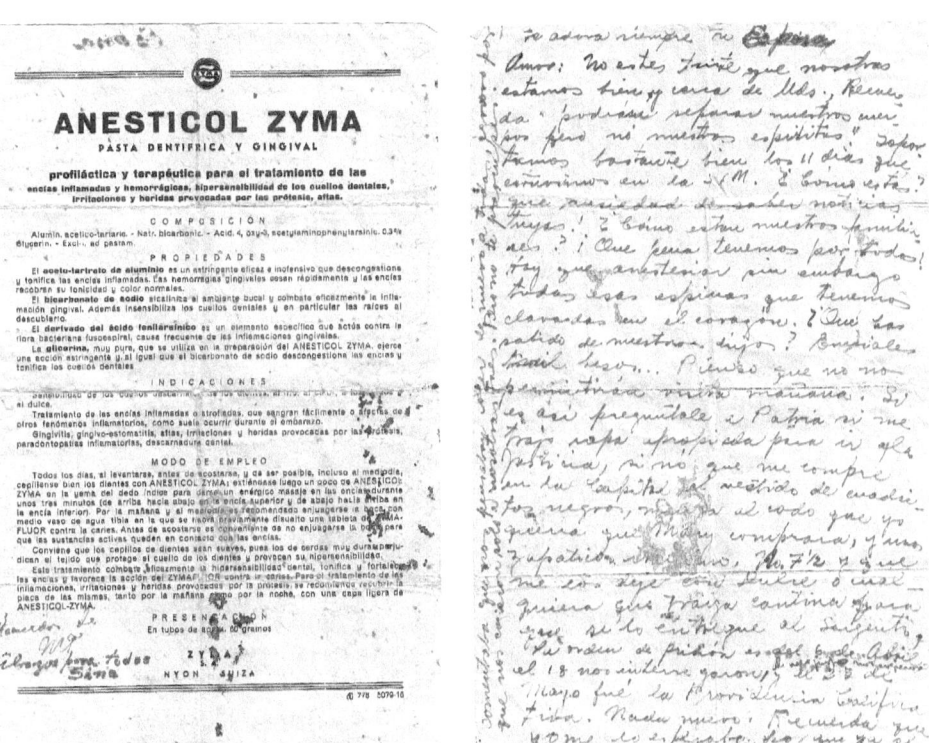

Figure 3.2. Letter from Minerva to Manolo, written in prison on the back of an insert for toothpaste, 1960. Courtesy of the Fundación Hermanas Mirabal.

Above: Figure 3.3. Letter from Manolo to Minerva, written in prison on paper from cigarette packaging, 1960. Courtesy of the Fundación Hermanas Mirabal.

Right: Figure 3.4. Bust of Minou that Minerva sculpted while in prison, 1960. Minou was three and a half years old at the time. Courtesy of the Fundación Hermanas Mirabal.

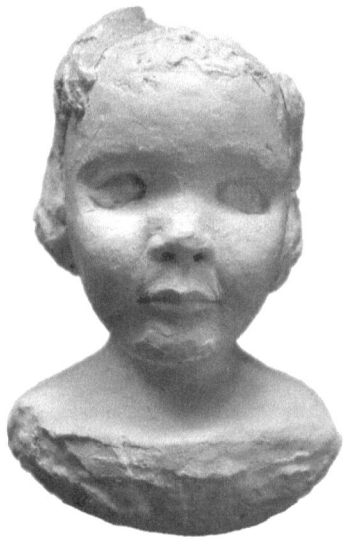

1959–1960

> Peace arrived too because I return
> to my land to fight,
> and as my heart is complete
> with the share of blood that you gave me
> for always,
> and as
> I go
> my hands full of your naked being,
> look at me,
> look at me,
> look at me across the sea, for I go radiant,
> look at me across the night through which I sail,
> and sea and night are those eyes of yours.[1]

I could begin to tell the story of these years in reverse. That is, I could go back to that August afternoon in 1961 when I made my First Communion at the Immaculate Conception School in La Vega, and my father, recently released from prison, came to pick me up and take me to live with him in a city that by then had recovered its name, Santo Domingo. We wouldn't separate again until he set off for Las Manaclas. Or perhaps I could begin even later, on that day in late December 1963 when I found out in the most absurd way that he would never come for me again, that he was dead. Such was the complexity of the events that yanked us out of private, family life and ultimately made my siblings and me orphans, when my parents and my aunts spilled their blood over the land where their sacrifices would take root and grow.

Much has been written and documented about the outset and the consequences of the intense political activism in which Papi and Mami were involved, together in flesh, spirit, and courage. Writing about them and about the movement they founded, numerous biographers and historians have narrated and analyzed the political timeline of those years. Looking back, I'm reminded once again that I was there, that my brother Manolo was there. As strange as it may seem, we were never left feeling abandoned by the constant absence of my parents, who would give their last breath for the political cause to which they were wholeheartedly committed. The spirit of justice surrounding their actions was that immense.

---

1   Neruda, "Letter on the Road," p. 149, with modifications to Devenish Walsh's translation in verses three through eight. (t.n.)

It is widely known that when the freedom fighters of the glorious Immortal Race[2] expedition arrived in Constanza, Maimón, and Estero Hondo on June 14 and 20, 1959, the heroism of the 198 revolutionaries, the cruelty with which they were met, and the execution of 192 of them, so wed indignation and hope in the hearts of Dominican youth opposing the regime.

From the outset, both Papi and Mami acted with complete awareness of what they were doing. They possessed extraordinary political and military lucidity and were prepared to lay down their lives, just as so many others who had died for having declared war on the tyrant. An essay titled "Memories of the Holy Spiritual Exercises that I Celebrated with Reverend Quevedo During My Last Year of School," which my mother wrote on February 3, 1946, while a student in La Vega, gives us a clue as to how important it was to 19-year-old Minerva to think about death and to live doing what needed to be done, aware of her human—and mortal—condition. The essay essentially summarizes the ideas, convictions, and principles that she wanted to maintain beyond graduation. "If I write this down, it is because I know that I am weak," she explains, eloquently detailing—at times in a playful tone—what she had learned and internalized through her spiritual training. One of her notes, set apart from the rest and written in a hasty Palmer-style penmanship bearing a striking resemblance to my own, echoes the Latin phrase *memento mori*: "Think each day: 'Remember that you will die.'"

Papi's awareness that he would meet certain death in the mountains has become legendary. He communicated as much to Mamá Dedé following the coup against Juan Bosch's constitutional government. Before going clandestine, he told her goodbye in Ojo de Agua and asked her to take care of us, his children.

Thus, the commitment they assumed on January 6, 1959, in the home of my Uncle Yuyo D'Alessandro, when Mami proposed collective action, was a life-or-death pact that the two of them made with their people, with our history, with their homeland. And so it began: clandestine meetings; the search for weapons; making contact with Dominicans in exile; trips to potential sites for implementing guerrilla warfare; articulation of principles and manifestos; closely following Radio Rumbo from Venezuela, Radio Rebelde, and the triumph of the Cuban Revolution; neglect of economic endeavors undertaken for the family's livelihood; prolonged absences; and the successful

---

2 Reference to the failed June 14, 1959, expedition of the National Liberation Army. (t.n.)

recruitment throughout the nation's territory of hundreds of young people who, like my parents, felt growing disillusionment, indignation, and rage in the face of such brutality. Aunt Teté (who had just given birth to Jacqueline), Uncle Leandro, Uncle Pedrito, Nina Patria, her son Nelson, Uncle Jaime Ricardo Socías, and several other family members also conspired. Anti-Trujillo sentiment was in our family's blood.

Simón Tomás Fernández tells me that in September or November 1959, Papi contacted him and assigned him the task of obtaining materials for making bombs. His position in the Ministry of Public Works allowed him to do so without raising suspicions. He completed the assignment but found it strange that there was a delay in follow-up contact. Concerned, he went in search of Cayeyo Grisanti and asked him if he had seen Manolo. Cayeyo told him that if he wanted to see Manolo, he need only go to Sunday morning Mass at the Santiago Cathedral, since that's where they used to meet and seize the opportunity to contact new allies for the cause.

The image of my parents as described by Simón Tomás is stunning: Minerva, beautiful, elegantly dressed with gloves and hat, together with Manolo in a formal suit, as if they had just stepped out of a movie from that era, walking down the center aisle of the church, the eyes of the congregation upon them. After Mass they used to talk with the priest and mingle with the congregation's poor, as well as with the posh men and women of Santiago's aristocracy.

The image etched in my childhood memory is a different one, however. I recall a slender woman standing in front of a mirror, trying on an olive-green uniform and beret over a "boyish" haircut. It is my mother.

The discovery of the plot against Trujillo conceived by the 14 of June Movement, led by Manolo and with Minerva as the backbone of its militancy, resulted in the imprisonment of hundreds of young people across the country. The women were the last to be arrested since the men, in spite of brutal torture, tried to protect their identities until the very end. Still, the names of the most active women were revealed.

Another very vivid memory that I have of my mother—who by that time had acquired the pseudonym "Butterfly"—was when, clinging to her legs and crying, I looked up at her from my height as a child, and she told me to be quiet. The caliés had come for her at my grandparents' house in Montecristi. One of my aunts took me in her arms as Mami asked her to give me chocolate. Mamá Fefa begged, "Let me go with her." But Minerva cut her off; "Don't ask for anything," she sharply replied as she hurriedly tried to release herself from my grasp and was taken off to prison.

The first woman to arrive at the terrifying prison called La 40 was Aunt Sina, who was subjected to horrifying physical and psychological torture. The next female "guests" to arrive at that cavern of human abuse, desperation and death—Minerva, María Teresa, Asela Morel, Dulce Tejada, Miram Morales and Fe Violeta Ortega—suffered torture of a different, though no less horrific, sort. I heard from the lips of Fausto Rodríguez Mesa, head of the 14 of June Movement in San Juan de la Maguana, that while he and his companions were in "the Coliseum," naked, waiting in line to be seated in the electric chair, the guards brought in various female prisoners to witness the torture inflicted upon their husbands and comrades. Minerva's presence was one of unimaginable poise amid such filth. Even the guards noticed and reacted by trying to break that upright person of unattainable dignity. The following is a transcription of how Mamá Dedé recalls the scene in her memoirs:

> Fausto Rodríguez Mesa [. . .] overheard one of the caliés tell Minerva to lose the haughtiness because maybe one day one of them might want to marry her. Minerva's response came flying like a bullet that shook them all: 'Don't worry. That will never happen because we don't like guards, especially if they're murderers like all of you.'[3]

What remains with me of that memory is don Fausto's view of my mother. It's his voice telling me that never in his life, before nor since, did he ever witness another presence that filled as much space with dignity as did Minerva's that one time long ago when he saw her in La 40.

The prisons were filled to capacity, and the country was like a pressure cooker with so many hundreds of prisoners, men and women from all regions of the country, young and not so young, from families with a history of opposing Trujillo, and sons and daughters of distinguished members of the regime, peasants, workers, professionals . . . As Aunt Teté commented to Tonó one day as they were sewing, ". . . but we almost brought him down." For the first time, the regime suffered a violent tremor of considerable proportions, one of the many likely reasons that the tyrant decided to release political prisoners on February 7.

"Freedom" was nothing more than house arrest under close surveillance, although one advantage was that my mother and aunts could visit their

---

3   Mirabal, *Vivas*, p. 170. (t.n.)

husbands, who had already been transferred to another penitentiary, La Victoria. And they could continue plotting. Minerva took advantage of each visit to La Victoria not only to see Manolo, but also to communicate with other prisoners in an attempt to reorganize the movement. For example, on one Thursday visit, she approached José Israel Cuello to ask him about his contacts who hadn't been captured. "Minerva was an extraordinary political leader whom Trujillo couldn't defeat since whether he kept her in prison or he released her, he was legitimizing her dissent."

Her release from prison also marked the beginning of our lives all together at the house in Conuco. Nina Patria's house in San José de Conuco had been completely destroyed, and Aunt Teté's home was ransacked and dismantled, as was ours. Mami was able to reach Montecristi in time to salvage a few precious things. She handed the home over to its owner on February 20, 1960, as if the certainty that she would never return were abundantly clear in her heart, and she were accepting the fate that awaited her. Except for Mamá Dedé, who was only three kilometers away in Ojo de Agua, the Mirabal sisters and almost all of their children took refuge under the maternal wings of Mamá Chea and Tonó at the house in Conuco. Their husbands and Patria's eldest son Nelson were still incarcerated. The sisters had begun their journey toward the point of no return.

All of our holdings had been expropriated. We were able to get by thanks to my grandmother's savings and to the clothes that my mother and aunts made and sold to whomever would dare buy them. It is essential to remember that anyone who came close to us fell immediately into disgrace. Those months were also marked by constant, huddled terror. I remember that when we used to get up at night to go to the bathroom or to the kitchen, we were supposed to duck down such that our heads remained below window level. The caliés would be out there all night, their damned footsteps sounding across the porch. They circled around the house, hiding in the shadows but always letting us know that they were there. To alleviate some of the pressure of life under surveillance, my grandmother decided to replace the modern glass windows with wooden ones, making it more difficult for them to peer in. I believe those large glass windows are still stored somewhere at the House Museum.

On May 18, while Aunt Teté was suffering from a bout of bronchitis, they returned for her and Mami and walked them off to what would be their final prison term. I remember as if it were yesterday that green blanket with white geometric shapes in which Mamá Chea wrapped Aunt Teté, begging at the top of her lungs that they not take her away with that 104° fever. They spent eleven days in La 40 and two and a half months in La Victoria. During this second round of arrests, they only detained the two of them and Aunt Sina. They arrived at La Victoria having already been sentenced and were held together in the same cell. There my mother would pass the time sculpting, embroidering, and sewing little clothes for my younger brother and me. When asking for plaster, fabric, thread, materials and instruments for working and distracting themselves, Minerva would insist that both she and Aunt Teté needed them more than they needed food. I'm also told that my mother would lift the spirits of the other prisoners with her out-of-tune songs. At the top of her lungs, so as to be heard beyond the women's wing, she would sing verses of "The Little Mouse Miguel": ". . . . *vaaaaaaamos a ver quién va a arrancarle a Misifú el corazón.*"[4]

I'll pause now. I'm trying to breathe. I'm accelerating inevitably toward the end of their correspondence and circling around it like someone who can't bear to enter into the verbal garden of my parents' final letters. Together with them, I, too, inhabit their cells.

The letters from La Victoria are tattered petals, bitten off by the beasts in that inferno of blood, death, and screams. My mother's letter, written with the sap of those thorns that she, with her characteristic nobility, sweetly resolved to numb. My father's letters, dictated by the fire that had tempered the steel in his body, turning it into a map of permanent scars to which they would add the tragic murder of the woman he loved. She, journeying toward him. He, journeying toward her. In that storm surge of their lives together, both of them prisoners in the same fortress of evil, reaching out to one another, unable to touch. They wrote to one another with their hands and with their thoughts. It occurs to me that though they couldn't be together, never were they closer than they were in that distance traversed by a few walls and some dismal bars.

From this minuscule part of their correspondence, we learn that treatment and life were especially hard during the first days in prison. Since the men had arrived first, they were already familiar with the inner workings of the place. Mami vehemently refused to make "deals" with their jailers in order to improve their living conditions. We also learn that reading helped them maintain their sanity. Books were divided up so that while some prisoners

---

4 "El ratoncito Miguel," by Cuban singer Félix B. Caignet. Some of its verses lend themselves to multiple interpretations, for example: "The thing is that [it / he] is terrifying and truly frightening . . ."

read one part, others read other parts. It moves me to know that this love of poetry that my parents left me as an immense legacy, in an almost intimate way, my way, also sustained them during their precarious days in confinement.

The memory of those exceptional witnesses who did not lose their lives is like a healing balm. Víctor Núñez told me a story that sends shivers down my spine. He formed part of The New Trinity (*La Nueva Trinitaria*), an opposition group based in the capital whose twelve members were incarcerated on November 8, 1959. One Saturday afternoon later that month, with only SIM[5] agents present in the courtroom, they were sentenced in a summary trial to thirty years in prison with hard labor. That means that when the first prisoners of the 14 of June Movement arrived at La Victoria at the end of January and beginning of February, 1960, they had already been imprisoned there for over two months and hadn't the faintest idea that, parallel to The New Trinity, an enormous opposition movement had formed throughout the country. With the arrival of so many new political prisoners, they, for the first time, were taken out of the two solitary cells in which they were being held and moved to Pavilion A with the general population. Their families, who after months without word had given them up for dead, were notified that they could visit them. In those subhuman spaces built to hold one prisoner there were initially six, and as they brought more and more political prisoners, they crammed up to twenty individuals in each cell. Inmates had to take turns in order to sleep.

Don Víctor says that one of the "good" prison guards (and there were some), one Sergeant Martínez, informed them one night that Mami, Aunt Teté, and Aunt Sina had been incarcerated. Around three a.m. the sergeant passed through the hallway of Pavilion A, where many of the *catorcistas*[6] were also being held, and dropped a comment that left them speechless: "That bastard even has women locked up now," and he asked them to give him some bed linens to bring them. They were happy to hand them over even though it had been only a few days since their families had been permitted to give them sheets and mosquito netting. Filled with emotion, he told me that it has always made him feel proud to think that perhaps my mother or Aunt Teté was able to cover herself with that sheet of his, which he gave up without a second thought, not entirely certain where it would end up.

But the part of his testimony that fills me with mixed emotions is when he

---

5   The regime's Servicio de Inteligencia Militar (Military Intelligence Service).
6   Collaborators in the 14 of June Movement. (t.n.)

refers to his contact with Mami and Papi in that wretched place. He shared with me that in June or July of 1960, when Manolo was already in Pavilion A, in the cell directly opposite his, one day when they passed in the hallway, don Víctor told my father that he had seen Mami through the bars of his cell window when they took her out to the patio. With deep sadness, Papi replied that he hadn't been able to see her even from afar since they put her back in prison more than a month prior. So, with the $25.00 that Mamá Fefita brought him each week to buy food, he began paying the guard to let him spend the day in Víctor's cell, from which he could see Mami from afar. The youngest cellmates took turns standing watch at the window to see when they brought the women out to the patio, which they did that very first day. Víctor Núñez couldn't hide his emotions when he recalled that first time that Papi climbed up to the window and called out, "Minerva!" Immediately, they heard Mami shout out in reply, "Manolo!" The guards allowed them to speak for a minute or so before taking her away. Lowering himself down from the window's iron bars, my father burst out weeping. I asked don Víctor if he recalled what they said during that minute. "Once they started talking with one another, we lowered ourselves from the bars, trying to give them a bit of privacy."

I believe that this is the incident to which Papi refers in one of his letters when he tells Mami how moved he was by the gesture that she sent him from a distance. Having felt up close the strength of this man who had endured the most horrific torture and taunting without bending, I tremble with consternation before the image that I glimpse through the sheer curtain of another's memory: my father, overcome by grief and his inability to get Mami out of there, to save her from that nightmare.

The following is don Víctor's description of my father's personality and of the role he played in prison:

> From the moment he arrived at the prison, even for those of us who didn't know him and didn't have any idea who he was, Manolo became the leader, the undisputable head of all of us anti-Trujillo fighters. He won us over with his simplicity and wise prudence, with his advice and with his ability to continue organizing the resistance on the outside. He had us all reading and studying. When they released me on July 14, 1960, he gave me assignments to carry out. It was impossible to do them because we were under constant surveillance. In fact, one day when Ildefonso Güemez Naut and I tried to go to the movies, a calié stopped us

from entering and sent us back home, asking us what we were thinking, that we had no right to those kinds of activities.

My mother, on the other hand, suffered for everyone: for her imprisoned husband, brothers-in-law and comrades; for those who had been disappeared and for those who had been executed; for her family suffering punishment and for everything she sensed in her premonitions. But more than anything, above all, for us, her two small children. She expresses this in the few, brief letters that she sent home. She avoided writing them for fear of reaching the end and having to ask about us. She embroidered a gown for her baby Manolito. With her eyes practically closed, she sculpted the bust of a little girl as if her Minou were there posing for her, alive and etched in her memory, a memory that couldn't—that absolutely refused—to be beaten down by the fateful plan.

When my mother and her comrades were released, contrary to what her instinct for survival must have deemed urgent, she ignored advice to save her own life by seeking asylum in an embassy. By remaining in the country and continuing her militant activism, contrary to the advice of those who wanted her to stay alive, Mami gave political witness and lived by example. In a way, I see in my mother's demonstration of courage, political conscience, and resistance the same contradiction that José Martí expresses with such beauty and pain in the prologue to *Ismaelillo:* "Son, frightened by everything, I seek refuge in you. I have faith in the betterment of mankind, in life to come, in the merit of virtue, and in you."[7] Paradoxically, her determination found its strength in what she always considered part of a broader concept of freedom, justice, and the future: in the deepest and most selfless love—that of her children—and in continuing to support spiritually and materially the only man she ever loved, my father. When her childhood friend, Tobías Emilio (Larry) Cabral, who had been exiled in the United States since 1950, suggested that she seek asylum in the Venezuelan or Argentine embassy, her reply makes her position very clear: "L. is absolutely right, but I run the risk of terrible reprisal. My children can live with my death, but I cannot live with theirs. M."

My mother, who always seemed to be the more disorganized one when it came to saving these chronicles of her love and desires, had a deeper awareness when it came to their correspondence in prison. Or maybe it was simply that after having found herself so nourished by Papi's letters during her incarceration, she learned to cherish them as if they were written on my father's

---

7   Book of poetry by the late nineteenth-century Cuban writer and revolutionary, José Martí. (t.n.)

bruised hands, on my father's beaten chest, on my father's burned arms and broken back . . . on his mouth, repeatedly degraded by the murderers' blows. In spite of my father's recommendations that she destroy his letters, she found the strength to defiantly hide them, God knows how, fully aware that if the guards spotted them, the punishment would be greater misery, more grief, further isolation in solitary confinement, deeper sorrow. And so, when she left prison, she carried with her these testimonies captured on fragments of dirty paper, on cigarette wrappers, and in the margins of instruction leaflets for medications. She left behind a clover that she had chiseled in the wall of one of the cells.

This is why the only remaining letters from their correspondence in prison are those that Papi sent Mami. Only one of the letters that Mami sent Papi remains. Full of clues that help us understand her, it is a treasure for the brevity with which her wounded words—harmed but not destroyed—are woven together. In my archaeological search for this correspondence, that letter appeared among the papers that remained in the home of my brother Nelson.

I also include in this chapter two other letters that Mami sent to Mamá Chea and to my aunts Patria and Dedé. Reading between the lines, we gain a more complete vision of those days, of that horrific space. Something that my father mentions and that was later confirmed by Alfredo Parra Beato and Miguel Feris Iglesias, among others, is that when the caliés caught Papi with one of Mami's letters, they put him in solitary confinement for several days. From that point on, he must have destroyed the other letters for security reasons, for both their sakes. As I said, rebellious Minerva ignored his recommendation and kept them. All the letters are from La Victoria.

The other two notes that I've included—from Puro Petit and from Jorge Tejada—have every right to their place in this book. My own mother gave them that right by saving them alongside Papi's letters, and they were written to calm her when Papi was isolated as punishment for having been caught with her correspondence.

According to Mamá Dedé, when she left prison for the last time, my mother smuggled the letters out in her undergarments. I found them in the mid-eighties, hidden in a discreet little pocket of an evening purse. Since none of them are dated, I've transcribed them in the order in which I found them.

Papi was imprisoned from January 13, 1960, until July 26, 1961. Mami and Aunt Teté were arrested and released on two occasions. On August 9, after having twice endured the dungeons, after two bogus trials and two sentences, they were released once more. We now know that the decision to release them from La Victoria and keep them under house arrest was part of the macabre plan directly orchestrated by Trujillo to eliminate them. The plan was realized on November 25, 1960, when they were murdered together with Nina Patria and Rufino de la Cruz.

From Manolo to Minerva. Written on half a page from a little notebook.

My Love,

You are not alone; my heart and all my thoughts are with you.

I send you this delightful book to help pass the time. May you feel all the infinite beauty that I send along with it, like an impassioned homage of my affection. Regards to Mery and your companions. We will be together soon.

Kisses,
Manolo

From Minerva to Manolo. Written on the back of an instruction leaflet for dental medication.

Love,

Don't feel sad. We're all right and are close to all of you. Remember: they may be able to separate our bodies, but not our spirits. We endured fairly well the 11 days in La 40. How are you? I'm so anxious to hear from you! How is our family? Our hearts break for all of them. However, we must numb all those thorns that are piercing our hearts. What have you heard about our children? Send them a thousand kisses . . . I don't think they're going to allow us to have visitors tomorrow. If that's the case, ask Patria if she brought me appropriate clothes for the hearing.[8] If not, ask her to go to the capital and buy me the dress I wanted with the little black squares and elbow-length sleeves, and some shoes, size 7 1/2. Tell her to leave them with Dulce or with anyone else who brings the meals so that they can give them to the sergeant.

---

8   At first, they were sentenced in the Criminal Court to 30 years for "conspiring against the security of the Dominican State," a sentence that on May 23 was reduced to five years. After the subsequent appeal, to which Minerva refers in this letter, and which took place on June 28, 1960, it was reduced to three years.

The arrest warrant was from April 6, we were interrogated on the 18th, and the preliminary hearing was on May 23. Nothing new. Remember that I was anticipating this because people were saying that they were thinking of arresting all the women again. I don't know whether the three of us are the only ones they arrested, but don't worry.

I adore you always,
Your Wife

On the back, in the spaces between the instructions, it reads:

Regards from MT

Hugs for everyone, SINA.

From Manolo to Minerva. Written on a torn, dirty piece of notebook paper.

My Darling,

A quick note to send you this pencil so that you can write to us. I wrote to you this morning and sent you a deck of cards to help you ladies pass the time. We're all right.

A thousand kisses,
M. Tavárez.

From Manolo to Minerva. On three little pieces of paper from a cigarette box.

My Love,

Yesterday I sent you a pencil so that you could write to me more regularly. I hope you've received it, as well as everything else we've sent you all. Let me know if you've received it. Today I'll send Mery a mosquito net, mine, as we've learned that she needs one. Tell me everything that you need, my angel. Don't refrain from telling me, thinking that you're keeping me from worrying. On the contrary, I prefer being kept well-informed rather than this uncertainty.

Tell me whether or not you are receiving meals. On Thursday, Patria and Dedé arranged for you two to receive them immediately. I've tried to send you food from Flaco's[9] kitchen, but it has been impossible. He's with me in my new cell along the same corridor where we were before. There are fewer of us now. We have beds and better food. You know how diligent Flaco is. Fortunately, he and everyone else are healthy.

You need not worry about me; I am all right, as are Leandro and Pedrito and our families. I asked the girls to bring us new photos of the children, both for you and for me. As soon as they arrive, I'll send them to you.

I'm going to try to send you something to read, among other things *Fabiola*[10] but under the condition that you keep it to yourselves. Hear me, my little demon? On Thursday Niño and Dulce were finally able to see each other during visitations. What joy and what pain! She told me to send you ladies her regards.

Thinking back on your words, we should numb all those thorns piercing our hearts, that is, with Machado[11]: "But that's not it—pain, I know you better: you are the longing for the happy days, the loneliness that fills the somber heart, that haunts the ship unfoundering and unstarred."[12] "You will go with me while my body projects a shadow, and while sand clings to my sandal."[13] What a beautiful and tender soul he has! That titan of intimism!

Regards to Mery and Sina, everyone here sends greetings and affection. For you, my angel, all my love,

Your Manolo

---

9 Nickname meaning "Skinny Guy." (t.n.)
10 According to José Israel Cuello, this is a reference to the novel *Fabiola; or the Church of the Catacombs,* by the Cardinal Nicholas Patrick Stephen Wiseman (1802–1865), which circulated among the prisoners and was very popular among them because they drew parallels between the persecution against the early Christians and their own struggle.
11 Antonio Machado (1875–1939) was one of Minerva's favorite poets. The first verses are from the poem "Es una tarde cenicienta y mustia…" / "This Withered, Ashen Afternoon," and the second set is from the poem "XXIX, Arde en tus ojos un misterio, virgen" / "A Mystery Burns within Your Eyes, Elusive Virgin," from his book *Soledades, galerías y otros poemas / Solitude, Galleries and Other Poems.*
12 Translation by Alan S. Trueblood, *Antonio Machado: Selected Poems,* 97. (t.n.)
13 Translation by Alice Jane McVan, reprinted in Bernard Sesé, 428. (t.n.)

From Manolo to Minerva. Written on half a sheet of notebook paper and on paper from a small cigarette box.

My Love,

How it fills my heart to know and feel that you are mine without reservations! That's what I said when I went out to the patio. I stood in front of the door for a long time in hopes of seeing you. Leandro said it was possible or that you two might see us. If so, and given that they take us outside every day for sunlight, maybe one day it will happen. I think I've become too romantic. Sometimes I'm afraid of being inappropriate considering the circumstances.

I sent you *Fabiola* and one *Selections*. I hope that you've received them. Again, I strongly advise against circulating them. As soon as you girls finish reading it, send it to me. Another thing: tear up everything I write you. Sometimes there are surprise inspections and they could catch us. The consequences are solitary confinement, with which you're already familiar, and loss of visitation rights, which we must avoid at all costs, more so for our family's sake than for our own . . . From time to time I'm overcome with worry thinking about this because I know you and how careless you are . . . Forgive me, *bien mío*, that I'm weighing you down with this sermon, but I have no choice. I need to take care of you, and I know that you need it too. Tell Mery that I'll try to send her Rodó,[14] part of it, because a comrade took the other part with him to another wing. I'm very grateful to all the comrades who have treated you both so well. Please express to them my gratitude. I'd like you to tell me everything that you two need and that you update me on the situation with the food or kitchen. I'm sure they'll let you do it since otherwise you'll not[15] be in communication with the outside. It seems that this is what they've been

---

14 Reference to *Ariel* by the Uruguayan politician and modernist writer José Enrique Rodó (1871–1917). They divided books into sections so they could read them and pass them back and forth between one cell and another.

15 Although it seems illogical given the context, the word "not" does appear in the original letter. Minou Tavárez agrees that this seems to have been Manolo's error and that the most logical understanding is this: that Manolo is quite sure that the prison guards will allow Minerva, María Teresa, and Sina (Tomasina) to set up their own space for cooking in their cell because that would eliminate the need for them to be in contact with the outside. Interview with Minou Tavárez Mirabal, Jan. 31, 2019. (t.n.)

trying to avoid. Yes, they canceled it since allowing the meal delivery meant publicly recognizing that you ladies were here . . . and even though everyone knows it, they make like they know nothing. These measures are typical of the prevailing "penal" system here. This is the first phase of incarceration. We have all gone through it. So don't worry thinking that these are special measures; nothing of the sort, my love, you can rest assured and be hopeful that we'll be together soon. I'm sending you these two magazines. They contain some very interesting articles, even though anything one reads here seems interesting. We're that bored.

Regards to Mery, my dear little sister, and to Sina. And to you, all of your husband's adoration.

---

*From Minerva and María Teresa to their family.
Written on a half sheet of paper.*

My Dear Loved Ones,

We were hoping to see you today. Now that seems impossible. Don't worry, though, we're all right. The sergeant told me that he had told Patria to file a request so that they'll allow us to see one another. I hope she hasn't done it. We don't want you to file a request of any kind. Sina says the same to her mother.

I tried to buy plaster but wasn't able. Send me a few pounds of it, not a lot; I don't want these people to be alarmed. Otherwise, send me some material to make an embroidered dress for Minou, the measurements, and some small, well-camouflaged scissors, but right away, I need something to do.

Send us the thermos and cigarettes, and tell the lady who prepares the meals to send us salad every day. As for the rest of it, whatever you want.

María Teresa also wants you to send her something to sew. In here we need that as much as food.

I know that my children are as well-cared-for, as if they were with me, but I miss them so immensely. You'll have to forgive me for not writing more right now. I simply cannot do it. It is the only thing that fills me with despair.

> To everyone, everyone, my affection and kisses,
> Mine

On the other side of the paper was María Teresa's note:

Dear Patria,

This is for you and everyone there, to tell you that I'm better now, thank God. Tell Mamá not to worry about me. It was laryngitis that I had, and now I'm totally healthy.

How is my Jacqueline? I hope that she's plump and learning a lot. I miss her immensely. We've received everything that you all have sent. Send me the red fabric that I bought in La Vega to make Jacqueline some little pants and send me the little green pants that were Pilin's, then Manolito's, and now hers for the size, since it's foreign. Also send red thread and if possible my scissors, the little ones that cut well. Regards to Antonia, Reyna, Ida, Margarita, Pedro, Uncle, Jaimito, Nelson and everyone who asks about us.

May you, Mamá, and Dedé feel the deep affection of your daughter and sister, who has not forgotten you and who loves you very much,

MT

Written by Minerva on a half sheet of paper. Signed "M and M," Minerva and María Teresa.

Dear Mamá, Patria, Dedé,

If only this note could reach you to let you know that we're all right, thank God. We're just sad thinking about your suffering and about our children, though we know that they are well-cared-for. Patria, don't lose hope for any reason; nothing human is eternal. There's never a moment when we don't think of you. We're happy that you finally have Nelson back with you.[16] We suppose the children are behaving themselves. You all say that they behave better when I'm not around. Sometimes I wonder if Minou realizes. Tell Antonia that I can imagine her telling me that Manolito calls for me. Take care of them for me, as always.

Give my best to her, Ida and Reina. Regards to Uncle and Jaimito and everyone else who is close to us. Write us a letter between the two layers of the box of oranges, not on a piece of cardboard like we used to, but

---

16 Nelson, Patria's eldest son, was imprisoned on February 1, 1960, before his 18th birthday. He was released on May 22, 1960.

rather lifting up the corner of one of the layers and going far inside. We dismantle everything you send from the outside. It has to be absolutely perfect, as you know how to do. We saw Noris that Thursday, and Toña. We were so excited! On Thursday we saw the baby, but from so far away!

Mary wrote a list of what you sent us. The meal delivery had its glitches but finally arrived yesterday. It seems that the matter is finally resolved. Sometimes we have the feeling that Mamá has been ill. Tell us how you all are. Again, don't worry; good people appear in all kinds of places and, anyway, we all have to carry our crosses. Thanks to God for giving us the courage to carry them.

Sending many, many hugs and kisses to everyone, whom we don't forget even for a moment,

M and M.

From Manolo to Minerva, written on four little papers from small cigarette boxes.

My Love,

I've felt calmer since receiving your letter. Now we know that you two are in good health and that for the time being you have enough to keep you from dying of hunger or of cold and loneliness and to endure with fortitude the cruel rigor that these circumstances have brought us.

I am with you, my angel. In each moment in time, my heart, my thoughts are more yours than mine. Nothing and no one can separate us because above all the iron bars, our souls are welded together in the sublimity of all our ideals . . . Today is Thursday, visitation day, and even though it is no longer what it was for me before, when you were there, when after a long week of waiting, I could look forward to the thrill of holding you in my arms, I'm not really sad because in spite of everything, I've been able to express my love to you, send you that book by Machado—whom you like so much—and the photo of our children. I'm feeling more sappy than what the dedication would lead you to believe, but, *bien mío,* I mean every word. I'm so very proud of my wife! What a shame that our children can't understand it yet! Mamy, wonderful news: they just brought Parra. We're so thrilled! Flaco and I were just talking about him. I set this letter aside to go to visitation. Dedé, Patria, Mamá and Edda came. Everyone is all right. They brought packages for you, and from what I learned, they'll deliver them to you today. Besides that, our children are doing quite well; don't worry about anything. I'll get you everything you've asked me to obtain.

I'm writing this in a rush because they're waiting for me so they can take it to you.

Sending you all my love.
Your husband, M.

P.S. Give my best to Mery and Sina. Jacqueline is on vacation at Dedé's.

From Manolo to Minerva. Written on a little cigarette wrapper.

My Love,

I'm giving the messenger two (2) boxes of cigarettes for you. I received your note yesterday. I don't know why you've become so laconic or maybe it's just the immensity of how much I need you.

Give my best to Sina and Mery. I'll write them today or tomorrow. I haven't done it yet because of how difficult it sometimes is to send them. Regards to all your other companions.

And for you, all of your husband's affection.

From Manolo to Minerva. The reference to the first pardon suggests it was written in early July. Written in pencil on half a sheet of notebook paper.

My Beloved Wife,

Though it may seem paradoxical, never before have I been as intimately close to you as I have in these last weeks. The pain and suffering have magnified our love. Today I can say with greater certainty and resolve that nothing and no one will ever manage to separate us. Therefore, *bien mío*, may it be entirely impossible that you're ever alone even for a moment of your life, which is mine. I'm with you, with all of you, we all are. There's so much I want to say to you! It's so hard to keep it inside!

Our separation or isolation is relative, and I can almost assure you that it will be brief. We will be together soon. You ladies are aware of the massive number of pardons that are being granted. To this date there have been more than three hundred political prisoners pardoned. We have reason to hope. Rumor has it that on the 11th and the 22nd of this month they will release two large groups. Things are looking good. In the meantime, have the patience and courage to keep your composure and your chin up as you endure the time we have left behind these horrendous walls and iron bars. Always remember Haydee S.,[17] remember the differences in means. For many reasons, prudence is imperative. Do you understand me? Let it guide all your actions and those of the other girls under the present circumstances. More intelligence than emotion! Dignity, prudence and intelligence! Discipline! Do you understand me? These must direct your conduct and that of the other girls. All the orientation you need to move forward through this crossroads of our destinies lies in a thorough understanding of these concepts.

The meal delivery situation worries me. If you don't get it resolved, try to get the sergeant or the sergeant major to buy you portable stoves, coal and oil, and cook for yourselves. They'll almost certainly agree to this. We'll take care of sending you all the necessary ingredients.

Tell me, my love, without hiding from me anything that you need. Some days ago, we sent you all $15.00 in cash, and a giant pillowcase full of cans, crackers and sweets. Yesterday I sent you two (2) boxes of cigarettes. I want you to always tell me what you've received from us to assure that nothing is lost.

Regards to Mery and Sina.
For you, all the adoration and respect of your husband.

From Manolo to Minerva. On wrinkled stationery, in pencil, and ending with illegible words.

Beloved Mamy,

I'm sure you've thought that I barely write you, and essentially, it's true. But if I don't write more often it's because after that incident (the letters they discovered), it's been more difficult for me. Never, *bien mío,* for lack of desire. You must sense that. Besides, I'm never satisfied with my letters since I'm unable to fully capture—to externalize—all my feelings, my thoughts. For example, how can I articulate the immense tenderness that you stirred in my soul with that delightful and loving embrace that you

---

17 Haydee Santamaría, Cuban revolutionary and guerrilla fighter, whose courage in the face of cruel torture in Cuban prisons following her participation in the assault on the Moncada Garrison was already legendary.

sent from afar and that had me dreaming all night . . . I don't know how to express that in writing. I'm unable to convey to you in the way that I want this raging river of feelings, longings and feverish desires. In a word, reveal myself, open myself up so that, reading these lines, you can experience the immense volcano that shakes me from within. I love you, I want you, I miss you so badly that sometimes I don't know how I can stand this torment of not having you with me . . . How unjust! How evil! Oh, the indignation that fills me after everything they've done to us!

I don't know how I would have been able to endure all this had I not gained complete control over my temperament. At least for everyone's sake, all these sacrifices haven't been in vain. But I can't help it (and it's only human), sometimes my passions get the best of me, especially rage and hate, and my calmness, my composure, falls crashing to the floor, shattering into a million pieces. After venting a little, it passes, and I'm back at the helm, once again the captain of my own destiny. In Chinese Buddhist philosophy there is the idea that: "All the wisdom of life can be condensed into knowing how to wait." This brief philosophical saying has taught me so much, my love. Whenever I become impatient, I remind myself of Lao Peng, the extraordinary character in *A Leaf in the Storm*.[18] Memories! I've read it again in here. What a human, moving, and beautiful book in spite of the misery, pain and destruction that pervade the setting in which it unfolds. The author's descriptive prowess and his deep understanding of the human heart are astonishingly genius. How masterfully developed his characters are, above all Malin, the poor, beautiful abandoned girl who unwittingly goes on giving of her body in an attempt to attain an honorable heart, a soul filled with love in whom she can take refuge, be saved from the cruel destiny that her proletarian status holds for her. Finally, after a series of trials, Lao Peng appears with his moral, intellectual and religious strength, and Malin manages to find herself. For the first time in her life, she has the chance to live her own life, to fully but in a heart-wrenching way attain self-realization. And then—What a beautiful miracle!—she becomes Tanni, a poem! What a romantic name for such a good woman. You are my Tanni, *dueña mía*,[19] and I'll be whatever you want, won't I? . . . I'm going to try to send you

---

18 Perhaps the most famous novel by the Chinese writer Lin Yutang (1895–1976). Papi had gifted this book to Mamá Dedé, telling her that it was a homage to courage, loyalty, and friendship, and he asked her to bring it to him in prison.

19 Literally "my owner," a term of endearment expressing total surrender. (t.n.)

something to read, here we have quite a bit. Unfortunately, they are large bound volumes, and they're hard to send because the carriers are rather cautious. But I'll try to send you everything pocket-sized, like *The Poem of the Cid*,[20] for example. I haven't read it, but I know you'll like it. I'll try to send the rest in sections, but I have to wait until everyone here finishes reading them. There's another one of Lin Yu Tang's works, *My Country and My People,* outstanding, like everything that man wrote before he sold his pen and became a despicable mercenary. We also have *Nine Dramas* by Eugene O'Neill. I'll try to send you all of it. Since the last group left on Thursday, among them Paquín, Lisandro Macarrulla, Cayeyo, Rodrigote, and Charlie Bogaert, our cells and these wings are almost empty. Between our cell and Pedrito's, which is across from us, there are barely 15 of us in all. We're lonelier but calmer. All the guys say hi. Tell our sister Sina that Paquín expressly ordered me to say hi to her on his behalf. To her and Mery I send a big, warm hug, and to you, Chiqui, all the good things that we have _____ although it may not be much _____ and all the love that _____ which, on the other hand, is great.

Yours

P.S. Our dear friend Parra, who is across from us, always asks me to tell you all hello. V.

From Jorge Tejada to Minerva. On a little piece of paper from a cigarette box.

My Dear Friend and Sister Minerva,

The guys haven't returned yet, but hopefully they'll be back by Thursday.

Yesterday I learned that you were all well, but if you need anything, I don't think I need to tell you that I'm here. You can come to me just as if I were Manolo.

How are Sina and María Teresa? Give them a hug for me.

Your brother,
Jorge Tejada

14 of June, 1960

---

20   Castilian epic poem *Cantar del Mío Cid,* of unknown authorship.

From Puro Petit Tavárez to Minerva. On a little piece of paper from a cigarette box.

Cousin,

Just a few lines to let you know that the guys are all fine. We are too. We're very thankful that everyone is physically and spiritually strong.

Hugs to everyone, and a very special one for the great Sina.

Your cousin,
(Puro)

From Manolo to Minerva. In pencil, on three little papers from cigarette boxes.

Beloved Mamy,

It's about five o'clock in the morning on another dreary, monotonous day. For the prisoner, each day is dreadfully like the last. However, today the morning struck me as beautiful, and here I am writing to you. My soul in search of yours. I'm reminded of a few verses from the little poem I wrote for you while you were a student living at the convent on Independence Avenue. Among other things, it said, "Your soul must be the twin of my soul, and your mouth a wild strawberry in the exquisite garden of my daydreams. How delightful it would be to know how to be a gardener!"

Today I tell you, my love, that the miracle has already occurred: our souls have become so intertwined that my soul is no longer mine, but ours. Love and the morning hours have me daydreaming. Isn't your husband a sappy romantic? It's your fault for having made yourself so deserving of being loved by me, by me alone . . . Oh, how jealous I'd become if another man tried! . . .

If only we had Cantinflas![21] This mail has become very economical. At least we saw each other sometimes in that television screen, but they want to take even that away from us. It's useless to try and separate us, to fail to understand that what God has made in his greatest moments of creative inspiration, man cannot ineptly destroy . . . Though he sadly stand in the way of it.

---

21 Stage name of Mario Moreno (1911–1993), an iconic comedian and actor of Mexico's Golden Age of cinema. (t.n.)

Before closing, I want to know what you ladies need. Whatever you need, send a list here. Allow me the pleasure of grappling to resolve your problems. Some days ago, I sent you all a small Palmolive soap with one of the regulars, and yesterday two more of the same kind, but bigger and with the official carrier. Thank you for the chickens and everything else. Leandro took charge of cooking it up just right, but the poor thing. Our dear friend Parra was the one who killed it. He grabbed it by the neck and electrocuted it. Remember how, along with other nicknames I had for him, I used to call him "Wired?" In here we joke around with him a lot and now after the chicken incident we've even written a song for our ensemble—our musical group—titled "Parra and the Chicken." When we tease him about it, he imitates a little palmchat[22] in springtime. Well you know him, so just picture it. Sometimes I think of how lucky I am to be with one of the people—perhaps *the* person—who most appreciates my strange sense of humor and who, by the way, just now made me laugh. He was darting across his cell, from the bed to the kitchen, and when I called out to him to say hi, he halted on one foot, lifted the other, and with lightning speed realized that I was writing to you. Then with gestures (waving his hand in your direction) told me to say hi to you all. And now there he goes without having said a word. Ah, my dear friend is one of a kind, irreplaceable. Before closing I want to recommend to you ladies that if you feel "well nourished," begin an exercise regimen. It will do you a lot of good. Warmest regards to my sisters, and to you I send all the very little that I am.

Yours,
Manolo

P.S. Tell Sina that I'll wear the hat outside to remind her of Paquín. V.

From Manolo to Minerva. On a single sheet of beat-up notebook paper with some parts rendered illegible.

Beloved Mamy,

Just a few lines in a rush since the pencil broke and I just now got hold of another one on loan from the cell across from us. Thank you for the

---

22   "*Cigüita*" is the diminutive of *cigua palmera* (palmchat), whose scientific name is *Dulus dominicus*. Native to the island, this is the national bird of the Dominican Republic.

succulent *sancocho*[23] that you ladies sent us. I swear it is the best one I've ever eaten, and I'm not the only one who says that; my companions say the same. You don't want to know the stir it created over here; everyone wanted some, but the demand was greater than what we could offer them. As a result, we've decided to buy some chickens and send you the supplies and all the other ingredients for you to make us another one. Our compliments to the chefs.

It was quite a scene today at the entrance. I've never enjoyed so much time and freedom for us to see one another. I'm happy. I have a lot of material to dream about and to revive our memories. How often I've longed for those days long ago in our humble home in Montecristi! We weren't in a rush, you were always near me, especially recently, rather, I was much closer to you, in the living room, in the garden, in the car, in the nighttime... Nearby, everywhere. We've certainly shared some very beautiful moments. And we'll share even better ones in the future... Oh, what hopes I have! I know that the struggle will be arduous and demanding but even so I'm yearning for it with such desire. How beautiful is this ideal of justice, freedom and peace! Anyway, I believe that soon we'll have a chance to talk and think...

Yesterday I wracked my brain wondering if part of your last letter got lost since it appeared unfinished. Regarding T.C., I'm sure it has to do with [his/her][24] own assets, like you said. Nobody else has suggested it to you? In any event, I don't think it's necessary to do it, and without that you'll be out of here, where we need to be. There are unconfirmed rumors that there is a general amnesty in the works for political prisoners. _____.

Elsa Justo was here yesterday. _____ but she wasn't able to see you. She asked me about you and told me to pass along her affection. Jaime too. I gave him instructions to sell everything that we discussed. What _____ decision with which I suppose Dedé will soon move forward because we're going to need that imminent _____. Everyone at home is in good health, _____ Mamá, Papá, Eduardo and everyone else send all of you their regards. If they don't come, it's because they can't. _____ with him, almost

---

23 Traditional Dominican stew made of meats, vegetables, and tubers. (t.n.)
24 Though T. C. may refer to Tomasina Cabral, that is uncertain, as is the gender of the individual being referenced. (t.n.)

on the floor, but [s]he went with her on an excursion to El Morro, your Morro[25] . . . My love.

Sending my best to your sisters, and to you, all my love. Tonight.

P.S. I'm sending a blank sheet of paper so you can reply to me, naturally it will be only one more page in the newspaper that I hope to receive from you. Kisses, many kisses.

From Manolo to Minerva. On a sheet of paper ripped from a notebook. It is the last of the letters that Minerva smuggled out of prison.

Beloved Mamy,

How often I've thought about the last night we spent together, full of premonitions, as you so accurately say! I've asked myself a thousand times if I shouldn't have done more to avoid being apprehended. It never occurred to me at the time that you could run the same risks. Had I considered that possibility, I assure you that perhaps we'd be far away from here. But I had too much faith in the courage and conscience of the comrades who preceded me; I believed they would follow through with what they had so often promised: remain silent even in the face of death. What an excruciating experience! My God! When I learned of your arrest and that of your companions, I wanted to die. I fervently begged God for it. That would have been easier than enduring the long, cruel and horrible moral torture that this has been for me. I don't know how I didn't lose my mind; there were times when I thought I'd go crazy. Death would have been liberation, but also cowardice. But who can possibly consider themselves morally and spiritually prepared for such trauma, such suffering? The thought that they would do the same to you ladies, give you the same treatment, was such a devastating blow for any man, especially when it comes to his wife and sisters . . . Only God knows how I've suffered. Oh! Those days and these long months that you've been in here are no small matter . . . But let's talk about something else, something more pleasant, less painful, something that brings us hope . . . and as it is, there are reasons to be hopeful. Forgive me for having shared that with you, but this experience forces us to think about everything. Besides, my beloved, you once told me and have always told me that you wanted to

---

25 Minerva came to love the mountain-hemmed beach of El Morro while she was living in Montecristi as a newlywed. (t.n.)

share in everything with me: my worries, my dreams, my thoughts and my sorrows. And I was thinking about all that and was saddened. But that is in the past, my love. I'm going to share with you what I'm thinking about now, what I'm desiring, dreaming: sleeping in your arms again, on your beautiful chest, drunk with the fresh scent of your body, the two of us intertwined in an intimate, tender, loving embrace. How I desire to be with you, *vida mía!* How many dreams! How beautiful our new life is going to be! Together with you. It seems that we'll be in here until the 16th. At least for those who get out, in the event that they leave us here. We must be prepared for all possible outcomes, even though all indicators suggest that we'll all be released. In regard to what you've told me about Sina, I had no idea that things had advanced that much. Tell me more, I'd love it if a connection[26] came out of this. They are two good candidates. It's her choice, although after what you told me, I wonder about her inclinations. My deepest affection to her and Mery. Hopefully we can get the money. We'll need it. Yes, you can imagine what for. Tell Sina, if you think it's all right. Mery's situation has been resolved.

Sending all my love. Yours,
Manolo

---

26 Sina Cabral had spoken with Minerva about her plan to seek asylum if they were released, which she, in fact, did. Three days after leaving prison, on August 12, 1960, she was granted asylum in the Argentine Embassy. This comment might refer to the notion that she could serve as a tie to organizations in exile, or it could be a light-hearted reference to a possible relationship with Paquín Noriega, to which various letters allude.

IV
The Final Letter

1960–1963

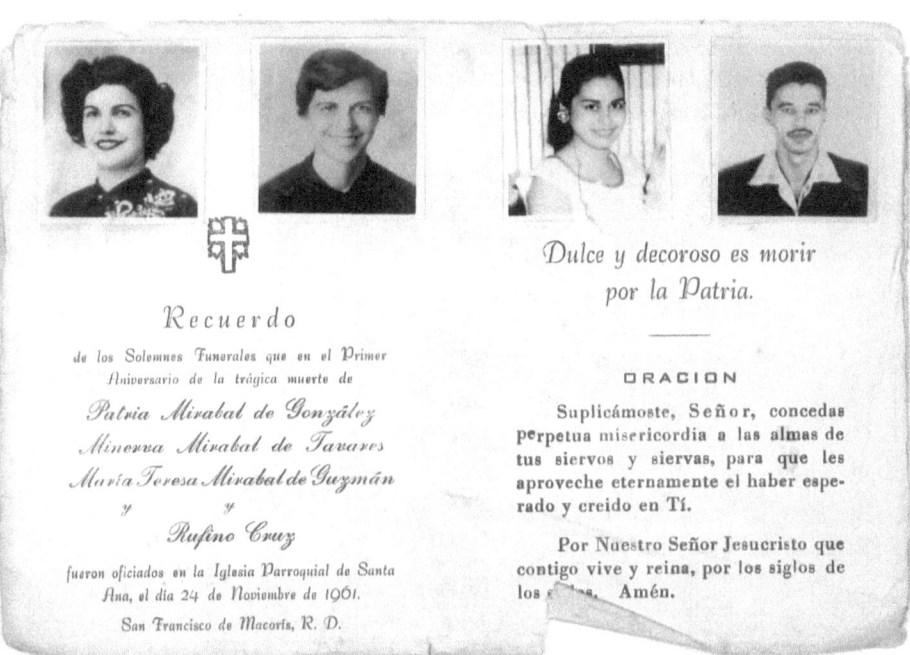

Figure 4.1. Memorial card from the Mass celebrated in San Francisco de Macorís on November 24, 1961, the first anniversary of the deaths of Patria, Minerva, and María Teresa Mirabal and Rufino de la Cruz. Courtesy of the Fundación Hermanas Mirabal.

Figure 4.2. The widowers of the Mirabal Sisters, Pedro González, Leandro Guzmán, and Manolo Tavárez, photographed in prison when they were presented to the commission of the Organization of American States that visited the country in June 1960. Courtesy of the Fundación Hermanas Mirabal.

Figure 4.3. Manolo and Minou on the day of her First Holy Communion in August, 1961. Courtesy of the Fundación Hermanas Mirabal.

Figure 4.4. Manolo addressing a crowd as leader of the 14 of June Political Party. Courtesy of Milvio Pérez.

Figure 4.5. Noris González Mirabal, Manolo, doña Chea, Jaime David Fernández Mirabal, Manolito, Jacqueline Guzmán Mirabal, and Raúl González Mirabal at the house in Conuco. Courtesy of the Fundación Hermanas Mirabal.

LIFE

> And so this letter ends
> without any sadness:
> my feet are firm upon the earth,
> my hand writes this letter on the road,
> and in the midst of life I shall be
> always
> beside the friend, facing the enemy,
> with your name on my lips
> and a kiss that never
> broke away from yours.[1]

All along this journey back to my parents through the letters they exchanged, I've felt that this book is not the place to retell the events that have most deeply hurt those of us who survive them. These events are too well-known, not only in our history, but in the world's. And in a way, the legacy of their lives, the memories of those of us who lived those events chronicled in books, articles, documentaries, and films over the past five decades exonerate me from detailing once again the ghastly murders of my parents and aunts. This is why last year, when I was invited to say a few words at the unveiling of the monument marking the spot where the Butterflies and Rufino de la Cruz were intercepted and murdered, I said, standing on the Marapicá Bridge, that my only wish was for that place to be erased from the face of the Earth. It's also what I felt as I made my way up to the place where my father was slain in the steep mountains of Quisqueya.

In the same spirit of love embodied by this correspondence, I prefer to contemplate a borrowed memory of the last time they saw each other in the prison in Puerto Plata. Mami, looking lovely, dressed up to visit him, perfumed and serene, and Papi eager to hold her, to squeeze her hands in his and to advise her to be prudent, knowing that it went against her profoundly indomitable nature. There they talked about a future that they believed they would build together and that, in effect, they would, though they would never know it.

In the early morning hours of that tragic night, Papi and Uncle Leandro were transferred to La 40 and isolated in a remote cell with Uncle Pedrito. On November 27, a supposed common criminal, whom they immediately

---

1 Neruda, "Letter on the Road," trans. Donald Devenish Walsh, p. 149. (t.n.)

identified as a calié, was put in their cell with them. He was there to observe their reactions when the henchmen passed through the iron bars a newspaper clipping from that day's *El Caribe*. It reported that the three sisters and their driver had died in an "accident." News of a death is never easy to believe. At first, it's hard to understand how someone who just recently was looking at us, speaking to us, touching us, is no longer there, is no longer waiting for us, and will never come for us again. But my father and uncles were denied experiencing that funeral that begins by accepting slowly and with certainty a pain that will last forever. Like someone who sadistically chafes an open wound, the henchmen planted doubt after doubt, weaving a newer, even more macabre plan: sewing in them a terrifying sense of distress.

At first, Papi, Uncle Leandro, and Uncle Pedrito couldn't—or wouldn't—believe it. It wasn't possible. What they had feared so much just simply couldn't be. Trujillo couldn't have gone that far. How paradoxical to think that the three of them fed their hopes by underestimating their executioners' cruelty. Overcome by the constant abuse and torture, they considered the news regarding the deaths of the girls and Rufino de la Cruz to be the latest and most twisted method of torture that their jailers had devised.

What I now understand is that Papi had to relive that experience of receiving the unfathomable news of my mother and aunts' murder. I can't imagine the relentless torment of uncertainty during all that time he spent in the dungeons until after Trujillo's execution, when he was the last one released.

There were no letters for anyone, no hugs, no visits, no replies, no condolences. Our families never heard another word about the widowers left by the girls, by the Mirabal sisters, by the Butterflies. So, in our home we lived through two funerals simultaneously: one knowing, and the other not. We carried Mami and my aunts to the cemetery not knowing if sooner or later we would have to do the same with their husbands. I know because I lived it. It became engraved in my childhood memory that Mamá Chea gave them up for dead as well, unlike Mamá Fefa, who during those long six months went tirelessly searching for them in almost every prison in the country.

Minerva's true funeral came for Manolo when he left prison and arrived at the house in Conuco, only to find her gone. His enormous humanity was shattered on the spot.

As word got around that Manolo was back, I remember that the house and garden filled with people. It turned into a political rally. Papi had to stand on the garden wall and address the crowd of followers. At some later point, he took me by the hand and led me through the hallway where I can still imagine my mother's silhouette advancing toward us. On the small back porch, it was just the two of us alone. He sat me, his little girl, on his lap to tell me everything that had happened during his absence. I saw the marks left by torture on his arms and chest, and I asked him what they were. He replied that they were where his torturers had struck him and put out their cigarettes on his flesh. He spoke to me of my mother, and I cried with him. I was not yet five years old.

Later on, during the years that I lived with him until he left for Las Manaclas, I only found that feeling of peace and intimacy between the two of us when, no matter what time he arrived home to our apartment, he would come to my bed to sing me the songs that he used to sing to Mami and to tell me about her. That's where I came to know the mother given to me as a gift of that immense love that existed between the two of them. Before history could recount her acts of heroism, my father had taken it upon himself to build an altar to Minerva in my soul.

But we would never again know true peace. Papi's galvanized political activism and the whirlwind that was life until 1963 never allowed him a moment's rest. He was always surrounded by more and more people. His friend and fellow party member Miguel Feris Iglesias told me about the time when Papi went to New York on a political mission in November 1961, and he received them there. Constantly surrounded by crowds, Papi asked him if they could escape out the hotel's back door. Finally out in the street, he recalls that Manolo seemed like a child, not exactly impressed by the Manhattan skyscrapers but rather by the chance to finally walk alone. He said to Miguel, "You won't believe this, but from the moment they first put me in prison up until now, I haven't been alone for a second. I haven't had a single moment to think, to enjoy some much-needed silence."

There were a bunch of us living in the apartment that we rented on Rosa Duarte Street. He shared a room with Uncle Leandro and I think sometimes Uncle Eduardo. I used to sleep with Auntie Emma, Auntie Elsa, my cousin Angelita, and I don't recall who else. Aunt Ángela and Uncle Jaime occupied the other bedroom. That apartment wasn't a house but a beehive. People were constantly coming and going. There were always meetings, visits, strategizing, proposals. The only freedom that Manolo knew, that freedom marked by a love that covered him like a blanket, would be forever left behind in the house in Montecristi, the last home he shared with us and with Minerva.

Beginning on November 25, 1960, my parents' story became everyone's history. For me, however, it would become history later on.

In the final days of 1963, I wandered around aimlessly, circling again and again throughout the area surrounding the house in Conuco. Kicking at the cacao leaves, I reached a patch of poppies in the cacao field and dropped to the ground. There I wept for the first time, distraught and without anyone around. I was an orphan.

I used to get up very early in the morning and read at the little green kitchen table where my mother used to do the same. Mamá Chea looked on, fearful and disapproving because of what she saw of Minerva in my affinities and because of all the apprehensions that my passion for reading stirred in her broken heart. Just like Mami, I wasn't much interested in anything beyond whatever book I was reading at the time. But one day, Genaro, one of the workers on the farm, indiscreetly made a comment that would change my life forever. He was talking with Reina, our cook, and in reference to Papi he called him not only by his name. No. He said, " . . . the *difunto* Manolo." I knew by the sound of the word and by the way he'd said it that it couldn't mean anything good, but I didn't know what it meant. So, I went to Mami's library and reached for an enormous dictionary on the top shelf. That's how I learned that my father was dead, that they had hidden it from me, and that in a sense, when I lost him, I lost them both.

Now that I look back, I must have heard Mamá Chea crying out a few days prior, "They killed him too! They killed my son!" But it never occurred to me that she was talking about Papi. Not him. He'd promised before that he'd come back for me, and he did. It was a long time before I came to understand that the snail's shell that he'd sent me with a message from Las Manaclas would be his final letter. And I realized that it wasn't just from him, but from both of them, from both my parents. And that little note wasn't written just for me, but for both his children, for my brother Manolo and me, and for the history of the Dominican people. Papi was able to *write to me tomorrow* because death didn't catch him off guard as it did Mami. When he went off into the hills, he knew without a doubt where he was headed.

That's why the discovery that I made in the dictionary left me feeling betrayed, and I did what many seven-year-olds would do after such a traumatic experience: I locked it up inside. All of it, including the tears, locked up inside for years, mourning in a way that the grieving adults around me barely understood. I think that moment shaped many aspects of my character. And I realize that neither my parents, nor that enormous love that "found territory" in them, nor this research into the love that united them, nor they themselves have anything to do with death, precisely because their greatest legacy was life. Life, that brevity and permanence of what we are and what we continue being, symbolized in two eternal gifts:

Minerva's gift: a prophetic codename: Butterfly. With a life that's fleeting but full of light, in the gardens that contain the world. Allegory of freedom and of perfect flight; woman in our imaginary; winged beam of colorful light.

Manolo's gift: the shell of a mountain snail, symbolizing a home that journeys with us, a refuge, an eternal country. A backpack that marches along with the beautiful mollusk that it protects. A shell filled with a mere eleven words that amount to an immense testament, a final letter that, even so, doesn't end, that is always being written.

Butterfly and Snail are with me. They're with all of us, here where they still speak generously and embrace us warmly with their lives, our lives.

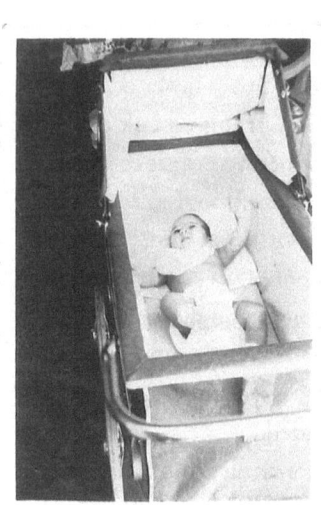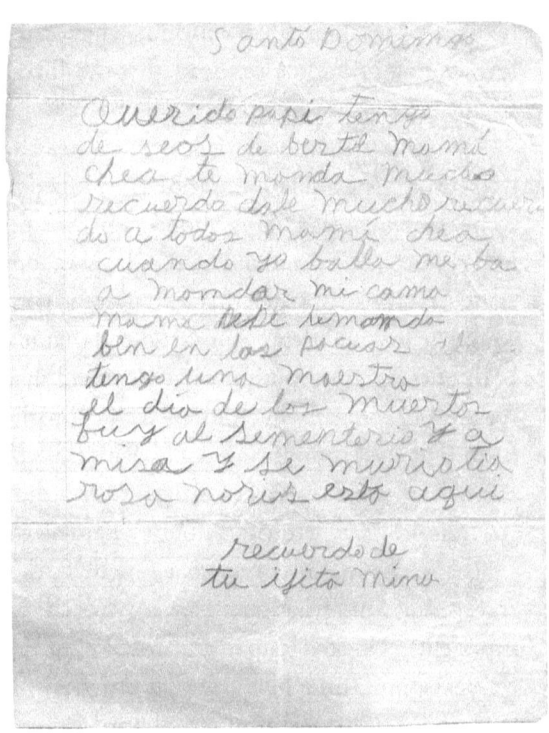

Figure 4.6. Photo of Minou at two months, which Manolo carried with him to Las Manaclas in November 1963. The letter that Minou wrote to her father that same month, just before his death. Courtesy of the Fundación Hermanas Mirabal.

From Minou to Manolo. Although it says Santo Domingo, it was written in Salcedo on November 2, 1963. Papi gave it to Josefina Peynado before going up into the mountains. He had it in his change purse along with a photo of me at two months old. On the photo it says: "Minou, Mte. Cty. (2 meses)" and "1J4" written in pencil.

Santo Domingo

Dear papi

I want to sea you mamá chea sends her best mamá chea wen I go shes going to send my bed
    Mamá Dedé says to Com at Cristmas I hav a teacher on the day of the dead I went to the sematery and to mass and aunt rosa died Noris is here
regards from your little dauter
minu

The Final Letter

From Manolo to Minou. Written on a snail's shell, hand-delivered from the steep, rugged mountains of Quisqueya. Sent about two hours before Manolo was viciously murdered.

12-21-63

To my little Minou, as a memento of a grand experience.
Manolo

Figure 4.7. The letter-snail sent by Manolo to his daughter Minou the day he was assassinated. Courtesy of the Fundación Hermanas Mirabal.

Figure 4.8. Doña Chea Reyes with her daughter Dedé and her nine grandchildren at the Mirabal Sisters House Museum in 1981. *Standing, from left to right*: Raúl González Mirabal, Minou Tavárez Mirabal, Noris González Mirabal, Dedé Mirabal, Manolo Tavárez Mirabal, Nelson González Mirabal, Jaime Enrique (*in back*) and Jimmy Fernández Mirabal; *keeling in front*: Jaime David Fernández Mirabal and Jacqueline Guzmán Mirabal. Courtesy of the Fundación Hermanas Mirabal.

Glossary

The names are listed as they appear in the letters and are arranged in alphabetical order. The names marked with an asterisk were added by the translator.

Acosta (Rafael Acosta)—Manolo's friend, fellow attorney, and witness at Manolo and Minerva's wedding. Manolo asked him to be Minou's godfather, but political circumstances prevented it.

Alba Divina del Socorro Marcial Silva—Hortensia's sister who lived in the United States. She was an interpreter with a great passion for opera.

Alfredo Parra Beato—See Parra.

Amaro (Dr. Bienvenido Amaro)—He and Antonio Guzmán, Esq., were long-time attorneys of the Mirabal family.

Amós Sabrás Gurrea—(1890–1976) A Republican from Spain. Professor of mathematics and algebra. During his exile in the Dominican Republic he lived in the home of Isabelita Tavárez, as did Minerva and Manolo. Minerva attended his lectures on mathematics even though they were not part of her prescribed curriculum.

Ana (doña Ana)—It seems she was the mother of one of Minerva's classmates.

Ángela Tavárez Justo—(b. Aug. 29, 1933) Manolo's sister. She was married to Jaime Ricardo Socías, Manolo's friend and companion in the political struggle. Following the execution of her husband and brother in 1963, she went to live in Spain with her daughter, Ángela Ricardo Tavárez. They both design jewelry.

Antonia (Ana Antonia) Rosario—Better known as "Tonó." She grew up and lived nearly her entire life in the Mirabal Reyes home. She was like a third mother to the Mirabal sisters' children.

Antonio Grullón Chávez—Lawyer from Montecristi.

Antonio Rosario—Besides being the owner of a bookstore in Moca, he was involved in the plot to assassinate the tyrant, as he testifies in his book *Moca and the 30th of May*.

Armando Óscar Pacheco—Lawyer, writer, and secretary of education under the regime. He was director of the María Martínez de Trujillo International Book Fair and author of Trujillo's *Work in Education* (1955). Joaquín Balaguer appointed him to the Civic-Military Council in 1962.

A. Óscar Pacheco—See Armando Óscar Pacheco.

Asela Morel—Minerva's gynecologist and companion in the 14 of June Movement. She was one of the seven women imprisoned in January 1960.

Avelina (Lina) Soriano—Manolo's classmate and fellow attorney. She also knew Minerva when they were students at Immaculate Conception High School in La Vega.

Bitín (Albertina) Marcial Silva—Hortensia's sister. Almost everyone in the Marcial Silva family played a musical instrument or sang, and thanks to her, Minerva developed a love of classical music, especially opera.

Camilo (Dr. José Amado; Cheché)—He was Jaimito's uncle and had a well-respected clinic in San Francisco de Macorís.

Carmen Marcial Silva—Hortensia's sister, in whose home the girls often studied and spent the night.

Carolina Pichardo—Minerva's classmate and friend. She was a nun.

Cayeyo (Carlos Aurelio) Grisanti—Manolo's friend and fellow inmate. A native of Montecristi, he assumed responsibility for the region of Santiago during the foundational meeting of the 14 of June Movement in Mao.

César Lithgow—Nephew of Enrique Lithgow Ceara and Isabelita Tavárez.

Chachita (María Teresa) Brito—Minerva's friend, also anti-Trujillo. A professional educator, she was the principal of the Salcedo Province High School for years. She gave Minerva advice on how to continue her studies when she was denied the right to register for classes in her second year at the university. To that end, she helped Minerva write her letter to Trujillo and the speech that she gave in Salcedo in November 1953.

Charlie (Carlos) Conrado Bogaert—Fellow prisoner with Manolo in La 40 and La Victoria. The 14 June Revolutionary Movement was officially constituted at a meeting held on his rice farm in Mao.

Chea (Mercedes) García—She worked for doña Chelito Conde, and the girls were very fond of her.

Chea (Mercedes) Reyes de Mirabal (Mamá Chea)—(Dec. 25, 1898–Jan. 21, 1981) Minerva's mother. She was the eldest daughter in a family known for their staunch opposition to the American invaders who occupied the Dominican Republic from 1916 to 1924. U.S. armed forces even torched the house where she lived with her mother and siblings. Throughout her entire life, she cultivated a sense of dignity and integrity that she instilled in her four daughters, and she accompanied Minerva in detainment on two occasions. Following the murder of three of her daughters, she, along with Dedé, the only surviving sister, became mother to the grandchildren left orphaned by the death of Patria, Minerva, and María Teresa.

Chelina Tavárez Miolán—Manolo's first cousin, daughter of Uncle Pasito and Aunt Tulia.

Chelito (Mercedes) Conde de Isa—Architect. Mother of Narciso and Tony Isa Conde. Minerva lived in her home from January until December, 1954. María Teresa did as well, from October until December of that same year, when she began her studies at the university. The house was located near the intersection of Saint Thomas Aquinas and Elvira de Mendoza Streets. They were forced to move due to pressure from General Miguel Rodríguez Reyes, who years later would participate in and lose his life in the Palma Sola Massacre.

Chiche (Francisco) Hernández—Known as "Chiche Bozo" thanks to his ample mustache. He was the driver of a bus belonging to Pedrito and Patria called "Patria Libre" ("Free Country"), which traveled to the capital. He later acquired his own vehicle to make the same public transportation route.

Chico (Tomás) Hidalgo Justo—Physician. Manolo's first cousin.

Clara Fernández de Paulino—The girls' cousin and Jaimito's sister.

Clarita Báez Pellerano—Minerva's friend and classmate, daughter of Professor Damián (Pachi) Báez and later the wife of Carlos Sánchez y Sánchez, professor of international American law at the university.

Curra (Martha B.) Reyes Ricardo—Niece of Jaime Ricardo. She met Minerva in Montecristi and loved her very much from then on. She died in adolescence.

Danilo Sagredo—Manolo's very bohemian friend. Together they sang and played the guitar. He's mentioned several times in the letters from back then, and he accompanied Manolo the night he went to see Minerva to convince her not to end their relationship after she discovered that he was younger than she.

Dedé (Bélgica Adela) Mirabal Reyes (Mamá Dedé)—(Mar. 1, 1925–Feb. 1, 2014) The second of four daughters born to Enrique Mirabal and Mercedes (Chea) Reyes. She was the only one to survive the tyrant's wrath. With her husband Jaimito Fernández Camilo she had three sons: Jaime Enrique, Jaime Rafael (Jimmy), and Jaime David Fernández Mirabal. Following Patria, Minerva, and María Teresa's murder, she dedicated herself to helping her mother raise her sisters' orphaned children, to preserving their memory, and to spreading their example, which she did by creating and maintaining the Mirabal Sisters

House Museum in Conuco, Mirabal Sisters Province. In 2009 she published her memoir titled *Vivas en su jardín* (*Alive in Their Garden*), in which she tells the story of her sisters' lives and of the horror that the family and country endured during the tyranny that oppressed them for more than three decades. Until her death at age 89, she welcomed hundreds of visitors each day at the museum, tirelessly answering their questions.

Delta Bonó—Friend of the Mirabal sisters, especially Dedé, in San Francisco de Macorís.

Díaz Belliard, Joaquín—Lawyer for the Tavárez Justo family and a close, trusted friend of don Manuel. Manolo began working with him in his office even before defending his thesis.

Domingo Antonio Peña (La Cuca)—Coach who organized athletic and cultural activities for The Blue Legion, a group of adolescents to which Manolo belonged while a teenager in Montecristi. He collaborated in the 14 of June Movement and was imprisoned on Beata Island.

Dulce Tejada de Álvarez—She participated in the foundational meeting of the 14 of June Movement in Mao and was imprisoned in January 1960. She was married to Niño Álvarez.

Edda Tavárez Justo—(Oct. 27, 1940–Feb. 18, 1998) One of Manolo's three sisters, Emma's twin. She was the girlfriend of Dr. Federico Cabrera, who was executed along with Manolo in Las Manaclas in 1963.

Eduardo Tavárez Justo—(Aug. 27, 1935–Aug. 25, 2015) Manolo's brother. After leaving the seminary, he studied finance at the University of Santo Domingo. He left the country following Manolo's uprising in 1963 and continued working in the United States until his retirement. He returned to the Dominican Republic, where he taught English in Montecristi and helped establish the Montecristi campus of the Central University of the East. He was a renowned poet.

El Rubio—A driver who regularly covered the route from the capital to San Francisco de Macorís.

Elba Rodríguez Chiappini—Sister of Dr. Ignacio Rodríguez Chiappini, a good friend of Manolo.

Elsa Justo González (Villa Vázquez)—(b. Dec. 6, 1931) Manolo's first cousin, who grew up with him in the Tavárez Justo home in Montecristi. After 1961 she lived with Manolo and his family in the apartment on Rosa Duarte Street. She was married to Juan B. Mejía, an antitrujillista in the 14 of June Movement who was incarcerated in 1960.

Emma Batlle Vda. Ginebra (Widow of Ginebra)—She had a boarding house on Crucero Ahrens Street in Santo Domingo. María Teresa's friend and classmate, Luly Caraballo, lived there. She demonstrated courage when standing up to doña Evangelista Mues, who went to Emma's boarding house to warn her about "how dangerous those women were" and to advise her against allowing María Teresa to study there with Luly because "they were enemies of the Chief." Emma told the girls this but said that they could continue studying in her home, which they did until they finished their education. In the interim, she moved her boarding house to the Malecón.

Emma Tavárez Justo—(Oct. 27, 1940–Jan. 9, 2000) Lawyer and journalist. Manolo's sister. She fought for freedoms and stands out for her significant participation as a constitutionalist combatant in the April 1965 Revolution. She was active in the 14 of June Movement and later in the Dominican Communist Party. During the first period of government under the Dominican Liberation Party (1996–2000) and until she passed away, she served as Director of ProComunidad, a government-affiliated organization that supports local initiatives and community development.

Enrique Mirabal Fernández—(June 5 or 6, 1895–Dec. 14, 1953) Successful merchant and landowner, he wed Mercedes Reyes Camilo on March 17, 1923. The father of Patria, Dedé, Minerva, and María Teresa, he was imprisoned on two occasions—in 1949 and in 1951—as a consequence of his daughter Minerva's having challenged the tyrant. The arrests, torture, and deprivations he suffered in prison had a significant impact on his health and led to his death in December 1953.

Eugenia—Domestic worker in the Tavárez Justo household.

Eva—Employee of a public institution dealing with the processing of exequaturs.

Evangelista Mues—Owner of the boarding house at 19 Felix Mariano Lluberes Street, where Minerva and María Teresa lived from January to April 1955. She was from San Francisco de Macorís and was the mother-in-law of Vincho Castillo.

Fausto Rodríguez Mesa*—Head of the 14 of June Movement in San Juan de la Maguana. Imprisoned during the massive detention of catorcistas in January 1960.

Fe Violeta Ortega—Odontologist from Salcedo. She was one of the seven women of the 14 of June Movement who were incarcerated in January 1960.

Fefa (Josefa) González de Garrido—(d. Aug. 3, 1954) Chea's cousin, but considered to be a beloved aunt of the Mirabal sisters. She was Patria's godmother.

Fefa (Fefita)—See Josefa Justo de Tavárez.

Fello, Rafael Rojas—Carpenter from Salcedo who often did repairs at the house in Ojo de Agua and later at the house in Conuco.

Flaco (Germán Ricardo) Ares Hevia (El Flaco)—Barber from Montecristi who was Manolo's cellmate in La Victoria.

Graciela Minaya—She lived in the home of the Marcial Silva family.

Gerardo—He worked with don Manuel on his farm in Montecristi.

Guerrero, Manuel A.—Dean of the law school. It is unclear whether or not he was also a professor of philosophy, which is what Minerva seems to suggest in one of her letters.

Héctor (Chery) Jiménez—Composer and Manolo's friend. He accompanied Manolo to serenade Minerva and years later wrote the music for the "Hymn of the 14 of June Movement."

Hilda Semán Mues—Classmate who graduated with Minerva. She was the daughter of Evangelista Mues.

Hipólito Herrera Billini—(1903–1965) Minerva's dissertation director. He was a judge, attorney, and professor of civil law and criminal procedure at the University of Santo Domingo over the course of several decades. He was attorney general of the republic and chief justice of the Supreme Court, among other things.

Horacio Geraldino—Bookbinder at the University of Santo Domingo in 1955.

Hortensia Marcial Silva—Lawyer and Minerva's classmate at the university. Besides María Teresa, she is the individual most frequently mentioned in all the letters remaining from Minerva and Manolo's courtship, and she wrote Manolo little notes in some of them.

Ida (Hida)—She grew up with doña Chea and worked for her for many years.

Ildefonso Güemez Naut—Member of The New Trinity opposition movement, who was already being held in La Victoria when the detained members of the 14 of June Movement arrived there.

Isabelita Tavárez*—Manolo's cousin. He lived in her home while he was a student. Minerva would later do the same until she graduated from the university in 1957.

Isaura Ventura—Medical student who was friends with Minerva and María Teresa. She lived with them at the home of Chelito Conde.

Isidro Marcial Thompson—Hortensia Marcial's father. He was fired from his job for no apparent reason, and Minerva suspected that it could have been because of his ties to her and María Teresa. She seems to refer to this in her Sept. 29, 1955, letter to Manolo.

Jacqueline Guzmán Mirabal—(b. Feb. 7, 1958) Only child of María Teresa Mirabal and Leandro Guzmán Rodríguez. She is currently an entrepreneur in the tourist industry. She and her husband, Dr. Fernando Albaine, have two children: María Teresa and Leandro Arturo.

Jaime David Fernández Mirabal—(b. Oct. 15, 1956) Physician, leader in the Dominican Liberation Party, and former vice president of the republic (1996–2000). He is the youngest son of Dedé Mirabal and Jaimito Fernández.

Jaime Enrique Fernández Mirabal—(Apr. 2, 1949–Mar. 14, 2021) Businessman, eldest son of Dedé and Jaimito.

Jaime Rafael (Jimmy) Fernández Mirabal—(May 3, 1951–Oct. 31, 2013) Engineer and businessman. Son of Dedé and Jaimito.

Jaime (Jaimito) Fernández Camilo—(1924–2012) Merchant and farmer. He was a cousin of the Mirabal sisters and was married to Dedé until 1981. He was the governor of Salcedo Province during the presidency of Antonio Guzmán. His sisters Millo, Olga, Lesbiolita, Clara, and Rosario were not only cousins but also close friends with Minerva and María Teresa.

Jaime Ricardo Socías—(Oct. 16, 1931–Dec. 21, 1963) Engineer, member of the 14 of June Movement, and husband of Ángela Tavárez Justo. He was Manolo's business partner and one of his best friends.

Jamín (Benjamín) Díaz—Employee at the Mirabal Reyes family's house and farm.

Joaquín—See Díaz Belliard, Joaquín.

Jorge A. Tejada C.—Student, Dulce Tejada's brother, and Manolo's cellmate at La Victoria.

José Israel Cuello—Engineer and collaborator in the 14 of June Movement. He was imprisoned at La Victoria in 1960.

José Reyes Camilo—Maternal uncle of the Mirabal sisters. From a young age he was opposed to the U.S. occupation and the Trujillo regime. He called the U.S. "the owner and master" and Trujillo "the master's dog." He exercised influence over Minerva's political sensibilities from a very young age.

Josefa Justo de Tavárez (Mamá Fefa; Mamá Fefita)—(Mar. 9, 1909–Mar. 11, 1982) Manolo's mother. She had a great artistic sensibility and enjoyed doing various kinds of handicrafts, above all ceramics. She never lost interest in learning, which is why as an older adult, while visiting her daughter Edda in the United States, she studied pottery and made the effort to learn English. She was a well-known seamstress in Montecristi and later in Santo Domingo. She married Manuel F. Tavárez Ramos, with whom she had five children: Manuel Aurelio (Manolo), Ángela, Eduardo, Edda, and Emma Tavárez Justo.

Josefina Peynado—Manolo's friend and comrade in the 14 of June Movement. Manolo entrusted her with Minou's letter, and she was the one who brought Minou the snail's shell that her father sent to her from the mountains the day they shot him.

Lala—The cook in the Tavárez Justo household.

Leandro Guzmán Rodríguez*—(March 13, 1932–June 5, 2021) Engineer, María Teresa's husband, and father of Jacqueline. One of the founding members of the 14 of June Movement, he was imprisoned during the massive detention of catorcistas in January 1960 and remained incarcerated until July 2, 1961.

Leda Garnes Sepúlveda—Classmate who graduated with Minerva.

Leoncio Ramos—Professor of Penal Law and author of the books *Criminology* and *Penal Law,* published by the University of Santo Domingo. He was Manolo's dissertation director.

Lesbiolita Fernández de Santos—The girls' cousin and Jaimito's sister.

Lila Piña de Mirabal—Wife of Uncle Fello Mirabal.

Lisandro Macarrulla—Manolo's friend, classmate, and comrade in the underground resistance.

Luis Espínola—Manolo's classmate and friend beginning in the days of the Democratic Youth.

Luly (Lourdes) Caraballo—María Teresa's friend and classmate at the university. One of her brothers, Óscar Caraballo, graduated with Minerva.

Machado (José Manuel Machado Gimbernard)—Professor of commercial law.

Mamá Chea—See Chea (Mercedes) Reyes de Mirabal.

Mamá Dedé—See Dedé Mirabal Reyes.

Mamá Fefita—See Josefa Justo de Tavárez.

Maney (Manuel) Socías—Relative of Jaime Ricardo Socías.

Manolito—See Manuel Enrique Tavárez Mirabal

Manuel Enrique (Manolo/Manolito) Tavárez Mirabal—(b. Aug. 14, 1958) Engineer and businessman. The younger of Minerva and Manolo's two children. He is married to Clara Vázquez and is father to Minerva Victoria, Minou, and Talía Tavárez Vázquez.

Manuel Francisco Tavárez Ramos (Papá Manuel)—(Dec. 17, 1890–July 1, 1975) Manolo's father. He studied odontology in Philadelphia. He was also a justice of the peace, farmer, and businessman in Montecristi. He was opposed to the U.S. invasion of 1916 and was against the Trujillo regime from the very start. His first marriage was to Isabel Mayer, with whom he had a daughter, Carmen

Tavárez de D'Alessandro. In the late twenties he married Josefa Justo Rousseau, with whom he had four children in addition to Manolo: Ángela, Eduardo, and the twins Emma and Edda Tavárez Justo.

Margot (Margarita) Mora—The cook at the Mirabal Reyes home in Ojo de Agua. She had also been nanny to Patria's eldest son, Nelson. Apparently, her mother had the same name as Pedrito's mother. In a letter to Manolo dated Sept. 14, 1955, Minerva refers to "Martina, Margot's mom." It was not possible to confirm this, however.

María Teresa Mirabal de Guzmán—(Oct. 15, 1935–Nov. 25, 1960) Just like her sisters, she was born in Ojo de Agua, Salcedo. She was baptized Antonia María Teresa. From a very young age she was known for her precociousness, her deep curiosity, and her excellent memory. She attended the Immaculate Conception School in La Vega until her third year of middle school and continued her education at the Evangelical High School in Santiago where she graduated with a diploma in natural science. While in Salcedo she also completed the requirements for a diploma in mathematics, which she needed in order to register at the University of Santo Domingo with a major in engineering. In 1958 she married Leandro Guzmán Rodríguez, an engineer. The following year, on February 7, 1959, she gave birth to her only child, Jacqueline Guzmán Mirabal. Together with her husband, her sister Minerva, and her brother-in-law Manolo, she participated in the January 6, 1959, meeting at the home of Yuyo D'Alessandro Tavárez, at which it was decided to organize a nationwide opposition movement that would put an end to the ignominious tyranny of Rafael Leónidas Trujillo. From that moment on, she became actively involved in the conspiracy in spite of being in the advanced stages of pregnancy and later on, in spite of having recently given birth. She was incarcerated on two occasions and was held in both the terrifying clandestine prison called La 40 and in La Victoria. On August 9, 1960, she was released along with Minerva and Sina Cabral, but the plot to murder the sisters had already been concocted. It was relentlessly carried out when, as she was returning from a visit to her husband Leandro and brother-in-law Manolo in Puerto Plata, she was murdered along with her sisters Patria and Minerva and their courageous driver Rufino de la Cruz.

Mela (Melania) González—Sister of Minada, the wife of Uncle José Reyes.

Melgen (Dr. Faroche Melgen Hazoury)—Ophthalmologist. Husband of Hilda Semán Mues, one of Evangelista Mues's daughters and one of Minerva's classmates.

Mercedes Reyes de Mirabal—See Chea.

Mery (Mary)—The affectionate nickname that Manolo and Minerva had for María Teresa.

Miguel Feris Iglesias*—Collaborator in the 14 of June Movement incarcerated in La Victoria in 1960.

Milagros Reyes Pérez—A classmate of Minerva.

Milita (Emilia) de Díaz—Employee in the Mirabal Reyes household. She was the wife of Jamín and the mother of Pedro and Rita Díaz, who are also mentioned in the letters.

Millo (Emilia) Fernández de Suazo—The girls' cousin and Jaimito's sister.

Minada (Iluminada) de Reyes—Wife of Uncle José Reyes.

Minerva Victoria Tavárez Vázquez—Granddaughter of Minerva and Manolo; eldest daughter of their son Manolo.

Miriam Morales, C.—Clerk. Member of the 14 of June Movement in Puerto Plata. She was imprisoned in January 1960.

Mon (Simeón) Mirabal Fernández—Paternal uncle of the Mirabal sisters. He lived in La Vega, and Minerva often spent her vacations at his home.

Monjas Carmelitas—University student residence on Independence Avenue, at the corner of Padre Pina Street. They later moved to another location on Independence Avenue and finally to Juan Sánchez Ramírez Street, near the intersection with Wenceslao Álvarez Street. Minerva lived at this residence her entire first year at the university, until December 1954. María Teresa lived there beginning in 1955.

Mundo (Raymundo) Garrido—Husband of cousin Fefa González. They were considered aunt and uncle to the Mirabal sisters and were dear to the family.

Nelson González Mirabal—(b. Feb. 2, 1941) Eldest son of Patria Mirabal and Pedro González. He has a degree in finance. At an early age he became actively involved in the conspiracy to bring down the Trujillo regime. In 1960, while still an adolescent, he endured several months of imprisonment and isolation in both La 40 and La Victoria. He is the father of Patricia, Nelson Enrique, Eva, and Sara.

Nelsy Tavárez—Dedé's friend and neighbor while she was living in San Francisco de Macorís.

Nina Patria—See Patria Mercedes Mirabal de González.

Niño (Luis) Álvarez Pereyra—Farmer from San Francisco de Macorís. Dulce Tejada's husband. Both of them participated in the seminal meeting of the 14 of June Movement in Mao on January 10, 1960.

Noris González Mirabal—(b. Oct. 8, 1942) Daughter of Patria Mirabal and Pedro González Cruz. Civil servant with the Ministry of the Environment. She is the mother of Patria Mercedes, Francis, and Enrique Román González. She volunteers with patriotic organizations such as the Memorial Museum of Dominican Resistance.

Olga Fernández de Noboa—The girls' cousin and Jaimito's sister. She accompanied Dedé to retrieve the bodies of her dead sisters.

Olga Rivas de Socías—Jaime Ricardo's cousin. Neighbor of the Tavárez Justo family. She became friends with Minerva when she was living in Montecristi.

Óscar Lara Rojas, Dr.—(d. June 4, 1955) Minerva's friend from their youth and Manolo's classmate. He died in an "accident" along the highway heading toward San Juan de la Maguana. His family insists that when they brought the casket to the family home in Moca, it contained someone else's body, but they were not permitted to open the casket.

Ozema Jiménez de Mirabal—Wife of Simeón (Mon) Mirabal, the girls' uncle.

Pachi (Damián) Báez Báez—Professor of penal law. He was the father of Clarita Báez, one of Minerva's classmates.

Papá Manuel—See Manuel Francisco Tavárez Ramos.

Papy (Reynaldo) Bisonó—Manolo's friend and business associate. His father, don Arturo Bisonó, owned a rice mill and provided financing for some of Manolo and don Manuel Tavárez's crops.

Paquín (Francisco) Noriega—Student. He belonged to the group from the capital. The letters from prison contain various references to him and to his relationship—or supposed relationship—with Sina Cabral.

Parra (Dr. Alfredo Parra Beato)—Lawyer from Montecristi, Manolo's friend, classmate, and companion in the resistance. They were cellmates in La Victoria, and he is mentioned various times in the letters from prison.

Patria Mercedes Mirabal de González—(Feb. 27, 1924–Nov. 25, 1960) Her parents baptized her with the name Patria because she was born on February 27, Dominican Independence Day. The eldest daughter of Enrique Mirabal and Mercedes (Chea) Reyes was known from a very young age for her sensibilities and artistic talent, which she developed along with a passion for gardening. At age 17 she married Pedro González Cruz, with whom she had three children: Nelson Enrique, Noris Mercedes, and Raúl Ernesto. She actively joined the 14 of June Movement and lent the use of her home to store arms and to host the group's first meeting. She herself was not imprisoned, but her husband and her eldest son, Nelson, were. Her house was confiscated and later destroyed, as well as all her belongings and properties. On November 24, 1960, she visited her husband in prison at La Victoria. The very next day, on November 25, 1960, she accompanied her sisters Minerva and María Teresa to visit their husbands, who had been transferred to a prison in Puerto Plata. She was brutally murdered along with them and Rufino de la Cruz.

Pedro Díaz—Son of Benjamín and Milita. He lived his entire life in the homes of doña Chea Reyes de Mirabal.

Pedro (Pedrito) González Cruz—(July 6, 1917–Dec. 23, 1972) Farmer. Husband of Patria Mirabal. He collaborated with the 14 of June Movement and lent the use of his house to hold the group's first, foundational meeting. He was in prison from January 1960 until July 2, 1961, when he was released along with Leandro Guzmán.

Puro (José Eugenio) Petit Tavárez—Manolo's first cousin and comrade in the 14 of June Movement. He was held prisoner in the same cell as Manolo in La Victoria.

Rafael David Henríquez—Registrar at the University of Santo Domingo.

Rafael Marcial Silva—Priest. Hortensia's brother.

Raúl—He was in charge of one of Enrique Mirabal's small farms.

Raúl González Mirabal—(b. 1958) Youngest son of Patria Mirabal and Pedro González Cruz. Engineer and businessman. He is married to Ana Amaya Hernández, with whom he has two children: Raúl Ernesto and Patria Marie. He serves on the board of directors of the Federation of Patriotic Foundations.

Reyna Mora—Cook at the house in Conuco.

Rita Díaz—Daughter of Benjamín and Milita. She worked as a nanny for Dedé Mirabal's children.

Rodrigote (Ramón A.) Rodríguez Cruz—Landowner. Founding member of the 14 of June Movement, in charge of the La Vega section. He was with Manolo in prison. He participated in the meeting in Mao.

Rosa Mirabal de González—(d. Nov. 2, 1963) Aunt Rosa, sister of Enrique Mirabal. Her patience was legendary in the family. Minou mentions her death in the letter that Manolo carried in his pocket as he headed up into the mountains to fight for a return to constitutional order and democracy in the Dominican Republic. Minou's indication that Rosa had died the previous day made it possible to determine when the letter was written.

Rosario Fernández de Escaño—The girls' cousin and Jaimito's sister. She and María Teresa were close friends.

Rosita—She seems to be a relative of Evangelista Mues, who lived in her home.

Rufino de la Cruz—In November 1960 he offered to drive Minerva, María Teresa, and Patria to visit Manolo and Leandro in Puerto Plata. He was brutally murdered along with them on November 25, 1960.

Sánchez Morcelo, Héctor—Criminal lawyer and Manolo's university professor. He later served as one of the prosecuting attorneys in the trial of the alleged perpetrators and accomplices in the murder of the Mirabal sisters and their driver, Rufino de la Cruz. The trial was held in the national criminal court.

Silverita Trujillo—Minerva's classmate at the Immaculate Conception School in La Vega.

Simón Tomás Fernández*—Collaborator in the 14 of June Movement.

Sina—See Tomasina Cabral.

Sully Martínez Bonnelly—Manolo's cousin. He lived in Santiago and was very close with the Tavárez family. One of Manolo's friends, Simón Tomás Fernández, was related to him through the marriage of a relative. His family had a house in Los Montones, very close to Las Manaclas. Manolo frequently vacationed there beginning in his adolescence. During those summers, he and his cousin and friends would go on outings throughout the area. According to Ángela Tavárez Justo, his familiarity with the terrain led Manolo to choose that particular area of the Central Mountain Range as the zone of operations for the Guerrilla Front in 1963.

Tamara Díaz de García—Minerva's neighbor and closest friend in Montecristi. She was married to Manolo's first cousin, Carlos García Tavárez. She shared with Minerva a love of painting and introduced her to the arts of sculpting and photography.

Tavares, Friolán Jr.—Professor of Roman Law and of Civil Procedure. Among his published works is *Elements of Dominican Civil Procedure*.

Teté—See María Teresa Mirabal de Guzmán.

Tobías Emilio (Larry) Cabral—Childhood friend of Minerva who lived in exile in the U.S. beginning in 1950.

Toca, Dr. Domingo—Lawyer from Salcedo.

Tomasina (Sina) Cabral—Engineer from Salcedo. Comrade in the resistance and cellmate of Minerva and María Teresa in La 40 and La Victoria from January to February 1960 and from May to August that same year. She is mentioned in all of the letters from prison.

Tonó—See Ana Antonia Rosario

Toña (Toñita; Antonia) Pantaleón Reyes—The girls' first cousin, daughter of Carmela Reyes Camilo.

Tulia Miolán—Manolo's aunt. She was married to Federico (Pasito) Tavárez Ramos, the youngest brother of Manuel Tavárez Ramos, Manolo's father.

Twins—A reference to Emma and Edda Tavárez Justo, Manolo's youngest sisters. Minerva refers to them fondly around the time when they spent a few weeks' vacation in Ojo de Agua in August 1954. This was during Minerva and Manolo's courtship.

V.*—Pseudonym with which Manolo signed some of his literary works, including poetry and a novel that he left unfinished.

Víctor Núñez—Member of the anti-Trujillo underground resistance called The New Trinity, he was incarcerated in November 1959. He was already in La Victoria when the mass number of catorcistas arrived in 1960.

Victoria Marcial Silva—Hortensia's sister. Medical doctor.

Virgilio Díaz Ordóñez—(1895–1968) Dominican lawyer, politician, and writer, known by his pen name, Ligio Vizardi. He was Minerva's philosophy professor and twice served as provost of the University of Santo Domingo. He also served as secretary of justice and legal counsel to the executive branch.

Víctor Núñez—Member of the anti-Trujillo opposition movement The New Trinity. He was being held in La Victoria when the imprisoned members of the 14 of June Movement arrived there.

Wadi Isaías—Hortensia Marcial's ex-boyfriend.

Yolanda Vallejo Pradel—Lawyer. Minerva's friend and classmate. She went with her to buy part of her bridal trousseau and along with other friends organized her bachelorette party at the Mario Restaurant.

Yuyo (Guido Emilio) D'Alessandro Tavárez—(1932–Apr. 18, 2011) Manolo's nephew. He was married to Josefina Ricart. It was at their home that on January 6, 1959, it was first proposed that they form a nationwide movement in opposition to the tyranny. He was related through marriage to Ramfis Trujillo, the dictator's son, as Yuyo's wife Josefina had a sister named Octavia (Chanchana) Ricart, who was Ramfis's first wife.

Bibliography

Alonso Romero, Mercedes. *Su nombre es Patria.* Santo Domingo: Editora Búho, 2011.

"Amós Sabrás Gurrea." *Diccionario Biográfico de la Real Academia de la Historia.* Real Academia de la Historia. Accessed January 29, 2019. https://dbe.rah.es/biografias/49099/amos-sabras-gurrea.

Barba Jacob, Porfirio. "Song of the Profound Life." Translated by Nicolás Suescún. 2006. *Poetry International.* The Poetry International Foundation. Accessed December 11, 2018. https://www.poetryinternational.com/en/poets-poems/poems/poem/103-7111_SONG-OF-THE-PROFOUND-LIFE.

Camilo, Pedro. "La Acción Clero Cultural, una organización de la resistencia antitrujillista." *Movimiento Revolucionario 14 de Junio.* Aug. 9, 2009. Accessed May 15, 2019. https://unojotacuatro.blogspot.com/2009/08/la-accion-clero-cultural-una.html.

Cassá, Roberto. "Algunos componentes del legado de Trujillo." *Iberoamericana* 1, no. 3 (2001): 113–27.

Code Name: Butterflies / Nombre secreto: Mariposas. Directed, written, and produced by Cecilia Domeyko. Accent Media (2008). Film.

Cruz Infante, José Abigail. *Hombres y mujeres de Trujillo. Isabel Mayer.* Santo Domingo: Argos, 2013.

Derby, Lauren. *The Dictator's Seduction: Politics and the Popular Imagination in the Era of Trujillo.* Durham: Duke University Press, 2009.

Galván, William. *Minerva Mirabal. Historia de una heroína.* Santo Domingo: Comisión Permanente de Efemérides Patrias, 2011.

Gelman, Juan. "Ahora." *Poesía reunida (1956–2010).* Barcelona: Seix Barral, 2012: 494.

Guzmán, Leandro. *1J4. De espigas y de fuegos. Aportes para la memoria necesaria. Testimonios de un militante.* Santo Domingo: Editora de Colores, 1998.

Horn, Maja. "Dictates of Dominican Democracy: Conceptualizing Caribbean Political Modernity." *Small Axe* 18, no. 2 (2014): 18–35.

———. *Masculinity after Trujillo: The Politics of Gender in Dominican Literature.* Gainesville: University Press of Florida, 2014.

Imbert Barrera, Antonio. "Entrevista al General Antonio Imbert Barrera, uno de los ajusticiadores de Trujillo." YouTube, uploaded by *El Día RD,* 31 May 2018. https://www.youtube.com/watch?v=iGGCN7kqONE.

Isalguéz, Hilarión. "Hoy se cumplen 54 años del fusilamiento de Manolo Tavárez Justo y 28 izquierdistas." *El nuevo diario,* December 21, 2017. https://elnuevodiario.com.do/hoy-se-cumplen-54-anos-del-fusilamiento-manolo-tavarez-justo-28-izquierdistas.

Machado, Antonio. "20. This Withered, Ashen Afternoon." *Antonio Machado: Selected Poems.* Translated by Alan S. Trueblood. Cambridge: Harvard University Press, 1982, 97.

———. "XXIX." *Antonio Machado.* Translated by Alice Jane McVan. New York: The Hispanic Society of America, 1959, n.p. in Bernard Sesé, "Alice Jane McVan, *Antonio Machado,*" 428.

Manley, Elizabeth. "Intimate Violations: Women and the *Ajusticiamiento* of Dictator Rafael Trujillo, 1944–1961." *The Americas* 69, no. 1 (2012): 65.

———. *The Paradox of Paternalism: Women and the Politics of Authoritarianism in the Dominican Republic.* Gainesville: University Press of Florida, 2017.

Mayes, April. *The Mulatto Republic: Class, Race and Dominican National Identity.* Gainesville: University Press of Florida, 2014.

Minaya, Héctor. "Dictador llegó al colmo de cambiar el nombre de la capital por Ciudad Trujillo." *El nacional,* May 26, 2016. Accessed May 13, 2019. https://elnacional.com.do/dictador-llego-al-colmo-de-cambiar-el-nombre-de-la-capital-por-ciudad-trujillo.

Mirabal, Dedé. *Vivas en su jardín. La verdadera historia de las hermanas Mirabal y su lucha por la libertad.* Vintage Español. New York: Random House, 2009.

Museo Memorial de la Resistencia Dominicana. "Juventud Revolucionaria. Juventud Democrática (J.D.)." Accessed May 15, 2020. http://www.museodelaresistencia.com/juventud-revolucionaria-juventud-democratica-j-d.

———. "Los Panfleteros de Santiago." Accessed May 15, 2020. http://www.museodelaresistencia.com/los-panfleteros-de-santiago.

———. "La resistencia del Exilio Dominicano. La solidaridad internacional." Accessed May 15, 2020. http://www.museodelaresistencia.com/la-resistencia-del-exilio-dominicano-la-solidaridad-internacional.

Neruda, Pablo. "Letter on the Road." *The Captain's Verses.* Translated by Donald Devenish Walsh. New York: New Directions, 1972, 142–51.

Ornes, Germán E. *Trujillo: Little Caesar of the Caribbean.* New York: Thomas Nelson & Sons, 1958.

Pérez, Milvio. *1J4. Del sacrificio (1959) a la inmolación (1963). Exposición Gráfica Movimiento Revolucionario 14 de Junio.* Dirección General de Aduanas, Dominican Republic. 2008. Print.

Peyrera, Emilia. "Auge y caída de Isabel Mayer, la incondicional de Trujillo." *Diario Libre,* Dec. 13, 2018. Accessed May 13, 2020. https://www.diariolibre.com/revista/cultura/auge-y-caida-de-isabel-mayer-la-incondicional-de-trujillo-JM11596618.

Robinson, Nancy. "Women's Political Participation in the Dominican Republic: The Case of the Mirabal Sisters." *Caribbean Quarterly*, 52, nos. 2–3 (2006): 172–83.

Roorda, Eric Paul. *The Dictator Next Door: The Good Neighbor Policy and the Trujillo Regime in the Dominican Republic, 1930–1945*. Durham: Duke University Press, 1998.

Sesé, Bernard. "Alice Jane McVan, *Antonio Machado*." *Bulletin Hispanique* 65.3–4 (1963): 426–28.

Tavárez Mirabal, Minou. *Mañana te escribiré otra vez. Minerva y Manolo. Cartas*. Santo Domingo: Editorial Santillana, 2014.

———. "Puesta en circulación de *Mañana te escribiré otra vez* de Minou Tavárez Mirabal en Higuey." Discurso 5ta Feria Gastronómica de la Yuca en la Provincia La Altagracia. YouTube. Uploaded by Opción Democrática, Jan. 24, 2018. https://www.youtube.com/watch?v=QAJ8EARb234.

Taveras, Rafael. "Entrevista con Rafael (Fafa) Taveras, Comunicador," *El día*. YouTube. Nov. 23, 2018. www.youtube.com/watch?v=4JgUzNtSMYg.

Tillman, Ellen D. *Dollar Diplomacy by Force: Nation-Building and Resistance in the Dominican Republic*. Durham, NC: Duke University Press, 2016.

Trujillo: 31 años de historia perdida. Fundación Rafael Leónidas Trujillo Molina. Unicaribe of Florida, 2010. Film. YouTube. Uploaded by Lavozdominicana, Aug. 30, 2020. https://www.youtube.com/watch?v=bJm7scU5fOM.

Turits, Richard Lee. *Foundations of Despotism: Peasants, the Trujillo Regime, and Modernity in Dominican History*. Stanford: Stanford University Press, 2003.

Wright, Micah. "Building an Occupation: Puerto Rican Laborers in the Dominican Republic, 1916–1924." *Labor: Studies in Working-Class History of the Americas*, 13, no. 3 (2016): 83–103.

Index

Accioli, Hildebrando, 97, 97n40; *Traité de Droit International Public,* 97
Acción Clero Cultural, 21–22
Acción Feminista Dominicana, 12, 16, 19
Adorable Creatures, 88
Aeschylus, 165; *Prometheus,* 165
Agrupación Política 14 de Junio (14 of June Political Association), 8, 30
Alba, Fucho, 211
Alegría, Ciro, 107, 114; *Broad and Alien Is the World,* 107
Alianza País, 1, 282
Almonte, Gumersindo, 220–21
Álvarez, Federico, 159
Álvarez, Julia, 3; *In the Time of the Butterflies,* 3
Anti-Haitianism, 14–15
Antitrujillistas, 4–6, 17, 18, 19–23, 231, 236, 268; and women, 16
Autonomous University of Santo Domingo, 217

Bachelet Jeria, Michelle, 1, 32, 43; background, 35
Balaguer, Joaquín, 30–31
Barba Jacob, Porfirio (Miguel Ángel Osorio), 37, 222, 224
Barroso, Mariano, 3
Baum, Vicki, 160, 160n87; *Headless Angel,* 160
Bisonó, Arturo, 158
Bisonó, Reynaldo (Papy), 158, 162
Bosch, Juan, 8, 128, 230
Bouzat, Pierre, 197; *Traité théorique et pratique de Droit Penal,* 197

Butterflies (Mariposas): as codenames, 3, 231, 262; murder of, 25–26, 29, 38, 239

Cabral, Tobías Emilio (Larry), 237, 277
Cabral, Tomasina (Sina), 24, 37–38, 232, 252n24, 254n26, 273, 275, 277
Cabrera, Neftalí (Lieutenant), 158
Caliés, 48, 48n1, 102, 128, 231–33, 236, 238, 259
Camilo, José Amado (Cheché), 128, 134–35, 266
Cantinflas (Mario Moreno), 250
Caraballo, Lourdes (Luly), 59, 128, 269, 272
Caribe, El, 17, 17n44, 127–28, 159, 206, 259
Carteles, 92, 92n38
Casa España, 144, 144n78
Cassá, Roberto, 31
Castillo, Marino Vinicio (Vincho), 83, 269
Castro, Fidel, 20
Catholic Church, 7, 21, 26
Caudillo rule, 10–11, 15
Cayo Confites expedition of 1947, 19
Cepillos, 17
Champollion, Jean-François, 63, 63n9
Coiscou, Abigail, 73, 73n15; *Código Penal y leyes que lo modifican y lo complementan,* 15
Cold War, 16, 19
Comisión Nacional de la Frontera (National Border Commission), 15, 20
Communism, 15–16, 19, 218, 220, 269; anti-, 27, 32, 143
Conde de Isa, Mercedes (Chelito), 82, 93, 267, 270
Cruz, Rufino de la, 7, 25, 239, 258–59, 273, 277

Cuba, 16, 18–20, 70
Cuban Revolution, 19, 218, 230

D'Alessandro, Guido Emilio (Yuyo), 19, 230, 278
Democracy, 30–32, 49; transition to, 30–32
Democratic Youth (Juventud Democrática), 4–5, 8, 17n43, 18, 216
Derby, Lauren, 13–14, 28, 29n76
Díaz, Junot, 3; *Brief Wondrous Life of Oscar Wao, The*, 3
Díaz de García, Tamara, 217, 223, 277
Díaz Ordóñez, Virgilio, 75–77, 278
Domeyko, Cecilia, 5; *Code Name: Butterflies*, 3n1, 5, 5n9, 25n64, 29n77
Dominican Republic, 1; colonial rule, 11; corruption, 16–17; economic history, 10–11; geography, 9; Haitian rule, 11; national identity, 14; national problems, 31–32; repression, 12; sovereignty of, 14, 28; Spanish US influence and occupation, 11, 13, 27; under Trujillo, 13–16, 31; white Dominican culture, 14–15; women's rights, 12
Durkheim, Émile, 148; *Règles de la Méthode Sociologique, Les*, 148n80

Espínola, Luis, 56, 272
Exile, 18, 19, 35, 70, 230, 237, 254n26

Fair of Peace and Fraternity of the Free World, 188, 188n101, 206, 212
Feris Iglesias, Miguel, 238, 260, 274
Fernández Camilo, Jaime (Jaimito), 101, 104, 128, 131, 134, 271
Fernández Mirabal, Jaime David, 32, 271
Fernández Moreno, Baldomero, 189, 190n102; "Invitation to Home," 189–90
Flaubert, Gustave, 185n99; *Salambó*, 185
"Foro Público" ("Public Forum"), 127, 157, 220
Fowler, Gene, 165; *Great Mouthpiece, The*, 165
Franco, Pericles, 4–6, 222

Galván, William, 4–7
García Lorca, Federico, 81, 89, 89n34

García Tavárez, Carlos, 217, 277
Garraud, Pierre, 107n44
Garraud, René, 152; *Traité théorique et pratique d'instruction criminelle et de procedure pénale*, 152, 152n85
Gelman, Juan, 49
Gender, dynamics, 27; ideals, 23–25; norms, 5, 22, 28; relations, 12, 12n23, 16
Gendered discourse, 28
Geraldino, Horacio, 128, 270
González, Francisco Aníbal (Pachico), 21
González Cruz, Ezequiel, 21
González Cruz, Pedro (Pedrito), 21–23, 275–76
González Mirabal, Nelson, 23, 274
González Mirabal family, 21
González Reyes, Antonio Ezequiel, 21
Grisanti, Carlos Aurelio (Cayeyo), 231, 266
Guillen Gómez, Wenceslao (Wen), 21
Guzmán Rodríguez, Leandro, 22–23, 25, 29, 220, 272

Haiti, 9, 11, 14–15
Hartlyn, Jonathan, 30–31
Healing, 2, 49, 235
Herrera Billini, Hipólito, 108–9, 270
Horn, Maja, 12, 28, 30–31
Hurricane San Zenón, 13

Imbert Barrera, Antonio (General), 25, 29
Israel Cuello, José, 233, 241n10, 271

Jiménez, Héctor (Chery), 59, 270
Josserand, Louis, 121, 121n59
June 1959 expedition, 7, 20, 22, 30, 230
Justo González, Elsa, 47, 252
Justo Rousseau, Josefa, 8, 273

La 40 (La Cuarenta), 8n16, 10, 20, 24, 174, 211, 232, 234, 239, 258
La Nueva Trinitaria (The New Trinity), 235
Lara Rojas, Óscar, 128, 134, 136, 275
La Victoria National Penitentiary, 10, 24, 234–35, 238
Letters, 26, 29, 84, 93; courtship, 36, 48,

55–206; marriage, 26, 207–25; to Minou, 38, 258–63; in prison, 24, 69, 227–54
Luperón expedition of 1949, 19

Machado, Antonio, 241, 245; *Soledades, galerías y otros poemas,* 241n11
Magallanes Moure, Manuel, 175
Magnificent Obsession, 87, 93
Mañana te escribiré otra vez, 1, 7, 32–33, 35–40
Manley, Elizabeth, 12, 12n23, 15–16, 27
Marcial Silva, Hortensia, 64–68, 70–71, 87, 98, 102, 196, 201, 270; correspondence to Manolo, 68, 71, 99, 111, 136, 142, 154; relationship trouble, 105
Marcial Silva, Rafael, 128, 138, 141, 276
Marcial Silva family, 128, 189
Martí, José, 219; *Ismaelillo,* 237
Martínez, Violeta, 4; arrest, 6
Martyrization, 1–2, 7, 26
Maternalism, 12, 15–16, 27
Mayer Tavárez, Isabel, 15, 19–20
Memorial Museum of Dominican Resistance, 2
Memory, 2, 31–32, 43, 46–47, 49, 76, 93, 173, 188, 211
Mirabal, Bélgica Adela (Dedé), 3–5, 10, 20, 43, 76; *Vivas en su jardín.,* 4, 43, 49, 123
Mirabal, María Teresa (Mary/Mery/Aunt Teté), 10, 22–24, 56, 61, 82–83, 102; death, 7, 10, 25
Mirabal, Patria, 3, 10, 67; activism, 23; death, 7, 10, 25; garden, 58, 60; letter to María Teresa and Minerva, 106
Mirabal Fernández, Enrique, 3, 4, 186, 188; arrest and death, 6, 75, 79
Mirabal Reyes de Tavárez, Maria Argentina Minerva, 1–3, 26; activism and opposition to Trujillo, 4–7, 19–20, 22, 25–27, 94, 97, 100, 213, 219, 229; concern for loved ones, 59, 66, 82, 105, 114; cultural and intellectual interests, 59, 66, 70, 73–74, 76–79, 84, 90, 104–5, 115, 135; death, 10, 25; depression, 75, 78, 105, 130–31, 159, 181, 185; early education, 4; graduation and law practice, 217–18; health problems, 81, 91, 93–94, 96, 100, 106, 125, 127, 131–33, 136, 138–39, 141, 214, 220–21; imprisonment, 6, 7, 10, 23–25, 55, 217, 232–37; interest in film, 79, 87–88, 96, 99, 161; interest in literature, 81, 90, 160, 165; law studies, 7, 10, 36–37, 55, 59, 70, 73–76, 90–91, 97, 107, 110, 142, 165, 211; law thesis, 216–17; leadership, 22, 28, 233; meets Manolo, 7, 55; as politically marked person, 59, 94, 103, 114, 128, 157, 187, 216–17; pregnancy, 187, 205–6, 212–13, 218, 220; sculpting and photography, 217, 237; values, 69–70, 72, 76, 79, 105; writing, 230
Mirabal Reyes family, 9, 18, 21, 26, 29, 76, 143, 216; as enemies of the regime, 216, 220; farm, 67, 185, 189; home, 9; meets Tavárez Justo family, 158, 169–70
Mirabal Sisters House Museum, 8, 49, 82, 167, 188, 212–13, 217, 233
Monroe Doctrine, 11
Monteverdi, Claudio, 93; *Coronation of Poppaea, The,* 93
Mora, Margarita (Margot), 58, 67–68, 86, 118
Morales, Miriam, 24
Morel, Asela, 24, 211, 221
Movimiento de Liberación Dominicana (Dominican Liberation Movement), 20, 23
Movimiento Revolucionario 14 de Junio (14 of June Revolutionary Movement), 7–8, 10, 20, 231; foundation, 22; goals of, 22–23; hymn, 59; imprisonment, 232–235; leadership, 22, 37, 232; women members, 24, 26, 28–29, 173, 211, 232
Mues, Evangelista, 83, 102, 109, 114–15, 269
Muhammad, Shams al-Din (pseud. Hafiz), 37, 222, 225
Mythification, 2

Nationhood, 12
Neocolonialism, 15
Neruda, Pablo, 40; "Carta en el camino, La," 40, 55n1; *Versos del capitán, Los,* 40
Nous sommes tous des assassins (We Are All Murderers), 79, 79n23, 93, 99
Núñez, Víctor, 235–36

October 1949 confrontation, 5–6, 27–28, 55, 75
O'Neill, Eugene, 249; *Nine Dramas,* 249
Opción Democrática, 1
Ortega, Fe Violeta, 24, 232, 269, 278

Pacheco, Armando Óscar, 107, 266
Panfleteros de Santiago, Los, 21
Parliamentarians for Global Action, 1
Parra Beato, Alfredo (Parra), 86, 238, 251, 275
Partido Democrático Revolucionario Dominicano, 18
Partido Dominicano, 16; sección feminista (feminist sector), 16
Partido Socialista Popular, 18
Pater, Walter, 150; *Renaissance, The,* 150
Paternalism, 15, 25, 27–28
Peña Castillo, Domingo Antonio (La Cuca), 173, 268
Petit Tavárez, José Eugenio (Puro), 37, 238; letter to Minerva, 250
Petit Tavárez family, 174
Pinochet, Augusto, 35
Planiol, Marcel, 90, 120; *Traité élémentaire de Droit civil,* 90n37
Poem of the Cid, The, 249

Quisqueya, 29–30, 258; as metaphor, 29–30, 48

Radio Rebelde, 230
Radio Rumbo, 230
Repression, 12, 15, 17–18, 31, 36, 82, 143, 157, 218–19
Resistance (to Trujillo's dictatorship), 1–2, 4–8, 18, 21–22, 25–28, 50, 213, 230–32
Reyes de Mirabal, Mercedes (Chea), 3, 21, 49–50, 82
Reynolds, Quentin, 66n10; *Courtroom,* 66
Ricart, Josefina, 19, 278
Ricart, Octavia, 19, 278
Robinson, Nancy, 23, 26
Rodó, José Enrique, 242; *Ariel,* 242
Rodríguez, Emma, 4; arrest, 6
Rodríguez Chiappini, Ignacio, 93
Rodríguez Mesa, Fausto, 232, 269

Rodríguez Reyes, Miguel (General), 82, 267
Rojas, Fello, 67–68, 270
Rolland, Romain, 78, 102, 104; *John Christopher, Vol. II,* 102; *Life of Beethoven, The,* 78, 78n20, 102, 105
Roorda, Eric, 11
Roosevelt, Theodore, 11
Roosevelt Corollary, 11
Rosario, Ana Antonia (Tonó), 76–77, 88, 205, 265
Rosario, Antonio, 201, 265

Sabina, Poppaea, 93–94
Sabrás Gurrea, Amós, 70, 71n13
Sánchez Cabral, Eduardo, 159
Sánchez Morcelo, Héctor, 152, 162, 190, 193, 197, 277
Santamaría, Haydee, 247, 247n17
Selecciones, 70, 73, 242
Servicio de Inteligencia Militar, 17, 23–24, 29, 36, 37, 48n1, 157, 235
Socías, Jaime Ricardo, 218, 231, 271
Soñé, Brunilda, 4, 20n49; arrest, 6
Soriano, Avelina (Lina), 56–57, 266
Spanish Civil War, 18
Stendhal, 89; *Rouge et le noir, Le,* 89, 89n33
Svich, Caridad, 3

Tavárez Justo, Ángela, 82
Tavárez Justo, Eduardo, 142, 146–47
Tavárez Justo, Emma, 20, 118, 118n56, 143
Tavárez Justo, Manuel Aurelio (Manolo), 1, 3, 8; affair, 221; agricultural enterprises, 162–63, 167, 191, 212, 215; childhood, 173–74, 176; cultural and intellectual interests, 89, 102, 248–49; death, 1, 8, 10, 82; education, 8; imprisonment, 1, 8, 10, 23–24, 232–37; law practice, 10, 37, 80, 106–7, 122, 124, 154–56, 191, 201, 212, 215n3; leader of armed resistance, 8, 10, 22, 38, 230–31; Mandatory Military Service and invitations, 153, 166, 188, 201; meets Minerva, 7, 55; as notary, 218; opposition to Trujillo, 20, 158; political activism and leadership, 8, 10, 30, 38, 219, 229; serenades Minerva, 59,

61n6, 62, 64; study of law, 8, 10, 79, 79n23, 82, 86 101; threats due to relationship with Minerva, 142–43, 154, 187
Tavárez Justo family, 9, 18, 143, 158, 216; conception of Minou, 206; first year of marriage, 211; home, 9; meets Mirabal Reyes family, 158, 169–70
Tavárez Mirabal, Jaime Enrique, 188
Tavárez Mirabal, Minerva Josefina (Minou), 2, 4, 6–7, 25, 29; background, 1; birth, 211; childhood, 213–14, 223, 229; letter to her parents, 44–50; narrative about her parents, 35–40; political activism, 30–33, 46
Tavárez Mirabal, Manuel Enrique (Manolo/Manolito), 7, 44; birth, 220
Tavárez Mirabal family, 32, 35, 39; legacy, 44, 49; marriage plans, 127, 157, 183, 187, 190, 192, 194, 199, 203; plans to have children, 200; wedding, 205
Tavárez Ramos, Manuel Francisco, 19, 82, 158, 162
Taveras, Rafael (Fafa), 21
Tejada, Jorge, 38, 238; letter to Minerva, 249
Tejada de Álvarez, Dulce, 22, 24, 232, 268
Telegrams, 55, 57–58, 65, 123, 154, 203–4
Three Kings' Day, 19
Tomás Fernández, Simón, 231, 277
Torture, 1, 8, 10, 24, 29, 35, 174, 232, 253, 259–60
Trauma, 2, 24, 253, 261
Triumvirate, 1, 8, 38
Trujillato (Era of Trujillo), 12–14, 28; October 1937 massacre, 14–15, 66n10
Trujillismo, 15, 19; discourse, 32; and feminism, 16, 19–20, 27; opposition, 19, 20, 23
Trujillo, Ramfis, 19
Trujillo, Silverita, 93

Trujillo Molina, Rafael Leónidas, 1, 5, 12, 25, 27, 37, 219; assassination, 25–26, 188n101; background, 12; misogyny, 27–29; political discourse, 31; release of political prisoners, 19, 26, 232; retaliation against the Mirabal family, 37, 56, 82–83, 94, 128, 218; as tíguere, 28
Turits, Richard Lee, 14–16

Unión de Grupos Independientes. *See* Panfleteros de Santiago
Ureña, Rafael Estrella, 12, 85

Vallejo Pradel, Yolanda, 204, 206, 278
Vargas, Ricardo (Malmente), 190
Vargas Llosa, Mario, 3; *Feast of the Goat, The,* 3
Vásquez Lajara, Horacio, 12–13
Ventura, Isaura, 93, 270
Vicini Burgos, Juan Bautista, 12
Vincent, Sténio, 14
Violence toward women, 26, 26n68

Walsh, Donald Devenish, 40
War of Dominican Independence (1844), 11
Ways of Love, The, 165
Wiseman, Nicholas Patrick Stephen, 241; *Fabiola; or the Church of the Catacombs,* 241–42
Women's activism and suffrage, 6, 16
Wyman, Jane, 93, 96–97

Yabal, Vicente (Priest), 109
Yutang, Lin, 248n18; *Leaf in the Storm, A,* 248

Zola, Emile, 84n29; "J'accuse," 84

MINOU TAVÁREZ MIRABAL is a political leader in the Dominican Republic and an internationally known human rights activist. She is the daughter of the martyred national heroes Minerva Mirabal and Manolo Tavárez. She has served as under-secretary of foreign relations, congresswoman, founder of the political party Opción Democrática, and vice president of the political party Alianza País. She also served as president of Parliamentarians for Global Action and is a member of the Board of Directors of the Trust Fund for Victims at the International Criminal Court. She is the author of *El camino que traigo conmigo* (2011). In *Mañana te escribiré otra vez. Minerva y Manolo. Cartas,* Minou Tavárez Mirabal seeks to better understand her late parents, their legacy, and what it means for a country that still struggles for democracy.

HEATHER HENNES is associate professor of Spanish at Saint Joseph's University.

www.ingramcontent.com/pod-product-compliance
Lightning Source LLC
Chambersburg PA
CBHW030818230426
43667CB00008B/1279